1966
and all that

UPDATED 40TH ANNIVERSARY EDITION
1966–2006

1 9 6 6
and all that

MY AUTOBIOGRAPHY

Geoff
Hurst

with Michael Hart

headline

First published in 2001
by HEADLINE BOOK PUBLISHING

First published in paperback in 2002
by HEADLINE BOOK PUBLISHING

This edition published in 2005
by HEADLINE BOOK PUBLISHING

1

A CIP catalogue record for this title is available
from the British Library

ISBN 0 7553 1454 9

Typeset in AGaramond by Avon DataSet Ltd,
Bidford-on-Avon, Warwickshire

Printed and bound in Great Britain by
Mackays of Chatham plc, Chatham, Kent

Headline's policy is to use papers that are natural, renewable and
recyclable products and made from wood grown in sustainable
forests. The logging and manufacturing processes are expected to
conform to the environmental regulations of the country of origin.

HEADLINE BOOK PUBLISHING
A division of Hodder Headline
338 Euston Road
London NW1 3BH

www.headline.co.uk
www.hodderheadline.com

To the women in my life: my wife Judith
and our daughters Claire, Joanne and Charlotte

Contents

Acknowledgements

I WOULD LIKE TO EXPRESS MY SINCERE THANKS AND GRATITUDE TO the following: My mum and dad, without whom none of this would have been possible; my wife Judith and our three daughters for a lifetime of love and support, in particular to Joanne for her help and contribution to the book; Ron Greenwood for opening my eyes and showing me what could be achieved; Sir Alf Ramsey for giving me the platform and the confidence;

Gordon, George, Bobby, Jack, Ray, Alan, Nobby, Bobby, Martin and Roger . . . simply the best;

The Scots for giving me so many happy memories!;

Michael Hart, a loyal friend for more than thirty years, who collaborated in the writing of my autobiography; Ian Marshall, Lorraine Jerram, Rebecca Purtell and all the team at Headline.

CHAPTER ONE

1966

WAS IT A GOAL? DID THE BALL CROSS THE LINE? THOSE TWO questions have haunted me for most of my adult life. They are the questions I'm asked most often – and I don't know the answers. I don't think I ever will. It's a controversy that will follow me to the grave. For those who played and those who watched that afternoon in 1966, and for those who have seen it since then, my second goal against West Germany is probably the most debated and questionable incident in World Cup history. It all happened nearly 40 years ago but hardly a week goes by even now without me being reminded about some aspect of the day England won the World Cup.

England's victory generated a whole range of emotions from jubilation and patriotism to anger and frustration, depending upon your loyalties. The German fury at the time has diminished over the years – but they've never forgiven us. In 1975, nearly ten years after their defeat, West Germany played England at Wembley in a friendly match. Franz Beckenbauer, who had played in the final in 1966, was still in the German team. The night before the game the Germans, as is customary, trained on the Wembley pitch. When they walked up the tunnel they noticed that the goalposts hadn't been erected, nor had the pitch been marked out. Beckenbauer turned to his team-mate Berti Vogts and said, 'See, Berti, they've removed the evidence!'

Franz was only half joking, unlike a countryman of his I had the misfortune to meet while holidaying in Marbella just after the 1982 World Cup. Early one morning we were the only people in the pool. We were swimming lengths from opposite ends of the pool and I noticed that each time we passed in the middle he took a long hard look at me. Eventually he stopped at one end and waited for me to join him.

'I am not happy with you,' he said with the harsh sort of German accent you used to hear from Nazi torturers in Hollywood movies.

'I'm sorry,' I said, genuinely puzzled. 'What have I done?'

'You scored the goal that wasn't a goal,' he said.

Initially, I was relieved, thinking that this would be another situation that I could joke my way out of, but he wasn't having that. He was a man on a mission, seriously bitter about a sporting event that had taken place all those years earlier. I tried to win him over with logic and gentle persuasion, but it was a pointless exercise.

What I told him is what I've told everyone, before and since, when asked. I can state without fear of contradiction that it was a goal because the record books say so. They say so because the man who mattered that day in 1966, the Swiss referee Gottfried Dienst, said it was a goal, the third in England's 4–2 victory over West Germany. It was his decision, after consultation with his Russian linesman Tofik Bakhramov, and one that turned a finely balanced match in England's favour.

Everyone understood the sense of anger and frustration felt by the West Germans. They believed they had been robbed unfairly of the most prestigious prize in world football. Perhaps they were.

I have to admit that I had a bit of sympathy for the Germans. They genuinely believed the ball had not crossed the line and they may be right. I can no more claim with certainty that the ball did cross the line than they can claim that it didn't. Having listened to all the arguments over the decades and watched the replay hundreds of times on TV, I have to admit that it looks as though the ball didn't cross the line. At the time, though, I desperately wanted to believe that it was a goal. It was the World Cup final. We were drawing 2–2 against formidable opposition. The whole nation was willing me to score. What would you want to believe if you hit a shot that struck the underside of the bar and came down on the line?

This controversy has run like an indelible stain through my playing career and my life after football. It's resurrected whenever England play Germany. Scotsmen creep up behind me in airport lounges and hiss, 'It never went in, wee man.' When I meet someone for the first time, I know that sooner or later I will be asked the same question – did the ball cross the line?

All the modern-day technology and computer wizardry has failed to produce conclusive evidence one way or another. Even the old Wembley Stadium, scene of the crime so to speak, has disappeared. So, I hold my hands up and accept that there will always be a big element of doubt. But until someone proves otherwise, I'm happy to go along with Herr Dienst and Tofik Bakhramov.

It's a long time now since England's one and only World Cup victory and it remains an abiding source of pride to me that I was part of that historic occasion. Gordon, Jack, Bobby, Martin and all the others feel the same pride too, even today, years later. We achieved something that was unique in English sport. People sometimes ask me whether I would prefer to be playing today and earning the money that seems to come so easily to players of even modest ability in the Premiership. Compared to the average working man, the top professional footballers of my era were well paid, but they were not seriously rich in the way that many of today's players are. All eleven who played at Wembley in 1966 would have loved to earn the fortunes available today but I don't think any would choose the big salary ahead of the honour of winning the World Cup for England.

Years ago playing for your country was considered a real honour. I'm not convinced that some of today's players view an England call-up in quite the same way. Some seem to have a more casual attitude. This would not have been tolerated by Sir Alf Ramsey, our manager in 1966. He expected loyalty and commitment from his players. He valued hard-nosed professionals. He wanted players who would not let him down. We, in turn, never took him, or a place in the England squad, for granted. I've never forgotten what he said to me at the end of England's victory banquet that day in 1966. Largely unmoved by the emotion of the occasion – at least in public – Alf wanted to ensure that his World Cup winners kept their feet on the ground. He had no use for hat-trick heroes with global-sized egos.

'See you soon, Alf,' I said at the end of the day that changed my life.

'Perhaps, Geoffrey, perhaps,' was his reply.

I played in Alf's England team for another six years but nothing again matched the sense of personal satisfaction I felt that day at Wembley. It won't surprise you to learn that I was smiling for days afterwards. In fact, even today I chuckle to myself when I think back all those years. Three goals in the World Cup final for a late developer who had been an unknown left-half at West Ham wasn't bad, was it?

Today a World Cup final hat-trick would be worth a fortune to the scorer, but that wasn't quite how it was then. Most of the 1966 squad had no idea what bonus – if any – we would receive from the Football Association if we won the World Cup. One or two of the senior players may have been aware of it beforehand, but I knew nothing about a bonus until the day after the final. During a quiet moment before we all went our separate ways, Alf told us that the 22 players in the squad were to share a bonus of £22,000. It was not a fortune but still a handsome sum in those days. Alf said that the FA felt that the money should be divided among the players according to how many games each had played in the tournament. This meant that players such as Gordon Banks, Bobby Moore and Bobby Charlton, who had played in all six games, would receive significantly more than someone like me, who had played in three, or John Connelly or Terry Paine who each played in only one match.

It speaks volumes for the sense of togetherness enjoyed by that squad of players that, within moments of Alf's announcement, the senior players got their heads together and persuaded Alf to change the arrangements. They were the ones who would have gained most from the initial terms, but they felt the money should be shared equally among all 22 players. So we each received £1,000.

Twenty-two of us were involved and those who didn't play were as important to our success as those who did. I came to realise years later in my career in coaching and management that those who don't play are often the ones who determine the mood and climate within a squad of players, especially when you are away from home for long periods of time.

In 1966 I think several of the lads in the squad – Ron Springett, Peter Bonetti, George Eastham and Gerry Byrne, for example – suspected from the outset that they wouldn't play unless Alf's plans were decimated by a catastrophic list of injuries. In the days immediately before the tournament, I was one of those wondering whether I'd get in the team. I had made my international debut just five months earlier. I was one of the newcomers, along with my West Ham team-mate Martin Peters who made his debut two games after me.

In that spring of 1966 I played in three consecutive wins. The first was against West Germany – my debut match at Wembley in the February – and the other two were against Scotland and Yugoslavia. When Alf announced his squad of 22 for the finals, I thought initially that I'd done enough to clinch a place in the starting line-up. The announcement of the shirt numbers seemed to confirm this. I was given No. 10. It looked as though I would partner Jimmy Greaves at the front in Alf's favoured 4–4–2 line-up. Jimmy was given No. 8 and the other front striker, Roger Hunt, had No. 21.

Then, just before the tournament started, I had a couple of indifferent games in warm-up matches in Finland and Denmark. I thought the final pre-tournament match – against Poland in Chorzow – would give the critical clue to Alf's intentions. This game was just six days before the World Cup kicked off. When Alf chose Jimmy and Roger as his front two I knew I wouldn't be in the starting line-up for the first World Cup game against Uruguay.

So, when he announced the team for that opening match at Wembley, without me in the side, I wasn't surprised. I didn't expect to play. I was just happy to be there. Jimmy and Roger played in the first three games against Uruguay, Mexico and France and I think would probably have stayed together had Jimmy not been injured against the French.

It was sad for Jim, who was one of the world's great strikers at the time, but for me it was an opportunity not to be missed. Alf put me in the side alongside Roger for the quarter-final against Argentina and the rest is history. I scored England's goal in that turbulent match and retained my place in the side for the semi-final with Portugal. We won that 2–1, with Bobby Charlton scoring both goals.

I remember wondering for two or three days afterwards whether I would be picked for the final against West Germany. Jimmy Greaves was fit again and, having scored 43 goals in his previous 54 matches for England, had every right to expect a recall. Jim said at the time that he couldn't imagine himself not playing in the World Cup final. In fact, no one could imagine him not playing. He played in my position and he was world class. No one admired him more than I did. When he moved from Chelsea to AC Milan he trained with West Ham for a few days. At the time I was a struggling midfield player. I was able to watch him at close-hand, and learn from him. He was a genius at getting into the penalty box and scoring goals. He was also a really nice guy.

But, to be honest, I wasn't going round at the time saying, 'Poor old Jimmy.' I was thinking to myself, 'Thank God I've got this chance.' I could understand how bitterly disappointed he was, but that's just the way football is at times.

I knew in the back of my mind that there was a very good chance that Alf would recall Jim for the final. You can imagine my elation, then, when Alf drifted over to me casually after a training session the day before the final and said, 'I want you to know that you'll be playing tomorrow. But, Geoffrey, keep it to yourself. I won't be telling the others.'

I was naïve enough to think that I was the only one who knew. I was determined to keep my secret to myself. I telephoned Judith, of course, but I was so immersed in my own sense of satisfaction, so bursting with anticipation and excitement, that I failed to notice one or two other players walking around smiling ridiculously to themselves. I must have looked exactly the same to them.

I was sharing a hotel room with Martin Peters, and later in the day, when we were in the room together, I just couldn't keep my good news bottled up any longer.

'Don't whisper it to a soul, Martin,' I said, 'but the boss has told me I'm playing tomorrow.'

'Great,' smiled Martin. 'So am I.'

On the morning of the final Jimmy, who shared a room with Bobby Moore, was packing his bags ready to leave. As soon as the match finished he left Wembley with his wife to go on holiday. I think his disenchantment with football began that day.

I shaved as normal on the morning of the World Cup final, read the papers, had a cup of tea and can remember a brief sense of frustration as I looked out at the grounds of the Hendon Hall Hotel in north London where the squad were staying.

It was a bright day, but it had been raining. That at least settled one issue in my mind. Whenever I played I preferred to wear boots with moulded rubber studs. I felt I was a bit quicker in moulded rubbers, but I couldn't wear those boots on a wet pitch because I would be sliding all over the place. When I saw the rain that morning, I knew that I'd have to wear boots with nylon screw-in studs. The studs were longer and gave a better grip on wet or soft surfaces.

I was one of the few players to wear moulded rubber studs at Wembley. I had never forgotten what Jimmy Greaves told me: 'Moulded rubbers give you an extra half-yard of pace,' he claimed.

Later that morning I went for a walk. I met Nobby Stiles on my way out of the hotel. He was on his way to church to say a few prayers. It was his usual practice – he probably felt that we'd need some special divine intervention that afternoon! I remember thinking to myself that he was lucky to find a Catholic church in Golders Green.

It's remarkable to think that he and I, and any other member of Sir Alf Ramsey's squad, could stroll about quite freely on the morning of the World Cup final. In similar circumstances today, the appearance of David Beckham or Michael Owen would bring Golders Green to a standstill.

At about midday we had lunch. I had my usual pre-match meal – beans on toast and a pot of tea – and then we set off to the stadium by coach. A handful of people were at the hotel exit to wave us on our way. As we stepped off the coach at Wembley an hour later and walked into the dressing-room, I had no idea of what awaited me out there on the pitch.

Sitting in that seething dressing-room at Wembley, I remember thinking to myself, 'Am I really part of all this?'

I've never forgotten the chaos in that dressing-room in the hour or so before kick-off. It was very un-Ramsey like. I was sitting next to Bobby Moore and he said to me, 'Have you counted the people in here?' The dressing-room was full of television crews, photographers, members of the various Football Association committees, members of the Wembley staff, even the man who made the tea was wandering around with his autograph book. I was puzzled by the red shirts hanging from the hooks. Why were we wearing red? One of the lads, I think it was George Cohen, pointed out that Wembley was technically a neutral venue. It was decided on the toss of a coin who should wear their home strip. The Germans won and chose to play in their traditional white shirts, so we wore red.

We'd had our team-talk at the hotel, but once Alf was alone in the dressing-room with his players he went to those he considered critical to his game plan to stress individual points. I recall him warning Bobby Charlton of the threat posed by Franz Beckenbauer. 'I want you to stay with him,' Alf told Bobby. At the same time the German manager Helmut Schoen was telling the young Beckenbauer, 'Bobby Charlton is their best player so you must mark him tight.' The consequence of this was that two wonderful players, probably the best two players on the pitch that day, cancelled each other out, which was a disappointment for the spectators.

As we walked up the tunnel to the pitch that afternoon the thought crossed my mind that the entire country would be watching. It sounded to me as though most of them were in the stadium. I noticed a big banner in the crowd, which read 'Nobby Stiles for Prime Minister'.

Odd thoughts run through your mind at times like that. Judith's dad had predicted before the match that I'd score a hat-trick. Ridiculous, I thought. I'd scored just two goals in my previous seven England matches. A single goal would be an achievement but, essentially, I wanted to get through the 90 minutes without embarrassing myself or betraying the faith Alf Ramsey had shown in me.

How different it turned out to be. My first goal, after 19 minutes, was a typical piece of West Ham opportunism, the sort of thing that Bobby, Martin and I had worked on over the years under Ron Greenwood at Upton Park. We were a goal behind when Bobby, fouled by Overath out on the left, quickly took a long, accurate free kick. I knew where he'd put the ball and he knew that I'd be running into that space. It was the sort of thing we'd worked on dozens of times for West Ham.

Sure enough, the pass from Bobby was perfection. I ran in from the right, met the ball with my head and steered it past Hans Tilkowski, the German goalkeeper. Almost from the kick-off I suspected that I'd get chances like that and cause the Germans problems in the air. They played with a sweeper, Willi Schulz, and three markers, Wolfgang Weber, Karl-Heinz Schnellinger and Horst Hottges. Weber was the only orthodox central defender and Hottges, a full-back, was given the job of marking me. When he latched on to me from the kick-off I thought that I might get a chance to show that I was a bit better than he was in the air.

I'd thought about this before the game. I reckoned that, with only one genuine central defender, they'd have trouble marking both Roger Hunt and myself. So, from the kick-off, it was my intention to take up positions that were unfamiliar to Hottges.

But it wasn't until 12 minutes from time that we finally took the lead. The Germans failed to clear a corner from Alan Ball, giving me the chance to hit a shot that struck Weber and flew into the air. As the ball fell, Martin Peters was the first to reach it and shot past the goalkeeper and two defenders standing on the line. The World Cup was in our grasp.

I thought it was all over at that point. The Germans thought otherwise and, with a minute of normal time remaining, Weber equalised. I was exhausted in the period just before the final whistle and suddenly to be faced with a further 30 minutes was a daunting prospect. As we prepared for extra time Alf told us not to lie down on the pitch. That's what the Germans were doing. 'Look at them,' he said. 'They're finished. They're flat out on their backs.' He told us that we'd won it once. 'Now go and win it again,' he said. So we did.

After ten minutes of extra time, Nobby Stiles hit a terrific ball from midfield out to the right. He had a reputation as a hard man, but I'd played with him in the England Youth team and knew that he had far more skill than most people acknowledged. Our other tigerish competitor that day, Alan Ball – my personal man of the match – was running along the right flank. Alan said later that he didn't think he was going to reach it. 'I was finished,' he said. He had already 'died twice'. But he did reach it, looked up and hit a first-time cross to the near post. He knew that the chances were I'd be running to the near post.

If anything I made my run a little too soon. This meant that instead of moving on to the ball it was falling slightly behind me. I needed to adjust my body and take a couple of touches to get the ball into a shooting position. To get the power required to strike it properly, I had to fall back. As it turned out I connected beautifully with the ball but, in doing so, toppled over. I therefore had probably the worst view in the ground when the ball struck the underside of the bar and bounced down on the line.

My next clear memory is of Roger Hunt, to my left, suddenly halting his forward run and raising an arm in the air. Had there been any doubt about the validity of the goal in Roger's mind, he would have continued his run and supplied the finishing touch. It would have been the easiest thing for him to do. Roger was a great player and the natural instinct of any striker in those circumstances is to put the ball in the net if he feels it necessary. Roger didn't think his intervention was necessary. At that moment, with the jubilation of the crowd pouring down upon us from the terraces, I had no doubt that it was a goal. But within seconds the German team were appealing to the referee. I sometimes wish Roger had applied the

10

coup de grâce and tapped the ball into the net. It would have avoided so much controversy.

Thankfully, my third goal meant that the final wasn't determined by the opinion of a Swiss referee and Russian linesman. Later, it gave me an overwhelming sense of relief to know that the disputed goal had not been the decisive one. The Russian linesman, a tall, distinguished figure, was ridiculed for weeks in the German media and, with hindsight, it would have been sensible not to have had a Russian official involved. The other linesman was from Czechoslovakia. In 1966, many people throughout Europe still nursed memories of the Second World War, and FIFA would have been better advised to select all the match officials from countries that had played no part in it.

There was a residue of lingering bitterness towards the Germans that, in my opinion, helped create the atmosphere in which the match was played. Judith's father had been a paratrooper and was in tears at the end of the game. Most of the players had relations who had fought in the war. It may be difficult for young people today to appreciate that this feeling still existed in the country in the mid-sixties.

Fortunately, there was no doubt about the validity of our fourth goal. Only a minute of extra time remained. The Germans had been knocking a stream of high balls into our area in a desperate search for the equaliser. The referee had the whistle in his mouth when another cross fell towards our penalty area, this from Schulz, the sweeper, who was now playing on the right wing.

Bobby Moore, untroubled and completely in control as usual, chested the ball down, played a short pass to Alan Ball, received the return and looked upfield to see where to play it next. I remember Jack Charlton screaming at him, 'Kick the f****** thing out of the ground!'

Instead, 'Mooro' turned back into the penalty box with the ball at his feet. Jack was going mad at him. The Germans were frantically trying to regain possession, but Mooro was a picture of composure. He looked up, carried the ball forward and then hit the killer pass upfield to me. It was the perfect ball. My first thought was not to give it away. We had to keep possession. I sensed that Overath was chasing me as I headed towards the German goal. Then I was aware of Schnellinger, having deserted Alan Ball for the first time in the match, coming at me from the side.

By this time I was about ten yards outside their box. I can't imagine where I got the strength from to make that run. I was exhausted, but had been flattered a few minutes earlier when, after another long run, Hottges had gestured to me to slow down. He was in a worse state than me.

The match was practically over. Kenneth Wolstenholme was telling a nation glued to their TV sets, 'Some people are on the pitch . . . they think it's all over.' I heard Ball calling me. He was chasing hard to support me. It was at this point that I decided to hit the ball with every last ounce of strength I had. I thought that if it flew over the bar and deep into the crowd it would waste a lot of time.

Funnily enough, just as I shaped to kick the ball it hit a divot, bouncing up fractionally higher than I was anticipating. This meant that I caught it on the hard part of my instep and it flew into the net. Wolstenholme continued his famous piece of commentary: 'It is now!'

Mooro was the first up the steps to the royal box. Judith's dad had been right. I was a hat-trick hero. I was exhausted and jubilant. It had been a wet afternoon and I remember, as I followed Bobby up the stairs to shake hands with the Queen, trying to dry my hands on my shorts. It was all happening at the speed of light. That night we dined lavishly in the Royal Garden Hotel in Kensington High Street. Limousines delivered the great and the good. We appeared with Alf above the hotel entrance and waved to the crowds below us. We were relaxed now but still didn't fully appreciate the significance of our achievement.

The strange thing about the official celebration dinner that night was that the players' wives weren't invited. The players and officials of the four semi-finalists were there, all the FA, World Cup and organising committee people – everyone was there, with the exception of the players' wives and, sadly, Jimmy Greaves. We all thought of Jim that evening but, while we celebrated, our wives ate separately in another part of the hotel.

None of us questioned it in those days. I was only a youngster who'd just broken into the team so I wouldn't have been consulted about after-match arrangements. It's possible that some of the senior players were asked for an opinion, but even then none of them would have questioned Alf Ramsey if it was his choice not to have the wives at the banquet. Alf's word was final, in all matters. If he was taking us out to the cinema for an evening and wanted to see a particular film, that was the film we watched. No one would challenge his decision. That was just the way it was in 1966.

It was a sumptuous, but stuffy, banquet and it had always been my intention that later in the evening Judith and I would go into the West End with some friends. We often went out after a match on a Saturday evening. I asked Martin Peters, Alan Ball, Nobby Stiles and John Connelly and their wives to come out with us to Danny La Rue's club in Hanover Square. It was one of the London hotspots at the time.

The wives waited for ages, tut-tutting as wives do, but at about midnight we all got in taxis and set off to Hanover Square with the exception of Martin and Kathy Peters, who decided not to come after all. The emotion of that day touched us all in different ways and, apart from that, Kathy had moved house while Martin was away preparing for the World Cup. It had been a long, exhausting day. Martin and I had been up since about 6 that morning because we couldn't sleep. In fact, I didn't sleep particularly well at any time throughout the tournament.

At Danny La Rue's they made us a cake and played 'When the Saints come marching in' but even at this point, with the other revellers applauding this little knot of World Cup heroes, it didn't strike me that we'd done anything special. It was all a bit unreal. We were back in the hotel by three.

So were most of the other lads. There were exceptions. Jack Charlton, the worse for wear, ended up spending the night on a sofa in the house of a complete stranger in Leytonstone in East London. Next morning a woman looked over the garden wall and said, 'Hello,

Jackie.' She was a neighbour of his, visiting relatives in London. They lived a few doors apart in the Northumberland coal-mining village of Ashington.

That Sunday morning most of us were back together again, reading the papers at breakfast and discussing where we'd been the night before. Judith and I went for a walk in Hyde Park. I remember a newspaper photographer who had been hanging around stopping us and asking if he could take a picture. About midday we were ferried to the ATV studios for a lunch hosted by Eamonn Andrews. It was during a quiet moment, just prior to lunch, that Alf told us the bonus arrangements.

Then it was all over and we went our separate ways. We'd spent eight weeks together, won the World Cup, and suddenly it was all over. It would never be repeated. We all went back to our lives, Judith and I to our semi-detached chalet bungalow, in Hornchurch, Essex, our first marital home. It cost us £5,050. Martin lived on the same estate, as did our West Ham team-mates Johnny Sissons, Ronnie Boyce and Brian Dear. It was here that I had to come to terms with my new status. Saturday, 30 July 1966 was the day that changed my life, but it didn't change overnight. It was a slow process and probably all the more enjoyable for that because, as life improved, Judith and I had the time to appreciate our changing circumstances.

There was a tremendous feeling of anti-climax when we got home. The whole thing had passed so quickly. We drove round to Judith's mum's to pick up Claire. She wasn't quite a year old. I cut the lawn because I hadn't been home for ages. Then I washed the car. It was pretty much like any other Sunday afternoon. I was a national hero but I didn't feel like one.

It might sound a bit pretentious, but for me it had been another football match, albeit a very important one. In those days the most important things were the sport and honour, doing your best and representing your country. It was also something I enjoyed, something I had always wanted to do. When you are out there on the pitch, doing the job, you focus on the game and are not aware of the enormity of the occasion for other people. It's just like another day at the office. People may find that hard to believe but that's how I recall it, and so do many of my team-mates at the time.

I think the legend of 1966 will continue to grow. I don't think it's overstating the case to say that, among today's kids, it's a date that will be remembered alongside far more important dates in history. It doesn't rank alongside the Battle of Hastings in 1066 for example, but the popularity of football and the lack of any significant achievement in the game since 1966 means that our success at Wembley is stitched into the folklore of the nation.

I'm as patriotic as the next Englishman and would love England to win the World Cup again. But from a purely selfish point of view, I don't want our success to be repeated. I'd be lying if I said that I wanted another English player to score a hat-trick in a World Cup final. It was – and still is – unique. Everyone I talk to remembers the day and what they were doing. But such is the media interest in football today that a modern England win would eclipse the triumph of 1966.

You may think that's a cynical view but I think it's realistic. When did Germany first win the World Cup? The answer is 1954. Few people remember that now because of their success in later World Cup tournaments. Our legend has survived because no England team, apart from Bobby Robson's semi-finalists in 1990, has got close to winning the World Cup in the last 35 years.

Can you imagine the frenzy that would accompany an England World Cup victory today? In my time, winning and losing football matches didn't dominate life and headlines in the way that it does today. The 1966 triumph was over quite quickly but the whole country teetered on the brink of collective madness when England beat Germany 1–0 in a group match in the 2000 European Championship in Belgium.

If Michael Owen scored a hat-trick in the World Cup final it would be worth millions to him but it would hardly change his life in the way that the World Cup changed mine in 1966. The difference is simply explained. He's already a millionaire. In purely financial terms the modern game has enabled him to achieve in a couple of years with Liverpool what took me the best part of a lifetime in football and business. Almost everything I've achieved in my sporting and business life has been as a direct result of winning the World Cup. That one game and those three goals have influenced almost every aspect of my life since then. Perhaps I was a shade fortunate with the second one, but you create your own luck in football. The golfing legend Gary Player used to say, 'The funny thing is, the harder I work the luckier I get.' He was right. I worked hard for my good fortune throughout my career.

When I went home that July afternoon I was unaware just how profoundly things were about to change. The events of 1966 helped shape the modern game in England and establish today's standard of living for footballing superstars.

CHAPTER TWO

Charlie

CHARLIE HURST WAS MY BOYHOOD HERO. OTHER KIDS IDOLISED Flash Gordon, Robin Hood or Davy Crockett, but I had only one hero – my dad.

I think I was privileged to have a father I could look up to as a genuine idol. Comparatively few people had television in the forties and fifties so we weren't force fed the kind of role models thrust at kids today. My life revolved around the backyard, the street outside our house and the school playground.

I loved football from as early an age as I can remember, but my only footballing hero was Charlie Hurst. Far better players existed at the time, of course, and I'd occasionally hear talk in the school playground of the big names – Matthews, Finney, Lofthouse and Wright. But in the eyes of the young Hurst, none of them could match my dad.

You have to scour the football record books to find a reference to him, but he's there. Born in Denton, Manchester, on 25 January 1919, my dad's footballing career embraced Bristol Rovers, Oldham Athletic and Rochdale before, having moved the family south, he played non-league with Chelmsford City.

A tough, lean, wiry man, he spent his whole career at centre-half, which I find surprising now considering he was only 5ft 8in. He took great pride in the fact that few got past him. He viewed losing the ball in the air as a personal affront.

'If I knew I couldn't outjump the centre-forward for a high ball, I always made a point of butting him in the back of the head,' he once told me with a mischievous grin.

That, perhaps, explains the massive, impenetrable Hurst forehead! Sadly, the Second World War took the best years of his playing career. He fought in France and was rescued from the beaches of Dunkirk but towards the end of the war, when his skills as a toolmaker were employed on the home front, he played regularly for Oldham Athletic.

Sometime during the war he played against Sir Stanley Matthews, who was in the RAF. My uncle Jack, who also served in the RAF, heard the match commentary on the mess wireless one day. According to family folklore, the match commentator told the nation, 'Charlie Hurst is playing the great Matthews as good as any defender I've ever seen.'

Although family history insists my dad was an outstanding all-round sportsman, his career as a soldier had few high points. He wasn't the most organised of men and consequently the discipline of army life didn't suit him. He was too easygoing, unreliable some would say, but I will always remember him as a great character with lots of friends. Everyone was his pal. A self-taught pianist, he was enormously popular in the pubs and regularly surprised my mother by bringing people home at all hours of the night.

She was a stoical, resilient lady. I'm glad that I inherited many of her qualities, but I think I got my sense of humour from my dad; that, and my determination to succeed whatever the problems. He was a dogged little footballer who wasn't easily intimidated and he taught me the value of hard work.

He wouldn't tolerate abusive behaviour of any kind and he taught me to stand up for myself and to guard against being led astray by outside influences. This was good advice and I was glad to have the benefits of an orderly home life. Bobby Moore, Martin Peters and I were from similar backgrounds and we grew up to share many of the same values.

Obviously my dad played an important role in my development and was particularly supportive in anything to do with football. I think it was as a sportsman that he felt most fulfilled and so it gave him enormous pleasure to see one of his sons progressing as a professional footballer.

I remember him telling me once how important it was to walk with short strides during a match. He believed that if you walked with short strides it was easier to adjust your feet to receive a pass. Players with long legs and long strides, he argued, were slower to adjust their body shape when receiving the ball. As a result of this little tip I started walking with short strides – everywhere! To train myself in this new discipline, I tried not to tread on the lines between the paving stones.

My mum, Evelyn, was one of four girls from Gloucestershire. Few outside the family realise this, but their maiden name was Blick. Their forebears were, yes, German. This I suspect would have made a few headlines in 1966 had it become public knowledge.

I was born in hospital in Ashton-under-Lyne, just outside Manchester, on 8 December 1941, and kicked my first ball about in the streets around our little terraced house in Denton.

Unlike my dad, my mum had a serious attitude to life. She was a complex woman with a feisty nature and didn't suffer fools gladly. I think she'd had a tough upbringing. She was sturdily built, a good tennis player, and I think I inherited my physique from her.

We weren't poor, just an ordinary working-class family from the north of England. My sister, Diane, was two years younger than me, my brother Robert four years younger. Both our parents worked, with Dad supplementing his wages as a toolmaker by playing football professionally in the old Third Division (North).

I was six when the family moved to Essex. My dad went south for work, but he was still able to play football. He took a job as a toolmaker in Chelmsford and played for the local team in the Southern League. Having found lodgings, he sent for Mum and she travelled from Lancashire with three young children to join him. I have memories of her, loaded with suitcases, trying to find our new home because Dad couldn't meet us.

We lived with a man called Ernie Hawkins, who used to give me a clip round the ear if my dad was out of the house. My mum eventually put her foot down and told Ernie what would happen to him if he ever touched her kids again. He never did.

After two years in lodgings we moved to a council house on an estate in Chelmsford. My dad carried on living there after he and Mum were divorced. When he remarried he lived there with his second wife, Joyce, until he died two days before his 80th birthday in 1999.

It was in the little back garden of this house in Avon Road, and in the local streets of the Chignall Estate, that I spent hours and hours playing football and honing the skills that would serve me so well in later years. My dad was a great teacher and did all he could to encourage me. He used to take me to the local gymnasium some evenings where I could train with older players.

His sister, my aunt Frances, bought me my first kit – shirt, shorts and socks, in the colours of no particular team. I didn't support any club at the time and had no favourite player, apart from my dad. Years later, my aunt and uncle Jack watched a lot of the games I played for West Ham and every time I scored a hat-trick they'd send me a £5 note. They also bought me my first cricket bat and ball. They were a lovely couple and became big fans.

I had a pair of Tom Finney boots that were my pride and joy. I spent hours cleaning them after matches. I was able to save enough from my weekly paper-round money – ten shillings (50p) – to buy a pair of shinpads.

Although I devoted every spare minute to football and cricket, I was a diligent pupil at school. I was disappointed to fail the 11-plus because my school reports at the time were encouraging. I can remember finishing third in a class of 40. I ended up going to the Rainsford Secondary Modern School in Chelmsford where I played in the football and cricket teams. I wasn't the best footballer in the school by any means. My pal Terry Copsey was a much better player but, like so many naturally talented kids, he didn't commit himself fully to the game.

I worked all the time because, in my early teens, I realised that I wanted to do one of two things with my life – play football or play cricket. This desire to improve became almost an obsession. Every evening after school I'd play in the street with Robert and the other kids. One neighbour used to write regularly to the council complaining about the unruly behaviour of the Hurst boys.

Another neighbour, whose children flew model aeroplanes, was so irritated by the regular arrival of our football in his garden that he took me to court for disturbing the peace. My dad came with me and had to pay a fine of £1. Years later the neighbour apologised for getting me in trouble with the law.

All these little aggravations must have been worth it because my skill level was improving and my football was getting noticed. Obviously, my dad talked a lot about me and a friend of his, Jock Redfearn, was sufficiently impressed to write to two of London's biggest clubs, suggesting they offer me a trial. He'd seen me playing in the park and took it upon himself to contact West Ham and Arsenal.

I was still at school and very flattered when I was invited by Ted Fenton, then the manager at Upton Park, to go to West Ham to play in a trial match. Arsenal eventually replied but by the time I received their letter I was already playing for West Ham boys.

My trial match was a bit of a disaster – a double disaster really. I missed the first trial altogether because I got lost on the Tube and arrived too late. They gave me another chance, thankfully, but the only thing I remember is hitting a back pass short, forcing our goalkeeper to scramble from his line just as one of the opposing strikers tried to intercept the ball. Unfortunately, our goalkeeper broke a thumb in the collision. I wasn't a very popular young hopeful at that moment.

That incident didn't do much for my confidence. Although I wasn't shy, I wasn't an extrovert. I couldn't honestly claim to be self-assured as a youngster. My sister Diane still tells the story of the day she brought her schoolmate to the house to meet me. She claims I just sat there with a newspaper, refusing to talk to the young lady, who fancied me. It was a different story when I met Judith Helen Harries. We went to the same secondary school and used to meet at the local youth centre. She thought I was a bighead because I was good at sport and in all the school's teams.

Anyway, there was something about her that I couldn't ignore. We used to go to the Odeon cinema together, or to the local dancehall. It was the Elvis Presley era, a great time to be young. We'd go home on the bus. I'd get off at my stop, she at hers. Eventually, I took her home to meet Mum and Dad. It took a while for her to be accepted. My mum didn't think she was good enough for me. How wrong she was. Judith was to become the backbone of my life.

However, at that stage, football was the priority. For about six months I trained with West Ham twice a week, being taught by players such as Noel Cantwell and Malcolm Allison. Many of the West Ham players of that era – Ken Brown, Dave Sexton, John Bond, Andy Nelson, John Lyall, Frank O'Farrell, John Cartwright, Cantwell and Allison among them – later became successful managers and coaches.

Occasionally I played in the club's fifth team and although this wasn't top-grade football, it was a higher standard than anything I was used to with my school, Chelmsford Boys, or my dad's works team for whom I had played the odd game.

I was 15 and about to leave school when Ted Fenton called me over after a training session one Thursday evening. He asked me if I would like to join the groundstaff as a young player the following season. I could join the club immediately, he said, but I would have to spend the summer months painting the grandstand at Upton Park. Of course I jumped at it and for weeks that summer travelled home to Chelmsford every evening splattered with green paint. I didn't mind. Perched high up on that ladder, I remember looking down at the pitch imagining what it would be like to play in front of a big crowd. Would I be good enough to make the grade?

So I went straight from school to West Ham, and eventually moved into lodgings with Mr and Mrs Foskett, a kindly couple who lived around the corner from Upton Park. I never really gave any thought to any other kind of job. I knew I wanted to be a footballer and, from day one, I told myself that I was going to be a good footballer. I may not have been bursting with confidence, but I had a very positive attitude. I wanted to succeed. I didn't allow myself to have any negative thoughts. I knew it was a tough, competitive profession, but my dad had taught me the value of applying myself. I wasn't naturally gifted like some of the other young players at the club, but I was determined to compensate for that with hard work. No one would work harder than me.

That first season we travelled all over the country to play because West Ham had no home ground for junior games. It was a hard apprenticeship. One of the highlights was the Saturday queue for the 'five shillings tea money' the club allowed the young players. None of us was earning very much and this five bob (25p) was a handy bit extra for those selected to play.

From time to time we'd turn up to find one of the seniors included in the team. This usually happened when a player had been injured and was playing his way back to full fitness. Even the reserve-team players were gods to us kids and having one of them on the pitch in the same team was enough to keep us happy for a week.

Similarly, if senior players such as Johnny Dick or Vic Keeble came to watch us in a midweek match at the Spotted Dog ground in Clapton, all the youngsters felt a great sense of elation. It was a wonderful incentive to play in front of some of our star names and it helped us feel we were all part of the same club. I was always impressed by the way the older players took an interest in the progress of the youngsters at West Ham. It wasn't that way at all clubs. Some apprentices I knew scuttled away like scared mice if a first-team player loomed into view.

The West Ham playing staff in those days reflected the local community. Most of the players were from within a five-mile radius of Upton Park. I was one of the exceptions, not because I came from Lancashire but because I came from Chelmsford, all of 30 miles away in rural Essex. I was considered a country boy and, because of that, was often the victim of the sort of horseplay that is so common among footballers. I remember how proud I felt one day when two of the first-team players asked me to help them practise a throw-in routine on the training pitch. I was to mark the centre-forward who was receiving the throw-in. From about six feet the thrower hurled the ball at the head of the centre-forward who ducked. I, of course, was standing right behind the centre-forward and the ball struck me hard in the face. The blood was pouring from my nose as the jokers wandered off chuckling to each other.

In the main, though, they were all good lads and I enjoyed learning from them. Vic Keeble, a great centre-forward of that era, was especially kind to me at the time, regularly driving me from the training ground home to Chelmsford in his white sports car. Like all young apprentices in those days, I didn't own a car and if I didn't get a lift I had to travel by bus, train or the old trolleybuses that ran from Forest Gate. I couldn't afford a car until I was 19 when I bought a pale blue Ford Anglia for £460 from a man I arranged to meet in a pub on the A127, the main road between London and Southend.

Judith, too, travelled by bus or train, all over East Anglia, watching me play football or cricket. She'd think nothing of sitting in a bus for two hours and it was at that time that she and Kathy, later to become the wife of Martin Peters, became lifelong friends.

Gradually Judith became my staunchest fan. She used to turn up for matches in her pleated tartan skirt and woolly jumper and throw peanuts at anyone abusing me or jeering from the stands. She worked in the local nursery close to our house in Chelmsford and would come by with three or four children. She used to have to wear a green, nylon uniform with a skirt that reached down to her ankles. It wasn't the most attractive of outfits, but I fancied her like mad nonetheless.

My mum remained convinced that I'd marry the daughter of a doctor or university lecturer. My dad used to telephone me at Judith's house at midnight and say, 'D'you know what time it is? When are you coming home?' He believed that girls and football didn't mix. He might have been partly right because, from the football viewpoint, I wasn't making the progress I wanted. It was a hard business.

Ted Fenton had faith in me and I will always be grateful to him for that. He gave me my first senior appearance for the club in a Southern Floodlight Cup tie against Fulham in December 1958. It was a wonderful experience. The crowd totalled 4,531 and I was in the team alongside some of West Ham's biggest stars – Johnny Dick, Vic Keeble, Ken Brown, John Bond and Phil Woosnam. We won 3–1, but I wasn't very impressive. I was learning, though, and kept working hard. Four months later the club offered me terms as a full professional. I was offered £7 a week and given a £20 signing-on fee.

Ted was one of the last of the old-style managers. A big, bluff, engaging character, he wore a trilby hat and a waistcoat and smoked a pipe. As a young player at West Ham in the thirties he was often sent to fetch beer for the manager, the legendary Syd King, who ran the club from 1902–32 and, sadly, committed suicide a few weeks after his dismissal. Nothing quite so dramatic happened to Ted, although he left in March 1961, after 11 years as manager at Upton Park, in circumstances that were never satisfactorily explained. He established the youth policy that was to prove so fruitful in the sixties and seventies and, in 1958, steered the club back into the First Division after an absence of 26 years.

Ted gave me my first taste of the big time. I knew I wasn't setting the place alight but in February 1960 he had so many injured players that he had no option but to use me for the visit to Nottingham Forest. I was a left-half of indifferent quality in those days and was given the No. 6 shirt. John Bond and Noel Cantwell, our regular full-back partnership, both played at the front because the two first-choice strikers, Keeble and Dick, were injured.

My contribution was insignificant. We lost 3–1 and I still have one of the reports from the following day's newspapers. The headline reads 'What a Stew-Mah!' which, if you haven't guessed already, is a rearrangement of the letters that make up West Ham.

I played two more games later in the season, but with so many good half-backs at the club – notably, of course, Bobby Moore – I was beginning to realise how difficult it would be to secure a regular first-team place. Andy Malcolm, John Smith, Bill Lansdowne, Malcolm Pike and Eddie Bovington were all pressing for first-team places, and there was a tall, thin lad from Plaistow called Peters who was gradually working his way up through the ranks. I was growing a little concerned and talked about my future to one of our most experienced professionals, Phil Woosnam, a university-educated Welsh international inside-forward who later became the very successful Commissioner of the North American Soccer League.

Phil felt Bobby Moore had made better progress than me because he was quicker to learn about the game. He thought that I wasn't grasping the subtleties of tactics and team play as easily as Bobby. His advice was simple – stick at it. That opinion was later reinforced by my dad.

The following season, 1960–61, I made just six first-team appearances. I was beginning to wonder whether I'd made the right choice. I was still playing cricket and was good enough to get into the Essex Second XI on a regular basis for three or four years. I was very happy at Essex and at one time cricket was a real option.

Then something happened that changed everything. Ted Fenton left and Ron Greenwood was appointed manager. I was 19 and still trying to make the grade. Bobby Moore had worked under Ron when he was coach to the England Under-23 team. Bobby thought it was a good thing when Ron took over. He respected him as a coach. 'You want to learn?' Bobby said. 'Well, there's no better teacher.'

CHAPTER THREE

Ron

It would not be overstating the case to say that the single most influential figure in my career in professional football was Ron Greenwood. My dad fuelled my boyish enthusiasm for the game and gave me a dream. Ted Fenton, the manager who signed me for West Ham, gave me the chance. He had belief in me when it mattered and gave shape and structure to my dream. But it was Ron Greenwood who opened the door to the world of modern-day football. He showed me what lay beyond. Like any good teacher, he showed me what could be achieved by hard work and self-belief.

Ron joined West Ham as manager in April 1961. I've never forgotten the date because during that month the Soviet cosmonaut Yuri Gagarin became the first man to fly in space. Ron's appointment didn't make the same headlines but, nonetheless, he created his own little piece of history by becoming the first West Ham manager to have no previous connection to the club.

Like me, he was from Lancashire. He was born in Burnley and had been a centre-half with Bradford, Brentford, Chelsea and Fulham, winning a league championship medal with Chelsea in 1954–55. I never saw him play but I'm told that he was a thoughtful defender. He wasn't tall for a centre-half, a bit like my dad, but unlike my dad, he found solutions to problems by force of intellect rather than just force.

Those who knew him as a player weren't surprised that he became such a respected, innovative manager. While chief coach at Arsenal, the Football Association offered him the part-time job of looking after the England Under-23 team, which is how Bobby Moore came to know him.

To me, though, he was an unknown quantity when he arrived at Upton Park to take over from Ted. I was a bit anxious, as any youngster would be in similar circumstances. I knew I still had a lot to prove and I just hoped that he would give me a fair crack of the whip. There was a lot of uncertainty among the players, inevitable at any club when there's a change of manager. Having not done too well under Ted, I wondered whether it would be better or worse for me now that Ron Greenwood had arrived. I remember him gathering all the players together in the old 'chicken run' stand – a primitive construction of corrugated iron and timber that had stood at the Boleyn Ground for most of the century – to tell us what he expected from us and what he hoped to achieve.

Within days of his arrival, the changes were quite dramatic. What the players noticed first were the new training programmes. Ted had been one of the old school. Under him, most of the work we did was physical – running, stretching, exercises to strengthen legs, arms and shoulders. Every day was much the same as every other day. He made us do a lot of sprinting and we had to wear running spikes for this. Each player had at least one set of spikes. It was quite common in football at the time. But when Ron turned up at our Grange Farm training ground the spikes went into the dustbin. He told us that, in future, everything we did would be done in football boots. We would no longer wear spikes for sprinting. Someone asked him, 'Why? We've always worn spikes.' Ron said that we couldn't wear spikes and kick a ball around and, in future, all training would involve the use of a ball. That is how it turned out. From that day on, practically all the training we did involved a ball.

We worked as hard as any other team in the country and most of us loved it. The game was changing, and coaching was becoming more important. Ron Greenwood was at the forefront of that change. He developed a reputation as something of an academic. Sure, he thought very deeply about the game but he was a practical coach, so keen to work with the players that I can remember days when he had to be dragged off the training pitch.

Years later, when he was appointed manager of England, the players found him as fresh and stimulating as I had done when he arrived at West Ham. He liked young players with open minds. He challenged them to learn. I took up the challenge. So did others.

It was no coincidence that Bobby Moore, Martin Peters and I were among those who flourished in the environment he created at West Ham in the early sixties. All three of us were disciplined. All three of us wanted to learn. Some, of course, ignored the opportunities he presented. There were other talented youngsters at the club, such as Johnny Sissons, Brian Dear and Trevor Dawkins who may have made it to the very top of the profession had they applied themselves more diligently.

Ron was a brilliant coach and could have improved any player who wanted to improve. He used to talk about 'bright minds and healthy bodies'. He liked his players to have 'pictures' in their minds when they played, by which he meant that players should always be aware of what was going on around them on the pitch.

When he was showing us some new tactic or passing movement on the training pitch, he'd walk us through it a few times. 'Penny numbers' he called it. I don't know why he called it that and nor did he. It simply meant that, in the first instance, we'd go through it slowly.

Much of what I learned from him in those days is still relevant today. When I'm watching games, situations arise on the pitch that often make me think of some of the things he used to tell us. For every tactical problem he had an answer. When I see a team with a problem I still think to myself, 'Ron would have solved it this way or that way.' For instance, a team may be having difficulty in bypassing opposing defenders. Ron taught us to create what he called 'two against one' situations all over the pitch. The object was to bypass defenders with a forward pass rather than a square one across the field. It was really the essence of West Ham's one-touch game and was dependent on the sharpness, vision and movement of our players. Too often today players accept second best with a square pass or high ball over the top of defenders simply because they've never been taught a passing strategy that carries them through the heart of the opposing team.

Ron impressed on all his new players the importance of good habits. This was nothing to do with holding a knife and fork properly. Players with good habits were those who consistently did the right thing on the pitch. The players with bad habits, who were inconsistent on the pitch, became bad players in his opinion.

When he joined the club my 'habits' on the pitch probably fell into the latter category. 'Horrible' was the word he used to describe one performance of mine at left-half. 'You're a horrible defender,' he told me. 'When the ball's behind you, you don't know where you are, where you're going or where you should be. We need to change that in you.' He did.

Fortunately, he must have seen something that he admired because he persevered when other managers might have given up with me. The fact that I was playing cricket throughout the summer months with Essex meant that I probably wasn't as fit as I should have been. In those days it was still just possible to play both sports seriously but the seasons did overlap and this often meant that I missed some of West Ham's pre-season training.

The first game I played for Ron was a 2–1 defeat by Burnley on the final day of season 1960–61. That summer I played cricket, reported back late for training, and wasn't considered for the opening games. Then Ron gave me a run in the side at left-half. I played 24 games that season and scored my first goal for the club in a 4–2 win over Wolves at Upton Park in December 1961.

In the summer of 1962, Ron took the team on tour to Ghana. I stayed behind to play cricket for Essex. In those days, cricket was still a gentleman's game and I found it difficult to reconcile its old-fashioned, leisurely tone with the harsher environment of professional football. Then Essex had a casual attitude to the county championship, which has changed dramatically in recent years. They're now as professional in their approach as any Premiership football club.

I loved the game and had I failed to make the grade at football there was a chance that, as a batsman of some potential, I would have tried cricket as a profession. But it was a sport that drove Judith to distraction. She was happy watching me play football but a day's cricket bored her to tears. The high point of my cricket career came in that summer of 1962 when an Essex side badly hit by injuries called me into first-team action. It was my one and only first-class game for Essex. I was 0 and 0 not out against Lancashire and, memorably, one of my team-mates that day was the great off-spinner Jim Laker.

Once again, because of my cricketing commitments, I missed part of West Ham's pre-season training and although I was given the No. 4 shirt for the opening match in 1962–63 – a 3–1 defeat by Aston Villa – I was grossly unfit. Not surprisingly, Ron sent me back to the reserves where I was left to contemplate my future.

Then in September, Ron produced the tactical masterstroke that completely changed the direction of my career. He had tried to accommodate me at right-half by letting Andy Malcolm go to Chelsea, but I'd obviously done nothing to change his opinion that I simply wasn't suited to the half-back role.

One Monday morning I feared the worst when I was told to report to his office after training. Two days earlier I'd played an appalling game in the reserve team against Shrewsbury. Nothing went right for me that day. I suspected that, having read the match report, the manager was about to give me a serious lecture – or worse.

I knew that some months earlier Ron had considered letting me go to Crystal Palace. When he was negotiating to buy Johnny Byrne, the Palace manager, Arthur Rowe, had suggested me in part exchange. Ron said 'no' but my dad knew Arthur from their days together at Chelmsford City and he felt a move down to a club in the Third Division might have given me the chance to establish myself as a first-team player.

Anyway, my fears were unjustified. What Ron said in his office that day surprised me. 'I gather you were terrible on Saturday,' he said. 'We can't go on like this. I want to do something about it. I want you to play in an attacking role. I want you to play up front against Liverpool tonight. I want you to try it. I won't hold it against you if it doesn't work. It's my judgement I'm risking, not your status within the club. Will you have a go at it?'

He convinced me that, if I had any future in football, it wouldn't be as a half-back. He had a memory, he said, from his days at Arsenal of me playing against them as a striker in a friendly match.

'I was impressed that day,' he said. 'You're good going forward, you know, but you're struggling with the defensive work in midfield. All I want you to do is play your natural game. Do the things you enjoy doing and, if you're any good, we'll add the rest in time.'

He wanted me to play at the front partly because he had no one else to do the job. Johnny Dick, the club's leading goalscorer in the previous two seasons, had left after the first two games to join Brentford for a fee of £17,500. So Geoff Hurst, the striker, was given Johnny Dick's No. 10 shirt for the first time on Monday, 3 September 1962. The crowd at Upton Park was 22,262. West Ham won 1–0 with Tony Scott scoring the goal. It was our first win of the season and I didn't do too badly. Ron was all smiles afterwards. I was absolutely exhausted and can remember wringing the sweat from my shorts in the dressing-room.

In all I played 27 games in the First Division that season, scoring 13 goals. I also helped set up a few chances for my striking partner Johnny Byrne, who scored nine goals in 30 matches. Considering I started the season as a half-back of dodgy quality, I was naturally thrilled with my goal tally. A goal every other game for a novice like me was quite sensational and, in the modern game, would guarantee overnight stardom and all that goes with it. But I wasn't foolish enough to think that a few goals in my debut season as a striker meant that I was the finished article. I still had a lot to learn, although I was proud that I had adapted to a new challenge.

Ron had given me this big chance and I didn't want to waste it. Nobody could have worked harder. I practised, and kept on practising. I learned to take the ball on the run, coming from behind me, I worked on my heading and shooting from all angles and distances. I worked hard to improve my control and to grasp the principles of creating and using space. Much of this I did on my own.

It was Ron who taught me how to drag my opponents out of position, creating space for others to exploit. Johnny Byrne – 'Budgie' to everyone in the dressing-room because he was such a chatterbox – was often the player who capitalised on my running. West Ham had paid £65,000 for him, a record at the time for a transfer deal between English clubs. They actually paid £58,000 but Ron Brett, valued at £7,000, went to Palace in part-exchange. It could have been me.

Slowly a partnership developed with Budgie. Initially, he was the star and I was the straight man, the guy who did the donkey work. Playing alongside him was one of the best things that could have happened to me. He was just 23 but already a big name, having made his debut for England while playing for Palace in the Third Division. Needle sharp and an incessant talker, he'd drive you mad in the dressing-room but, once on the pitch, you just stood back and admired a rare talent.

In the penalty box he was as clever and cute as the Artful Dodger. He'd score goals and you'd scratch your head, wondering how he did it. Much of what I learned from him proved to be of great value later in my career. I was the pupil and he was the master.

We were opposite in appearance – me sturdy and powerful, him shorter, dapper, cheeky, with instant control and a burst of pace that carried him beyond defenders. It was the contrast, I think, that made us such an effective partnership.

There were several elements of his game that I particularly admired and I strived to add them to my own rather thin repertoire of tricks and skills. His volleying was outstanding and I worked hard on this technique in training. He had wonderful close control and I tried to copy that too. He had a marvellous knack of controlling the ball with his chest. However hard it was driven at him, he could cushion the pass on his chest and have the ball at his feet within fractions of a second. I worked hard to copy that.

Within a year we both knew where the other would be on the pitch at any given time and we both knew exactly where the goal was. In our first season together as West Ham's striking partnership we shared 29 goals in first-team matches. That was just the start. The following season, 1963–64, we shared 59 goals, then 48, then 57. In our first four seasons together I scored a total of 100 goals in 191 first-team matches and Budgie scored 93 in 163 matches. In today's game a goalscoring combination of such reliability would be beyond price.

Ron once said that Budgie and I were as complementary 'as bacon and eggs'. Others, too, were beginning to take notice. I recall Jimmy Hill, then the high priest of television football, putting together a 15-minute montage that illustrated the strengths of my game. He pointed out to the viewers what I was doing and why – the decoy runs, the one-touch lay-offs to a team-mate, the sprints to the wings to give an attack width. He highlighted what he thought was an instinctive awareness I had for the positioning of team-mates during a match. Much was made of my 'peripheral vision' but what it simply meant was that, with or without the ball, I was constantly looking around for the options available to me and my team-mates. I took it as a compliment when the Spurs manager Bill Nicholson sent his new signing Martin Chivers to watch me and study the way I played.

I was flattered by such attention. As Jim pointed out at the time, did the fans on the terraces always appreciate what I was doing? Sometimes I don't think they did.

Ron, though, knew exactly what I was doing, and he made sure that I knew and understood too. In the space of two or three years he turned me from a run-of-the-mill left-half into a centre-forward who was good enough to lead the England attack at a time when Sir Alf Ramsey had an abundance of strikers from whom to choose. I never considered myself a world-class player like Bobby Moore or Bobby Charlton, even at my peak. But I was comfortable in world-class company and that was good enough for me.

Why did I flourish like that after such inauspicious beginnings? I think there were three main reasons. The first was my own determination to succeed. The second was Ron's faith and the third was the time he devoted to improving my game. I felt I had to repay him.

Initially, he showed faith in all his players. He believed in people. In football, as in business, you need to show people that you believe in what they're doing. He wanted players to accept responsibility for themselves. But there are risks involved, as he discovered during his 16 years at the club. Players let him down. Some let him down spectacularly, none more so than Bobby Moore, Jimmy Greaves, Brian Dear and Clyde Best who went to a nightclub on the eve of an FA Cup tie in January 1971. I think when you give players as much responsibility for their own destiny as he did, on occasions you are bound to be let down. That's human nature.

His nature was always to give players the benefit of the doubt. I remember there was once a move in the dressing-room to introduce a regular golf day into the training schedule. Whether he would have agreed to it or not I don't know, but he asked all the players for an opinion. He valued their opinions. Mine was strongly against a golf day.

But Ron would always consider any new idea. He was a progressive thinker with an open mind. He would hear something, read something or see something in a game that impressed him and talk to his coaches about it. Like most of his players, the coaches were eager to learn. Then we would try it on the training pitch and, if the players liked it, we'd try it during matches.

He had been profoundly impressed by the Hungarians in the mid-fifties. The Mighty Magyars were the 1952 Olympic champions when they beat England 6–3 at Wembley in November 1953. They were the first foreign team to win at Wembley and Ron had been in the crowd. For years afterwards he spoke about their vision, their exquisite control and movement to anyone who would listen.

What he took specifically from the Hungarians was the near-post cross, a tactic that was to become one of West Ham's trademarks during my time with the club. One day he put cones down in wide positions on the training pitch. The cones were to act as full-backs, he said. The wingers had to run and cross the ball before they reached their cone. They had to bend their pass around the cone so that the ball landed in the space between the opposing goalkeeper and his back line of defenders. It was the task of forwards like me to get into that space and attack the ball before the goalkeeper or any of the defenders could reach it.

Harry Redknapp, a popular, flame-haired winger who made his first-team debut in 1965, and Johnny Sissons eventually had the crossing off to perfection. But Ron made sure we were all capable of crossing to the near post. I spent hours crossing the ball. Martin Peters, Bobby Moore, everyone, practised until Ron was satisfied that his near-post ploy would work regardless of which of his players were involved.

Some years later, Sir Alf Ramsey was particularly grateful to Ron when Martin supplied a near-post cross for me to score against Argentina at Wembley. Those hours spent on the training ground at Chadwell Heath were instrumental in breaching one of the best defences in the World Cup and securing England's progress in 1966.

We worked for months at West Ham until we perfected the technique. Once we had it right, it was a tactic that was very difficult for the opposition to counter. David Beckham is currently the best exponent of the early pass from the right wing. I remember playing against Manchester City at a time when Malcolm Allison, a former West Ham player and a big Greenwood fan, was the first-team coach. Malcolm told me afterwards that he had stressed the dangers of the near-post cross to his team before the match. It made no difference. West Ham won 2–1. I crossed one for Martin Peters to score at the near post and he crossed one for me to score. When we got it right, there was little the opposition could do.

Ron was one of the new breed of coaches who believed that we could learn from the development of the game in other countries. It wasn't a matter of simply emulating their style of play. What he wanted to do was take the good elements from the foreign game and add them to the traditional English style of play.

For him, the best way to complete the education of his players was to test them against foreign teams. Competitive European club football was still in its infancy so in the summer of 1963, he decided to take us abroad – to New York.

America wasn't a footballing hotbed by any means but Ron jumped at the chance when invited to take part in an international club tournament on Randall's Island. The prospect of pitting the skills of his players against opponents from Brazil, Germany and Italy among others on hard pitches in the summer heat of New York intrigued him. How would we cope in that sort of company?

Burnley had faced problems in the tournament the previous summer and Ron warned us that it wouldn't be a picnic. Having established myself in the first team, cricket was no longer an option for me so when the rest of the lads flew out to America I was with them.

We flew in one of those great, lumbering aircraft with propellers, stopping at Prestwick to pick up the players of Kilmarnock. The flight took about 14 hours and when we landed in New York, we were each given five dollars by the club. This was to be our daily allowance for as long as we remained in the tournament.

The clubs involved were split into two groups, with the winners of each due to meet in the final. We played six games in our group, losing just one, to Mantova of Italy. They were a skilful team and beat us 4–2. We drew 3–3 with Kilmarnock, beat Oro of Mexico 3–1, Valenciennes of France 3–1, Prussen Munster of West Germany 2–0 and drew 1–1 with Recife of Brazil.

We knew a draw in our last group game against Recife would be good enough to qualify for the final. It was a hot, humid night and we had to play the game at a slower tempo than usual. At the end the Brazilian coach, who had been given a handful of West Ham badges, threw them at Ron. Typically, Ron simply smiled back.

We flew home for three weeks while the second group was played and then returned to America to meet the winners in the final. The players asked Ron if we could take the wives and girlfriends and, although it was a costly business, the club agreed. From a team spirit point of view, it was a wonderful move. We had a lot of fun looking after ourselves in our self-catering apartments on the corner of East 86th and Madison. The best suite was the penthouse on the top floor. I shared that with Martin Peters and Ronnie Boyce because we were the three unmarried members of the party. Martin showed me how to get four cups of tea out of one tea bag by winding the little string round the bag and pulling it tight. As he rightly pointed out, five dollars a day wasn't a lot, especially when you were saving to get married!

When we arrived for the final, Ron explained to the wives and girlfriends that victory would mean an extra week in America because the organisers wanted to stage a special Challenge Cup match against the previous year's winners, Dukla of Prague.

But first we had to play a two-legged final against Gornik of Poland, a busy, thoughtful team who included in their ranks an unknown 17-year-old called Wlodimierz Lubanski, who was already a full international and would become one of the all-time greats of Polish football.

We drew the first leg 1–1. In the second leg, Polish immigrants in the crowd poured on to the pitch and attacked the referee. Ron led us all off and, when we finally returned, Gornik seemed deflated by the incident.

I scored the goal in the 1–0 win that meant we now had to play Dukla, over two legs, for the Challenge Cup. The first leg was to be played in Chicago and, as the wives were staying behind in New York, there was quite a scene when we departed with the boys cheering and the girls secretly delighted to be left on their own.

Dukla were the best side we played in America. They had five men who had played for Czechoslovakia in the World Cup final the previous summer, among them the great Josef Masopust. They beat us 1–0 in Chicago and although we played much better in the second leg in New York they held us to a 1–1 draw.

Although we didn't win the Challenge Cup, it would have taken two or three years at home to gain the experience we squeezed into one month in America. The education we received on that trip was priceless. We learned to appreciate different attitudes, different rule interpretations and different techniques and strategies. Most of us were kids playing against great players. It was an eye opener. It prepared us for football in Europe. It was no coincidence that we won the Cup-Winners' Cup at our first attempt. I don't think we would have achieved that without our trip to America.

The trip helped put West Ham on the map and from my point of view it meant that when I was selected to play for England I already had some knowledge of foreign teams and foreign players. It would not be overstating the case, in my opinion, to say that some of the goals England scored in the 1966 World Cup were the result of what happened on the dusty pitches of Randall's Island that summer.

I blossomed on that trip and so did my relationship with Johnny Byrne. I scored nine goals in ten games. During the previous one or two summers I'd played cricket and wondered what sort of reception awaited me in pre-season training. But this time, as I flew home from New York with Judith, I was full of confidence and couldn't wait for the season to start. Ron Greenwood had given me belief in myself.

In the next three seasons I would be on the winning side at Wembley in three finals of increasing significance – the FA Cup, the European Cup-Winners' Cup and the World Cup.

Ron was one of the most influential coaches of his generation and although the style of play he developed may not have been conducive to the nine-month slog of the league championship race, some of the football West Ham played in his time was the most attractive and memorable in the world. The Upton Park loyalists appreciated the way we played and, most tellingly, came back year after year because they knew they would see a good game of football. West Ham had a well-deserved reputation for high-quality attacking football and Ron was responsible for that.

Some in the game, Brian Clough for instance, who had an opinion about everything, felt that a West Ham team with Hurst, Moore and Peters should have had greater success. Ron was criticised, too, for the number of goals we conceded. What few understood outside West Ham was that Ron Greenwood cared more about football's finer values than about winning for winning's sake. He was a man of principle and he cared about the sport in a way that many would not understand in the modern game.

Twenty years after we had both left West Ham, we met at a game at Upton Park. Ron was deep into his retirement, a little more portly perhaps, but he still enjoyed watching football.

'How's Judith?' he asked me.

'She's here,' I replied. 'In fact, she's in the Ron Greenwood lounge. Let's go and find her.'

So Ron and I set out along the maze of corridors at Upton Park to surprise Judith in the hospitality suite that had been named in Ron's honour. When we reached the entrance to the lounge, a uniformed steward held up his hand like a policeman stopping traffic and said, 'Can't come in here, mate, without a pass.'

'But this is Ron Greenwood,' I said to him.

'Oh yeah,' he said, 'and I suppose you're Geoff Hurst!'

'Well, actually . . .'

Before I finished the sentence a senior steward stepped forward to avert any further embarrassment.

'I think you'd better let these gentlemen through,' he said.

It was an unfortunate incident and one that I hope hasn't been repeated. West Ham owe a huge debt of gratitude to Ron Greenwood and, had I anything to do with it, I'd have erected a statue in his honour when he finally handed control of the team to John Lyall in 1974. There's nothing to stop them doing it now.

As a coach he was unrivalled and had a positive and lasting influence not just on the club but on the game as a whole. How many coaches can truly have that said of them?

CHAPTER FOUR

A footnote
in history

As an exercise in bonding and strengthening team spirit, the two trips across the Atlantic had been an enormous success. It had been a physically demanding summer, not the sort of programme any club manager would seriously consider today, but as we prepared for season 1963–64 there was a mood of optimism in the dressing-room that I hadn't noticed before. Perhaps I'd been too busy playing cricket.

Now at last I felt part of the West Ham first team. I felt as though I belonged. This confidence grew in me, and the rest of the team, as the season progressed. It became the bedrock upon which we built our passing game and our reputation as one of the most attractive, attacking teams of the time. The fact that we won the 1964 FA Cup can be traced back to the quality football and dressing-room harmony that took root in New York that summer.

Today, West Ham's victory at Wembley in 1964 is no more than a footnote in history, but that team demonstrates how the game has changed in the last 40 years. Most of the players were Londoners and all of them were English. Since then, I don't think that any club – with the exception of West Ham again in 1975 – has won the FA

Cup with an all-English team. Ron didn't specifically want to play an all-English team. The players he inherited when he took over were all from England and most were from the East End of London. In fact, he and I were the only members of the dressing-room without an accent that was obviously from the London or Essex areas.

West Ham, at the time, drew its players and supporters from the local area. It had been that way for the best part of a century. Formed in 1895 from among the 6,000 local men employed by the Thames Ironworks shipyard, the club became an integral part of the daily life of the surrounding community. It was the focal point for the emotional loyalties of thousands of working-class residents in that part of East London and that is why, over the years, the fans on the terraces invariably developed a close affection for the youngsters who rose through the ranks at the club.

On his arrival, Ron found an abundance of promising talent, most of it drawn to the club from the local communities, and it was from these players that he built the team that won the 1964 FA Cup. Jack Burkett, Eddie Bovington, Ken Brown, Bobby Moore, Ronnie Boyce and John Sissons were all London boys who had emerged from the youth team at Upton Park. John Bond came from Colchester and played for no other league team before making his West Ham debut in 1952. Jim Standen, the goalkeeper, was born in Edmonton. He had played for Arsenal, but joined West Ham from Luton in 1962.

Peter Brabrook was born not far from Upton Park and supported West Ham as a child but somehow slipped through the net. Ron eventually signed him from Chelsea for £35,000 in 1962. Johnny Byrne came from West Horsley in Surrey.

I was therefore the only member of that team who didn't have some attachment to the London area, but any Lancashire accent I had developed as a child had long since disappeared. My roots were elsewhere, but by this time I felt at least an honorary Londoner.

East Enders – honorary or otherwise – are far less common in the modern West Ham team. I'm pleased that my old team-mate Harry Redknapp, the West Ham manager between 1994 and 2001, tried to reverse the current trend. Although he signed his share of foreign players, he also encouraged the emergence of youngsters such as Rio Ferdinand, Frank Lampard, Joe Cole and Michael Carrick. But in general terms, the emotional ties that bound the fans to the players have been loosened in the last couple of decades, an inevitable consequence of modern society and, specifically, the changes made to the framework and structure of professional football throughout the world.

The majority of West Ham's players can no longer claim to represent the local community in the way that they did years ago, any more than Liverpool players can claim to represent the people of Merseyside. The influx of foreign players has changed all that – dramatically and for ever. I can't envisage a day, for instance, when another all-English team wins the FA Cup.

As a former England footballer, proud to represent his country, I am concerned that increasing numbers of foreigners in the Premiership will inevitably diminish the value of the domestic game as a source of players for the national teams at all levels. Kevin Keegan, the former England coach, is only one of a number of national team managers to have voiced an opinion about the threat facing the international game.

In England there are more than 300 foreign players appearing regularly in the Premiership. Twenty years ago British players would have filled those places, the great majority of them qualifying to play for England. Foreign players in such large numbers inevitably hamper the progress of local youngsters trying to make the grade. If they are not getting the chance to play regular first-team football, there is little prospect for them at international level. I have nothing against the principle of foreign players but they are detrimental to the English game when they are brought here in such large numbers.

This is a serious problem for the sport's authorities who, I suspect, have been outmanoeuvred by global changes in the laws relating to the right of the individual to live and work wherever he likes. There is no easy solution and many of today's fans may not even consider it to be a problem. Could you seriously argue with Chelsea supporters, for instance, that Gianfranco Zola has been bad for the game? Zola is a wonderful player and enhanced the entertainment spectacle for all those who watched him when he was at Stamford Bridge.

You could say the same about Eric Cantona at Manchester United, Paolo Di Canio at West Ham, Jurgen Klinsmann at Tottenham or Dennis Bergkamp at Arsenal. The best of the foreign players have enhanced the status of, not just their clubs, but the Premiership in general. I have no doubt about that. Over a period of five years in the nineties, Klinsmann, Cantona, Zola, Bergkamp and David Ginola won the coveted Footballer of the Year award in successive seasons. They were recognised as the best players in the Premiership in each of those seasons and it was hard to argue with the choices made by the nation's leading football writers.

What is interesting is that each player had a creative role, either scoring or making goals. They were very important elements in the successes enjoyed by their teams. Many of the foreign players in the English game are brought here to provide the creative impetus. This means that few young English lads now get the chance to make any progress in the key positions. In recent years we have not produced players with the skill of Cantona or Zola, though I have hopes for some of England's young lions like Joe Cole, Michael Carrick, Steven Gerrard and Michael Owen. If the English youngsters are good enough they will keep out the foreign players, won't they?

The last truly creative English midfield player was probably Paul Gascoigne and we have not seen anyone remotely close to him in the last few years, with the possible exception of Joe Cole at Chelsea. To have any realistic chance of success the England manager needs players who can create in midfield. Keegan and his predecessors all complained with increasing regularity about the disappearance of this type of player.

The long-term problem concerns not just players but coaches too. The fewer English players there are, the fewer English coaches there will be in the future. That was already becoming obvious when the Football Association appointed Kevin Keegan in 1999. The former England captain was top of an FA short list of precisely one. There were no other serious English-born contenders for the job. When he suddenly resigned in the autumn of 2000, the FA insisted there were no suitably qualified English candidates, so they gave the job to a foreign coach for the first time – Sven-Goran Eriksson, the Swede who led Lazio to the *Serie A* title in Italy in 1999–2000.

I believe the game in England needs to concentrate more resources on developing home-grown players while, at the same time, keeping the best of the foreign players. Someone like Zola, for instance, is a shining example to all youngsters, whatever their nationality. I've watched him several times and have met him a couple of times and he has become a favourite of mine. It is not simply a matter of his skill, which is sublime, but his attitude on and off the field of play. Once, not so many years ago, English sportsmanship was admired throughout the world. Players such as Stanley Matthews, Bobby Charlton and Trevor Brooking were looked upon as fine, upstanding sportsmen. Professional football still has some English gentlemen, and not all foreigners are angels, but Zola, so forgiving, so sporting, so ready to smile and offer his hand to an opponent, embraces many of the virtues that were once considered the exclusive domain of the Englishman. He provided us with a wonderful example of how the game should be played and how players should conduct themselves. It's a shame he isn't English!

I know Ron Greenwood would have loved a player of Zola's skill and temperament in his West Ham team in the sixties. He often talked about introducing foreign players to the English game. I don't think he envisaged bringing players from abroad in their hundreds, but he knew that the technique of good foreigners, their close control and passing skills, would give West Ham a fresh dimension. At the time, the Football League were responsible for such matters and their regulations, combined with the immigration laws, meant that the prospect of a foreigner playing professionally in England was about as bright as a foggy night in the Blackwall Tunnel.

Nonetheless, Ron was not a man easily dissuaded and, had he had his way, he would probably have been responsible for introducing some of the first foreign players to the old Football League. I remember, for instance, his attempts to convince Alan Hardaker that West Ham should be allowed to sign Mordechai Spiegler.

Hardaker was a stubborn, diligent and enormously powerful

secretary of the League for 22 years. Spiegler, of Russian ancestry, was the captain of Israel, an attacking midfield player of perception, skill and enthusiasm – all the qualities Ron loved.

Although professional in his approach to the game, Mordechai was an amateur and Ron believed that this would overcome the residential and employment regulations. Hardaker, though, refused to register him under any circumstances. Mordechai was terribly disappointed. After training with us for some weeks, he joined Paris St Germain. Ron felt West Ham, and the English game as a whole, had missed a great opportunity.

None of those who trained with him at West Ham had any doubt that he would have become an influential figure in the old First Division. Built like Martin Peters, he had wonderful technique and boundless energy and played for Israel in the 1970 World Cup in Mexico. But in 1964, the English game had no room for Mordechai, or any other foreign players, although it was obvious to Ron that, in time, this would change.

Quite what it's like in a modern dressing-room at clubs like Arsenal, Chelsea or Liverpool is hard for me to imagine. At West Ham, there was a strong sense of loyalty between the players, club and supporters. It was, and remains to some extent, a family club in which the Pratt or Cearns families have had a boardroom connection for more than a century. Few clubs can have had a more stable background. When Ron arrived he was only the fourth – yes, fourth – manager in West Ham's history. No other club, not Manchester United, not Liverpool, not Arsenal, could match that stability. This all contributed to the atmosphere at the club. The dressing-room was a happy place most of the time and, even when we weren't winning, the fans usually went home satisfied that they had seen an entertaining game of football.

The fact that so many of the boys forcing themselves into the first team were East Enders from similar backgrounds, boys who had developed together through the youth scheme, ensured that team spirit was good. It also meant that by the time Ron introduced a youngster to the first team he was well versed in West Ham's playing style and the individual characteristics of many of his team-mates.

Much credit for this should go to one of the club's unsung heroes. Wally St Pier's long and loyal service contributed to West Ham's stability. A boy from Becontree Heath, in the suburbs of East London, he joined West Ham as a centre-half in 1929, but spent most of his career in the reserves. It wasn't until he retired from playing, after just 24 first-team matches, that he found his true vocation. The manager at the time, Charlie Paynter, appointed him as chief scout, a role he held with growing distinction for 40 years.

A large avuncular man with a powerful handshake and principles to match, Wally cultivated schoolmasters and the coaches of amateur teams and did a wonderful job 'selling' West Ham to the parents of promising young players. He even put West Ham's mediocre record to good use, claiming that it meant youngsters would have a better chance of first-team football than they would with a successful club.

Other clubs might offer illicit inducements. Wally simply offered his good name and West Ham's reputation. He played with a straight bat and his influence within the football community in London was immense.

He wasn't always successful and one or two big names escaped him. Everyone assumed, for instance, that Jimmy Greaves and Terry Venables, both great schoolboy players in the East End, would go to Upton Park when they left school. Everyone was wrong. They both went to Chelsea.

The loss of both of them irritated Wally. Years later I recall Terry Venables saying, 'Wally was like a smashing grandad. When I joined Chelsea the only thing that bothered me was that Wally would be upset.'

Wally was responsible for introducing young players to the West Ham production line. He recommended the raw material. He watched youngsters, including Bobby, Martin and me, before suggesting to the management that we be offered places on the staff. Once on the conveyor belt, others took over. I particularly remember Tom Russell, a schoolteacher from Leyton who had a part-time job as a coach at West Ham, and Bill Robinson who managed the A team that played in the old Metropolitan League.

Bill was Ted Fenton's assistant and, with Wally, was largely responsible for establishing West Ham's youth development programme. He came from Whitburn in the north east and was as hard as nails. If he pushed his trilby to the back of his head, you knew you were in trouble with him. Few will remember today but he held West Ham's post-war goalscoring record – 26 in 40 league games – until Johnny Dick surpassed him in 1957–58. He also played for Sunderland and was in Charlton Athletic's FA Cup-winning team in 1947.

Sadly, like Wally St Pier's, his contribution to West Ham's rise is largely forgotten. There is no doubt that they were significant figures in the creation of the team that won the FA Cup in 1964.

Some of us had played in the FA Youth Cup final teams of 1959 and 1963. Most importantly, we were all pals who spent much of our youth together. John Lyall, Martin Peters, Ronnie Boyce, Joe Kirkup and I often shared a pot of tea after training in Cassettari's, a family-run Italian café round the corner from Upton Park. We'd spend hours in there, talking about football with the likes of Noel Cantwell, Malcolm Allison and John Bond.

Cassettari's became *the* place for any young West Ham player who wanted to learn about the game. They did a delicious egg, bacon, chips and sausage. It would be frowned upon in the modern game but a good fry-up with bread and butter became the number one choice for most of us after a long training session. This was accompanied by pots of tea until, finally, the tables were cleared of everything except the salt and pepper pots and the sauce bottles. These were the essential props in our long discussions on tactics and strategies, usually led by the senior players. We, the pupils, listened and learned and were honoured to be involved.

Similarly, after home matches, a big group of us regularly went out together on Saturday evenings with wives and girlfriends. The favourite venue at the time was the Moby Dick, a big restaurant and pub on the Eastern Avenue running out of London towards Romford in Essex. On those occasions, too, tactics frequently dominated the evening. It's no surprise that so many of the West Ham players of that era went on to enjoy successful careers in coaching and management.

I was still at the fledgling stage with much to learn, so was happy to listen to more experienced players. The American trip that summer had filled me with fresh enthusiasm and confidence but by October it was beginning to fade a little. We had won only three of our opening 13 games and I had scored just one goal.

It was a curious period for us. We knew we were capable of playing better than our results suggested and I wondered whether the two long trips to the States had robbed some of the players of the chance to recharge their batteries during the summer break.

Ron kept faith with us. We had long dressing-room discussions. The theme was usually 'Do you believe in what we're trying to achieve?' He was convinced that if we believed in his methods and the way we were playing, the results would improve.

I wasn't really surprised when he left me out for four games and when I returned, for a home match against Everton, I scored in a 4–2 victory. Slowly I began to find some consistent form – two goals against West Bromwich Albion, another against Leicester, another against Bolton and, all the time, I was helping to create more goals for Johnny Byrne. It was our first full season together and I scored 14 goals in 37 First Division matches and he scored 24 in 33.

But the real drama that season unfolded in the FA Cup. Our form in the First Division had been no better than mediocre. When we were drawn to play at home to Charlton Athletic in the third round on 4 January we felt that a game against Second Division opposition might provide us with the tonic we needed to lift flagging spirits.

That theory was to be tested to the full because, on Boxing Day, we were beaten 8–2 at Upton Park by Blackburn Rovers. They were at the top of the First Division and included in their ranks England players Bryan Douglas, Ronnie Clayton and Fred Pickering, who scored a hat-trick. I was marked that day by Mike England, a young centre-half who went on to captain Tottenham and Wales.

It was a heavy pitch but that was no excuse. Blackburn murdered us and most of us expected to be left out of the side for the next game. In those days, the fixtures were arranged home and away over the holiday period, so two days later we travelled to Blackburn. How many would Ron drop from the team?

In the end, he decided to make only one change. He left out Martin Peters and gave his place in midfield to Eddie Bovington. Remarkably, this time we beat Blackburn 3–1 with Johnny Byrne getting two goals and me the other. Unfortunately, it was to prove a significant result for Martin.

A week later Ron announced an unchanged team for the FA Cup tie against Charlton. It was a decision that haunted Martin for the rest of that season and still irritates him today. We beat Charlton 3–0, with goals from Peter Brabrook, Johnny Sissons and myself, and Ron decided to retain an unchanged team for the fourth-round tie against our East London neighbours Leyton Orient at their Brisbane Road ground. It was a tough game that finished 1–1. The same 11 took the field for the replay at Upton Park. I scored two and Johnny Byrne the other in our 3–0 win.

Ron kept the same team throughout that Cup run. The same 11 players appeared in all seven FA Cup ties from the third round to the final at Wembley. Martin sat and watched. 'I didn't think I was the only bad player against Blackburn,' I recall him telling the rest of us one day after the team list had been pinned on the noticeboard.

At least Martin had a future in the game, unlike our friend John Lyall. He had become someone I could talk to about my football problems and so I was upset when he learned one January morning that he would never play again. John was a hard, uncompromising full-back who had played for the England youth team and, but for his injuries, may have graduated to the senior side. He had his first knee ligament operation at the age of 18 and spent most of the next three years in the reserves, in and out of hospital or on the treatment table at Upton Park. Finally, after another comeback match against the Metropolitan Police at Imber Court, his knee popped out of joint again. This time the injury was inoperable.

John was 23 years old. He had a wife, a son and a mortgage and within a few months he would probably have no income. A young professional's salary in those days didn't allow for any serious investment so an injury prematurely ending a career was a real blow. Typically, John took it all in his stride. He began coaching children at Stepney School five afternoons a week and took a part-time job in the wages department at West Ham.

I knew how painful the injury had become for John because, on several occasions, I'd been in the medical room when our physiotherapist, Bill Jenkins, was treating him. John endured some very distressing treatment for a long time. By comparison with today, a football club's medical room was primitive.

Bill Jenkins was an enormously popular figure with the players and worked for months – no, years – to get John Lyall fit. John appreciated the time and energy Bill had devoted to him and, like the rest of us, was really upset when he died of a heart attack in 1966. Bill had a special place in the hearts of Ron Greenwood and the West Ham players at the time. He was succeeded by his son, Rob, who became just as popular at Upton Park.

Bill was from the bucket and sponge era and, as a medical orderly in the army, had once saved a soldier's life by cutting his throat to bypass a blockage, enabling him to breathe. He was a man's man and he would often tell young players whom he was treating for the first time about some of his army exploits. If this was intended to help them relax, it didn't work!

Budgie Byrne lived in fear of the day he would have to be treated by Bill. Budgie teased and tormented him endlessly. Bill referred to him as 'A Pile'. It was light-hearted but Budgie could get on your nerves and Bill always told him ominously, 'For your own sake, Budgie, don't get injured.'

Strangely, Bill was the one who got injured. One night, after a game, we'd had a few drinks and, as was invariably the case, Budgie was annoying Bill as we walked back to our car. Suddenly, Bill made a lunge but Budgie was quick enough on his feet to avoid his bull-like charge. Bill missed him but stumbled forward, cutting his head on the end of a scaffolding tube. It was a bad cut, pumping blood. We held some padding to Bill's head and helped him into Budgie's car. As Budgie drove off to the hospital, I sat in the back with Bill, trying to stem the bleeding. 'Where are we going?' he demanded to know. When we told him we were going to the hospital, he replied, 'No we're not. Take me home. Connie can sew me up.'

Bill was a tough man. So, too, was John Lyall. Although he must have been terribly upset that his career had ended so suddenly, he remained defiantly optimistic. His bullish attitude was an example to all of us and made him a very popular figure around the club. He was a good friend to all of us, particularly Bobby. They used to go dancing together at the Ilford Palais in their shiny mohair suits and, if they were late, John would often stay at Bobby's parents' house in Barking.

Typically, Ron wanted to keep John involved. He knew he would have a vacancy on the coaching staff in the summer because Tom Russell was going to Uganda, so he offered John the job of youth-team coach. Eleven years later, John succeeded Ron as manager of the club.

Ron used John's traumatic experience as a motivational tool in the team-talks. He used to tell us how lucky we were compared to John Lyall. He also told us that a trip to Wembley for the FA Cup final would ensure John a bumper testimonial match at the end of the season.

By the time we travelled to Swindon Town, another Second Division side, for a fifth-round tie on 15 January we were all committed to securing a big testimonial night for John Lyall. We won 3–1. I scored two and Johnny Byrne scored the other and afterwards I can remember thinking for the first time that season that I was playing well. I felt that at last I was grasping the tactics and subtleties of the game. I was making my runs into the right place at the right time – a double triumph! I felt that I had an understanding of the role Ron Greenwood wanted me to play in the team. All the things he had taught me were coming together and beginning to make sense.

The quarter-final promised to be a difficult game. We were drawn to meet Burnley at home and Ron sent John to prepare a report on them. At the time, Burnley were one of the First Division's most accomplished teams and, two seasons earlier, had finished as runners-up in both the championship and the FA Cup. They took the lead against us through John Connelly, but Budgie had a storming game, scoring twice and setting up another for Johnny Sissons in our 3–2 win. We were now just one match away from the FA Cup final.

The other three semi-finalists were Matt Busby's mighty Manchester United and two Second Division sides – Swansea and Preston. We all hoped that we'd be drawn against one of the Second Division sides. However, we had to face Manchester United at Hillsborough on 14 March. A week before that we met them in the First Division at Upton Park. Busby, hoping not to give too much away, fielded a team with seven youngsters, and left out established players including Bobby Charlton, Denis Law, George Best, Bill Foulkes and Maurice Setters. They still beat us 2–0.

Charlton, Law, Best and the rest were back for the semi-final a week later and, as we had just been beaten by Leicester City in the semi-final of the League Cup, popular opinion suggested that we would have no more than a supporting role to play on the big day at Hillsborough.

The media at the time didn't give us a chance but Ron and John had done their homework. They conceded that United had a quality forward line but, Ron said, if we cut the supply to them we could win. The instructions were simple – deny them the time and space they needed to dictate the pattern of the game. We did just that. Our pride had been hurt and on a wet, grey afternoon we showed the nation just how good we could be. Little Johnny Sissons did an outstanding job chasing the imposing figure of Pat Crerand. Bobby Moore was immaculate and Ronnie Boyce, who only ever scored goals that really mattered, hit two, one of them almost from the halfway line.

We called Ronnie 'Ticker' because he made our midfield run like clockwork. If he played well, we all played well. He wasn't a natural athlete but he was a perceptive reader of the game, an exceptional passer and always used the ball intelligently.

I got our third and decisive goal, a gem set up by Bobby Moore from his corner of the pitch with good control in a tight situation. He carried the ball forward for some distance on a heavy pitch and then hit the perfect pass. I had seen him do something similar so many times before and he did exactly the same again in the World Cup final in 1966.

It was an epic match at Hillsborough and we won 3–1. In all the excitement immediately afterwards, the team coach left the ground for Sheffield railway station without Ron, who had been busy giving an interview to BBC radio. He caught up with the rest of the party at the station. The train ride back to London was madness that night. Ron had reserved a dining carriage for the team and officials, and we were all in the mood to celebrate. Before the train pulled out of Sheffield, our carriage was overrun with jubilant fans. The introduction of security men, who now travel with Premiership teams, was still light years away.

Nothing could diminish the sense of achievement we all shared. West Ham at Wembley! It was a big deal in the East End of London that spring. We were going to Wembley and our opponents were to be Preston North End who had beaten Swansea 2–1 at Villa Park in the other semi-final.

Ron did his homework on Preston. When the big day finally arrived we could not have been better prepared. Few of us at the time realised the poignancy of the occasion for Ron, who had worked in the stadium during his teenage years as a sign writer on the maintenance staff.

I'm sure there have been better finals before and since 1964. We were clear favourites but played poorly, especially in the first half. We gave Preston too much room in midfield and among those to profit from this was Howard Kendall, who at 17 years and 345 days became the century's youngest FA Cup finalist at the time.

We spent most of the 90 minutes chasing the game. Young Kendall set up the opening goal for Preston's crafty winger Doug Holden in the ninth minute. Johnny Sissons equalised 60 seconds later but, just before the interval, Alex Dawson scored with a powerful header to put Preston back in front.

Ron made a few tactical observations at half-time and suggested to Bobby Moore and Eddie Bovington that they push further forward. The changes worked. Soon after the restart I scored with a header that hit the underside of the bar and bounced down on the line (as usual!). It remained deadlocked at 2–2 until the last seconds of the match.

The thrilling, dramatic finale probably rescued the event as a spectacle for the fans. I remember ploughing forward, shrugging off a couple of tackles, before passing to Peter Brabrook out on the right wing. He swung over a centre that Ronnie Boyce met with his head. It was one of Ronnie's specials.

That night we had a bit of a do at the Hilton and the following morning devoured the Sunday newspapers. Preston were portrayed as the gallant losers and one paper carried a lovely photograph of Johnny Sissons leaving the pitch with a consoling arm around Howard Kendall.

John, still only 18 himself, was one of the truly outstanding young talents of that generation. He should have played for England and it remains a mystery to me why he didn't achieve his full potential. No one questioned his dedication. He worked hard at the game, had a wonderful left foot and the sort of pace that Ron Greenwood believed put him in George Best's class. Great things were expected of him but, in the end, Ron sold him to Sheffield Wednesday.

On that Sunday morning, Johnny Sissons was a hero. It seemed as though the entire East End of London was out on the streets in their Sunday best to greet our open-topped bus on the journey back to Upton Park. It was West Ham's first FA Cup final victory and I remember thinking to myself how much it mattered to the people on the pavement.

It mattered to us, too. We had made a breakthrough. No longer could we be considered simply as a team that played good-quality football. We had won the FA Cup. We had to be taken seriously. We had also qualified to play in the following season's European Cup-Winners' Cup. The challenge of European club football, still at a relatively early stage in its development, was something we all wanted to experience.

Not surprisingly, I felt satisfied with life, a situation that was further improved when I scored in a 3–1 win over Manchester United at Upton Park in the second game of the new season. Life couldn't get much better, it seemed to me, but it did.

On 13 October 1964, squeezed between a 3–0 win over Aston Villa and a 2–2 draw at Liverpool, Judith and I were married in

Chelmsford Cathedral. I sold my car, a little grey Morris 1100, to raise the deposit for our first house. We spent our first night together in a motel in Forest Gate.

All my team-mates were at the wedding and Eddie Presland was best man. Eddie was a full-back at West Ham and a very good cricketer, playing for England boys and for Essex as a professional. In fact, he was a far better cricketer than I was, but he had to go to Crystal Palace to become a regular first-team footballer. He later moved to Colchester and, encouraged by Ron, went into coaching when his playing days ended. He played a handful of first-team games for West Ham, scoring on his debut in a 2–1 win over Liverpool at Upton Park four months after my wedding. A copy of the BBC 'Match of the Day' video recording of that match is among his prized possessions.

I know from personal experience how difficult it is to score against Liverpool but four days after the wedding we drew with them at Anfield and I scored both our goals. Married life clearly agreed with me!

That season we finished ninth in the First Division, with Budgie and I sharing 42 goals, but it was the novelty of European football that appealed to us most. At the time, Bill Nicholson's Tottenham were the only English winners of any European title, having beaten Atletico Madrid 5–1 in the Cup-Winners' Cup final in Rotterdam in 1963.

Could West Ham become the second English club to win a European crown? Ron thought so. He was convinced that at our best we would be a match for anyone in Europe. He personally watched our opposition as soon as each draw was made. He prepared a little dossier for the players, telling each what to expect from their opposite number.

Our first trip, by coach, train, boat and coach again, took us to Ghent in Belgium, via Ostend. Ronnie Boyce scored our only goal in a 1–0 win over La Gantoise and an indifferent 1–1 draw at home was sufficient to put us into round two.

Sparta Prague, the pacemakers at the top of the Czech First Division, provided the opposition this time. We were without Bobby

Moore for both matches. Ron gambled with Ronnie Boyce and played him as a sweeper in both games. Ronnie was brilliant in that position, an influential figure in ensuring that we didn't concede a goal at home. We won 2–0 at Upton Park and although we lost 2–1 in Prague, we progressed to round three.

Next we played Lausanne, winning the first leg 2–1 in Switzerland with goals by Johnny Byrne and Brian Dear, a local West Ham boy who, despite a record of a goal every other game, played only sporadically in the first team. In fact, he was lucky to be playing at all that night because earlier in the day he could have drowned. He was wading through the shallow end of the hotel swimming pool when he suddenly disappeared under the water. He wasn't prepared for the steep descent into the deep end and, as a non-swimmer, he was in trouble. I was the only other person in the pool and pulled him out, spluttering and gasping for breath.

Anyway, he was on top form that night and again in the second leg at Upton Park where he scored two in a thrilling 4–3 victory. So, we were through to the semi-finals.

I had played in all our European matches but it was becoming something of a frustration because I hadn't scored a single goal. This was partly because Ron felt some tactical modification was needed if we were to adapt successfully to the different challenges. Bobby Moore, for instance, would often play the sweeper role, acting as a spare man at the back and, for our away matches, Ron preferred to play just one striker at the front. His choice for this job was Johnny Byrne. I played a withdrawn role, behind Budgie, thus reinforcing our strength in midfield. Ron also liked to have two wingers, usually Johnny Sissons and Alan Sealey, because not only did they give us width going forward but they prevented the opposing full-backs attacking on our flanks.

It was a new experience and it was working for us. In the first leg of the semi-final we beat Zaragoza of Spain 2–1 at Upton Park with Byrne and Dear scoring the goals. Dear, known as 'Stag' to all the lads in the dressing-room, was on fire, probably enjoying his best period at West Ham. A few days after this game he scored five goals in 20 minutes in a 6–1 win over West Bromwich Albion.

A week after that remarkable First Division match we took our slender 2–1 lead to Spain for the second leg of the semi-final. Zaragoza were a good, attacking team with a forward line known locally as 'The Magnificent Five'. Ron told us beforehand that chances would be few and we had to make the most of them. Zaragoza scored first but when a half-chance fell to Johnny Sissons, he took it well. A tremendous match ended 1–1, giving us a 3–2 aggregate victory and a place in a second Wembley final.

The decision to play the final at Wembley, taken earlier in the season, was obviously to our advantage. So was the fact that we had, as a squad of players, watched our opponents, TSV Munich 1860, twice that season. During the pre-season, while on tour in Europe, we had passed through Munich where Tommy Docherty's Chelsea were playing them. As we knew they were in the Cup-Winners' Cup, Ron suggested we watch them.

Then, eight months later after we had beaten Zaragoza, Munich 1860 had to meet Torino in a semi-final play-off in Zurich. Ron suggested we all go. 'It's too good an opportunity to miss,' he insisted. So we all went to Zurich, sat in the open in a violent thunderstorm and watched Munich 1860 beat the Italians 2–0. It's not often that a manager has the chance to take his team to watch the opposition in action. From the players' point of view it gave us an invaluable insight into the individual strengths and weaknesses of the team we were going to face.

The final itself was an unforgettable evening. There were several changes to the team that had won the FA Cup a year earlier. The whole right flank had changed with Joe Kirkup replacing John Bond at right-back, Martin Peters replacing Eddie Bovington at right-half and Alan Sealey selected ahead of Peter Brabrook on the right wing. Sadly, Budgie was a non-starter having injured a knee playing for England against Scotland at Wembley. His place went to Brian Dear and although we were playing at Wembley, Ron asked me to operate in a deeper role again.

It was a truly tremendous match, ranked by many as one of the best games ever played at Wembley. The Germans were well organised, defensively disciplined and technically accomplished.

But we were better and some of the football we played was magnificent.

We won with two second-half goals by Alan Sealey, who was a great striker of the ball with his right foot. His first was a thudding drive but he poached the second, the result of a free-kick routine we often tried in training. It was a goal that demonstrated the value of team play. I ran over the ball to deceive the defenders and Bobby Moore floated the free kick into the penalty area where Martin Peters, making a late run, connected perfectly. But the ball came back out off the goalkeeper and Alan was there to hit the rebound home.

Bobby had a great game that evening, so did Jack Burkett at left-back and Jim Standen in the West Ham goal. Jim saved one with his legs; a certain goal, I thought, but somehow he stopped it. He invariably did well on the big occasion. He was an accomplished goalkeeper and cricketer. He won the county championship with Worcestershire and topped the bowling averages.

The real hero, of course, was Alan Sealey. Another East Ender, from Canning Town, he was a very popular figure, known to all the players as 'Sammy' (the seal). In the end, though, he demonstrated to all of us just how fleeting fame and celebrity could be. A few weeks after the Cup-Winners' Cup triumph we were all back at our training ground at Chadwell Heath preparing for the new season. During an impromptu game of cricket Sammy tripped over a long, wooden school form while running to take a catch and broke a leg. He never fully recovered from that injury and he played only four more games for West Ham before moving to Plymouth in 1967. He played a handful of games for them and ended up with Romford in the Southern League. Sadly, Sammy died in 1996 at the age of 54 but I occasionally see his younger cousin Les, who played in goal for Coventry City, Luton Town, Manchester United and West Ham, among other clubs.

Sammy's two goals at Wembley ensured his place in West Ham folk history. You could argue that he provided Ron with the most glorious moment of his entire career. It wasn't just the result but the manner of our win that pleased him. He felt that his principles had been justified. We had shown that football, at its best, is a game of beauty and intelligence. For Ron Greenwood, it was the fulfilment of a dream. He knew that European football was the way ahead. He knew that every First Division coach would want to emulate what he and Bill Nicholson had achieved.

It took Matt Busby and Manchester United six attempts to win their first European title. It took Bill Shankly and Liverpool nine attempts. Ron Greenwood won his first European title at his first attempt.

Suddenly, the bubbles were flying high around Upton Park.

CHAPTER FIVE

Memories of Mansfield

SOME THINGS STICK IN YOUR MIND, ESPECIALLY PEOPLE AND places. I'll never forget Pele and Bobby Moore, for instance, nor Wembley, Hampden Park, the Maracana in Rio, the Azteca in Mexico City, nor the Field Mill Ground at Mansfield. The good people of Mansfield have never let me forget Field Mill. I have tried.

The style of game Ron encouraged us to play meant that we were always among the favourites for the knockout competitions. The prospect of testing our status caused great excitement if we were drawn to play a team from one of the smaller footballing communities of the Football League. In this respect Mansfield, a coalmining town on the eastern flank of the Pennines, was no different from any other small town with dreams of FA Cup glory.

Most of Ron's coaching focused on attacking football, making forward runs, sustaining an offensive momentum and creating space. We worked hard on the training ground, season after season, to devise new ways of making space. I felt that in this one particular aspect of the game we had no rivals at the time.

Our passing game was built on confidence, and when we were confident we were full of running. Our one-touch football was pure and simple and our movement off the ball ensured there was always space to move in to. But there was a downside. When we lost possession of the ball we had almost always created space for the opposition to exploit.

This was our Achilles heel. This is what made West Ham vulnerable, and unsuited to grinding out 1–0 wins or goalless draws away from home, results that form the backbone of any successful league championship bid. The football West Ham played was conducive to six-goal thrillers. The crowds appreciated the entertainment and, most of the time, the lads at the club loved to play the West Ham way.

The trouble was, lots of our opponents loved the West Ham way, too. They considered us a soft touch and I have to admit that there were times when we were muscled out of games by opponents whose values were totally different from ours. Their game plan, quite simply, was to stop us playing. It worked on several occasions and for a while we were the First Division team all the lower clubs wanted to meet in the FA Cup. Some emerged triumphant, securing a little footnote in the FA Cup record books with their giant-killing exploits.

Mansfield were among the most notable conquerors of West Ham in the days when the scalps of Moore, Hurst and Peters were highly prized. They provided the biggest FA Cup upset of season 1968–69 when they beat us 3–0 in the fifth round on a damp February day at Field Mill. At the time they were a Third Division club, just avoiding relegation that season, while we were in fourth place in the First.

Three months earlier we had beaten Bolton 7–2 in the League Cup and Sunderland 8–0 in a league match at Upton Park. I scored three against Bolton but really hit the jackpot against Sunderland with six goals, equalling the club's individual goalscoring record set by Vic Watson in 1929. At the time, the only striker to have scored more in a First Division match in the twentieth century was the legendary Arsenal centre-forward Ted Drake, who scored seven against Aston Villa in December 1935. I felt sorry for the Republic of Ireland centre-half Charlie Hurley, who was marking me that day, but by the end three or four other players had tried as well. We were playing so well at the time that few defences could have withstood our attacking momentum for long.

Even so, I have to admit that I helped the first goal in with my hand. I confessed to the media, soon after the match, and in the newspapers the next morning they made more fuss of the one I handled than the five I scored legitimately. My dad's disappointment at the coverage was so deep that he actually ticked me off for being honest.

'To score six goals was a hell of an achievement,' he said. 'But the papers made more of the fact that you handled the ball. That's what you get for being honest with them!'

Early in the New Year, we cruised through the first two rounds of the FA Cup against Bristol City and Huddersfield. I remember the Bristol City tie particularly because it coincided with the opening of the new East Terrace, replacing the old chicken run.

Originally we were drawn to visit Mansfield on 8 February, but the winter weather was so severe that day that the entire FA Cup programme was postponed, plus all but four league matches. The game was re-arranged for 19 February and this too was postponed. After one further postponement we finally played on 26 February by which time, I suspect, Mansfield were desperate to test themselves against the big shots from London. A crowd of 21,117 squeezed into their little Field Mill ground in Quarry Lane to make life as uncomfortable as possible for the strolling players from Upton Park.

We had all our star names in action including three big-money signings Ron had made to strengthen our defence. These were Scotland's Bobby Ferguson, whose £65,000 fee was a record for a goalkeeper, Billy Bonds, who played at right-back, and Alan Stephenson, who played at centre-half. Moore, Hurst and Peters were also on the teamsheet along with the emerging Trevor Brooking and two wingers, John Sissons and Harry Redknapp. On our day we would have beaten anyone, but it was not our day.

Mansfield chased and harried and knocked us out of our stride. In those days, too, pitches often cut up badly in mid-winter and this didn't suit our passing game. Dudley Roberts, Ray Keeley and

Dominic Sharkey scored the goals and we returned to London with our tails between our legs.

There were other moments of bitter Cup disappointment and recrimination – Rotherham, Swindon, Huddersfield and Blackpool spring to mind – but West Ham's defeat at Mansfield is the one of which I am most often reminded. It's amazing how many Mansfield fans there are in the country. Whenever I meet them they remind me of that game and, without exception, they were all there in Quarry Lane that day – or so they tell me. There must have been about 150,000 in the ground to witness the downfall of the Hammers.

This is all part of the tradition of the FA Cup and well worth preserving in my opinion. I think the FA Cup has a special place within the fabric of our sporting heritage largely because there is always the chance that the little team will overcome the odds and beat the big team. This is the romance of the FA Cup and explains why there have been so many imitators since the inauguration of the competition in 1871–72. It's a fact that people like to see the mighty humbled. Can you imagine the reaction had Wycombe Wanderers knocked Liverpool, the eventual winners, out of the 2001 FA Cup in the semi-finals? Their progress captured the imagination of all football fans. You could sense the nation-wide disappointment when Liverpool beat them 2–1 at Villa Park. The Second Division club still deserved an enormous pat on the back because they earned a place of honour in the history of FA Cup giant-killing with victories over Leicester City, from the Premiership, and Wimbledon and Wolves from the old First Division.

West Ham may have suffered more than other big clubs in this respect but the fact is that in Mansfield, for instance, that defeat of more than 30 years ago is still spoken about. This is part of football's folklore. It helps keep the game vibrant and, in that respect, is good for the sport's long-term health.

I didn't look upon it in that way at the time, of course. It annoyed me that some people thought we were pushovers. We worked as hard as anyone, both in matches and on the training ground, but most of our effort went into the skills of the game. Ron was a purist with high ideals. He encouraged us to enjoy the game.

I think, deep down, most of us realised that we were never likely to win the league championship, something Ron conceded publicly only after he stepped down as West Ham's manager. I accepted that was the reality of the situation. I was happy with that because I loved playing for West Ham. Initially, most of my team-mates felt the same, but I think a time came when Martin, for instance, felt that he would have to move to another club if he was to have any chance of winning the major prizes in club football.

From time to time we registered an outstanding victory that provoked a lot of soul-searching among the players. 'Why can't we play like this every week?' was a familiar complaint from within the dressing-room. One of our most memorable triumphs came in the League Cup – again not the League – in November 1966. West Ham won 7–0. Remarkably, our victims that day were Leeds United, one of the great club sides of the era.

We had already brushed past Tottenham and Arsenal – I scored twice in a 3–1 win at Highbury – when Don Revie's mighty team came to Upton Park on a chilly autumn evening for a fourth-round tie. Revie's squad read like a Who's Who of international football. It included Billy Bremner, Johnny Giles, Peter Lorimer, Eddie Gray, Jack Charlton, Terry Cooper, Paul Madeley, Paul Reaney and Norman Hunter.

Like Ron Greenwood, Revie had devoted much time and energy to developing his team through the youth ranks at Elland Road. Unlike Ron, he favoured a more cynical tactical approach to the game and would turn a blind eye to the kind of physical excesses that Ron abhorred. Nonetheless, it would be churlish of me not to acknowledge that, when they put their mind to it, Leeds United were one of the most talented teams in Europe.

This made our victory all the more astonishing. We were in a world-beating mood that night and in the opening minute the Leeds goalkeeper David Harvey had to make good saves from Johnny Byrne and Ken Brown. Within two minutes the first goal went in from Johnny Sissons, who completed a hat-trick inside 35 minutes.

Budgie Byrne played one of the greatest games of his career that night and had a part in all of my three goals. Leeds made the mistake of marking me with a full-back called Willie Bell, who shortly afterwards moved to Leicester City. I remember thinking back to the World Cup final when another full-back, Horst Hottges, similarly unfamiliar with shadowing a central striker, had tried to mark me.

Perhaps Martin Peters scored the best goal on that memorable night. He dribbled past two defenders before driving a thudding right-foot shot beyond the disconsolate Harvey.

I heard later from Jack Charlton that Revie kept his players up until the early hours of the morning discussing the biggest defeat of his managerial career. Leeds were not used to losing, and certainly not by seven goals.

The ill-feeling that took root at Upton Park that night lingered for years. Leeds showed us no mercy in the following seasons and we didn't beat them again until 1971–72 when, in the last days of my West Ham career, we knocked them out of the League Cup.

Years later, when Revie was the England manager, he visited Ron at Upton Park. 'Remember that night you beat us 7–0?' said Revie. 'I went into your dressing-room and congratulated you and all you could say to me was, "Thank you very much." I found your attitude hurtful and went back to our dressing-room and told the players, "You'll never lose to that man's team again."'

Five days after the 7–0 win over Leeds we went to White Hart Lane and, with Tottenham playing a full part in a spectacular contest, produced one of the great First Division games of the sixties. Like us, Spurs at the time valued their reputation as entertainers. Bill Nicholson's wonderful team included Jimmy Greaves, Alan Gilzean, Cliff Jones, Dave Mackay, Mike England, Alan Mullery and Pat Jennings.

It was an epic, enthralling match, locked at 3–3 until 13 minutes from the end when Sissons and Peter Brabrook combined to provide me with a headed goal. We won 4–3, and more than 57,000 people filed out of the ground at the end having witnessed a stirring, memorable game.

Such occasions inevitably sharpened the appetites of some of my team-mates who perhaps believed that their own careers would be enhanced by a move to a bigger club with a more realistic chance of the major honours. I never felt that way.

When you're playing for a team that can score seven one day and four the next it's really quite good fun. When job satisfaction is that high, why should you want to play for anyone else? I think most of us were quite happy to play for Ron and observe the beliefs that he cherished.

Just think about this for a moment. West Ham's team play at this time was so good that for a period in the autumn of 1966 I was scoring at the rate of nearly two goals a game. In a run of 14 first-team fixtures I scored 22 goals. Ironically, I just couldn't find the net in the next game at Chelsea – a 5–5 draw!

Goals were the hard currency of my career and I realised that the secret was to score them at a consistent rate – easier said than done. In that season of 1967–68, I scored a couple more in a 3–1 win at Blackpool in the fifth round of the League Cup and then, for no obvious reason, the flow began to slow.

That is always a concern to a player whose prime job is to score goals. But I consoled myself with the thought that I was more than merely a goalscorer. I had learned the game and now appreciated the value of team play. I knew that, if I didn't score, I could still make a substantial contribution during the course of 90 minutes by holding the ball, drawing team-mates into the play and creating space and opportunities for others.

Kenny Dalglish was perhaps the best exponent of this art. A prolific marksman with Celtic, Liverpool and Scotland, his all-round play was such that, even when he wasn't scoring, his value to the team was beyond price.

We lost seven of our last eight First Division games that season – I didn't score in any of them – but what really hurt was the League Cup semi-final defeat by West Bromwich Albion. They'd beaten us in the final the previous season and this time took a 4–0 lead in the first leg at the Hawthorns. The 2–2 draw in the second leg at Upton Park was little consolation for missing the first League Cup final to be played at Wembley. For Bobby and I, a place in the final would have meant a fourth consecutive Wembley appearance, each in a different competition.

It was at the end of this season that Ron, perhaps against his better judgement, decided that he needed a tougher presence in the heart of the West Ham defence. Ken Brown had moved to Torquay and Ron bought an uncompromising Scottish centre-half, John Cushley, from Celtic for £25,000.

John was enormously likeable, but he was as tough as old boots and tackled as ferociously as any defender. It was becoming an increasingly aggressive game and I think Ron initially felt that we had to have a more intimidating presence alongside Bobby Moore in the heart of the defence. That feeling didn't last for long, though. I think John was reprimanded once or twice for over-zealous tackling. Ron's intention was always to create rather than destroy and I wasn't surprised when John returned to Scotland to play for Dunfermline after 46 first-team games.

It's a fact that all successful teams have one or two hard-edged individuals, but that particular era produced a cast list of hundreds of seriously tough competitors whose chief, and sometimes only, function was to prevent the opposition from playing. Ron wanted no part in these roughhouse tactics, nor did he appreciate those who did employ them. He taught us that there were finer values in football than winning simply for the sake of winning. It might be hard to preach such a gospel in the modern game but I believe he was right.

Winning is important, and was no less so when I was playing, but the spirit in which the game is played is important, too. In the sixties and seventies, Ron felt that many coaches and players ignored the finer values. In fact, the values established in those days were part of the sport's evolution and inevitably influenced the climate and structure of the modern game.

In a sense, the football played by Revie's Leeds United epitomised many of the problems of the time. Their success, or lack of it, was bewildering. Under Revie they finished runners-up in the First Division five times and out of four FA Cup finals won once. The harder they tried, the more painful the failure. They could play great football, but relied too often on their physical commitment and defensive discipline. Their disciplinary record was appalling and I can say from personal experience that they had some of the hardest players of that era. Johnny Giles was an exceptionally talented midfield player but an acknowledged expert in some of the game's darker tactics. Other notable exponents of these questionable tactics were Billy Bremner, Allan Clarke and Norman Hunter.

The genuinely tough guy in that Leeds team was Jack Charlton, who marked me on many occasions. His job was to stop opponents playing and although he was as hard as nails he was fair. If your health was a matter of some interest, Jack wasn't the one you'd be most concerned about when you played Leeds. There were others you'd worry about first. Jack always conceded that he was a hard player but it was his opinion that Leeds United's fearsome reputation was based largely on the tackling of Johnny Giles, rather than himself, Bremner, Clarke or Hunter.

In those days, football was full of players who were not quick, mobile or technically proficient, but they could tackle. The laws of the game still allowed tackling from behind and this, of course, allowed heavyweight defenders to win the ball in a way they couldn't today.

People complain these days about violent or ungentlemanly conduct on the field of play but changes to the laws have outlawed many of the questionable practices that I had to contend with as a striker. In my opinion, the game was physically more demanding when I played and what was accepted as an everyday challenge, all part of a man's game, would today attract an immediate yellow card from the referee.

In my twenties I was strong and sharp and had the build of a light heavyweight. I needed the bulk to withstand some of the challenges that came my way every Saturday afternoon. Without those physical attributes I wouldn't have had a 17-year playing career with West Ham, Stoke and West Bromwich Albion. I also learned to distinguish between the challenge that I could win and the challenge that was going to cause me some damage. I didn't pull out of much but you do learn to recognise the tackle that is going to hurt you more than your opponent.

It also helped to be aware of exactly where you were on the pitch and the consequences of winning or losing a tackle. For a striker like me, for instance, losing a tackle in the centre circle was of far less significance than winning a tackle in the opposition's penalty area. When the ball was in our opponent's penalty box, I was expected to challenge for it whatever the risks. This I did, of course, but I have to admit that there were times in the centre circle when I wasn't averse to getting out of the way. I was never naïve enough to go into a tackle I knew I had no chance of winning. It was no good to my team or me if I was carried off on a stretcher and put in hospital for a month.

That didn't happen but I had my share of injuries, which was probably the inevitable consequence of playing against some of the toughest footballers of the last 50 years. Among these I would include Ron Yeats, Tommy Smith, Maurice Setters, Gerry Byrne, Ronnie Harris, Johnny Giles, Vic Mobley, John McGrath, George Curtis and Peter Storey. This is not intended to be a rogue's gallery, merely a personal recollection of some of the toughest defenders I played against. They made my life difficult; if asked, they would probably say the same about me.

Although defenders were a rougher breed they weren't as sly as some are today. There was far less of the cheating, shirt-pulling, play-acting and feigning injury that so annoys me about the modern game. It should be a joy to play today, especially for the forwards who are the main beneficiaries of the rule changes designed to encourage attacking football. The rule changes have particularly benefited the many foreign players who like to hold the ball, something they couldn't have done so easily years ago.

I would have loved playing in the modern game but I suspect many of my old adversaries might have struggled. Stripped of many of their weapons by the rule changes, I think many old-time defenders would have failed to cope with the pace and movement of the modern game. Some, though, would have adapted successfully. As intimidating as they were at times, I had great respect for most of the defenders who marked me. I hope the feeling was mutual.

One defender I actually looked forward to meeting each season was Chelsea's Ronnie Harris. My former England team-mate Peter Osgood always reckoned that his club captain at Chelsea was the hardest player he'd ever met. Ron was affectionately known to the Stamford Bridge fans as 'Chopper' Harris. But confidants such as Ossie and the other Chelsea players at the time always referred to him as 'Buller'. I knew why they called him Chopper, but never discovered the origin of Buller. Although he wasn't the First Division's most intimidating physical specimen, Chopper tackled like a runaway train.

I can still recall the crunching sound as he deflected Johnny Ayris into the sixth row at Upton Park on a sunny autumn day in 1971. John was a lightweight winger from Wapping, just 18 at the time. He'd played a handful of first-team games and, after his collision with Buller, played just a handful more before joining Wimbledon on a free transfer.

Jimmy Greaves didn't like playing against Buller either. He invariably found himself marked out of the game whenever he faced Chelsea and Buller was the man responsible. I always played well against him and often scored. But I didn't call him Buller or Chopper. I called him Sir!

CHAPTER SIX

The three of us

ON NEW YEAR'S DAY 1966 BOBBY MOORE, MARTIN PETERS AND I played in the West Ham team that lost 3–0 to Nottingham Forest in a First Division match at Upton Park. We had won just six games in the opening half of the season and Martin and I had never played for England. The World Cup final was more than six months away and, over dinner after that Forest defeat, Martin and I discussed possible holiday destinations in the summer. The World Cup? Forget it!

Bobby, of course, would be involved. He was already long established as the England captain with 35 international caps to his credit. Martin and I assumed that when West Ham's season ended in May we would be free to do what most footballers did during the summer months in those days – very little.

The three of us – Moore, Hurst and Peters – were already friends but the events of the six months that followed bound us together in a way that remains unique in the history of British sport. The public assumption is, and always has been, that we three were the very best of friends. That was never the case. We were team-mates, pals who spent a lot of time together, but I don't think you could say we were best friends.

Bobby Moore didn't have 'best' friends. He had plenty of mates and, at the height of his fame, more hangers-on than any other footballer I've known. But he was, essentially, a private man. He wasn't shy, but he kept himself to himself. Some people mistakenly thought he was aloof. He wasn't that either, but he'd rarely confide in you. If he bought a new sweater or a new pair of shoes it just wouldn't occur to him to tell anyone. Why should it? He simply assumed that no one else would be interested in the trivia of his everyday life.

After matches, Martin or I or one of the other lads would often invite him out to dinner. 'I'm not sure,' he'd reply. 'I've made provisional arrangements.' Within his circle of friends he was famous for his 'provisional arrangements'. I was with him on one occasion when Terry Venables said, 'Tell me, Mooro, what exactly are these provisional arrangements?'

'I'm not sure,' he replied.

What cannot be disputed is that Bobby Moore was a star, and not simply in the football context. The late sixties were the golden age of English football and Mooro was the golden boy. He was a sporting hero, an incomparable stylist, graceful and gracious both on and off the pitch. He carried out the match ball, resting on his hip, with the kind of panache that no other captain could manage.

His appeal extended beyond the playing field and the training ground. At a time when television was just beginning to beam the world into everyone's living room, Bobby's fame and success elevated him to international celebrity status. Whatever his broader appeal, there is no doubt that he was one of the most significant figures in English sport in the last century.

He was eight months older than me and joined West Ham a year before I did, but in terms of the pecking order at the club he was light years ahead of me. I'd only just established myself in the first team when he was playing for England alongside the likes of Johnny Haynes, Jimmy Greaves, Jimmy Armfield and Bryan Douglas in the World Cup finals in Chile in 1962.

The fan mail the players received reflected their status quite accurately. The staff at the training ground used to lay out three piles of letters for the players. The biggest pile was for Bobby Moore. The second biggest pile was for Budgie Byrne. The third was for the rest of us.

My couple of letters a week invariably used to say, 'Dear Geoff, You were brilliant on Saturday. D'you think you could get me Bobby Moore's autograph and send it back in the envelope provided?'

Bobby was 21 when he made his England debut and, once in the team, he was determined to stay. His determination was awesome. People talk about his composure, but it was an iron will that underpinned his whole career and helped him enormously in the last, difficult years of his life.

I remember how impressed I'd been with this blond-haired youngster from Barking when I first started training at West Ham. When we were doing exercises to strengthen the stomach muscles we had to lie on our backs, raise our legs in the air and hold them there. Try it yourself. If you are not used to it you will quickly discover how painful this can be. Of the 50 or so players doing this exercise the last to lower his legs was Bobby Moore. Always. His will power was tremendous, and when he was dropped from the first team to make way for me his pride was bruised. I knew that I wouldn't keep him out of the side for long.

Initially, Bobby, Martin and I were all rivals for midfield places. Bobby was the regular left-half, wearing the No. 6 shirt, when Ted Fenton's reign as manager ended in March 1961. Phil Woosnam, one of the senior players, was asked to select the team and he immediately dropped Bobby and gave his No. 6 shirt to me. I played two games before Ron Greenwood took over as manager and he immediately reinstated Bobby at left-half. Ron had worked with him in the England Youth and Under-23 teams and told Bobby that he thought he could build the team around him. Perhaps Ron's masterstroke was moving Bobby from left-half to the centre of the defence.

Of the three of us, I think Ron realised that Martin was the most naturally gifted footballer. He was versatile enough to play anywhere and he did. In my time at West Ham, he wore all 11 shirts – yes, even goalkeeper. He was given the No. 3 shirt in his third match for

West Ham at Cardiff in April 1962, but ended up in goal. Our goalkeeper that day was Brian Rhodes, who was making a rare first-team appearance because Lawrie Leslie was injured. Brian, who sadly died of leukaemia in New Zealand at the age of 55, dislocated his collarbone after an hour of the match at Ninian Park and was replaced by Martin. Despite his heroics, we lost 3–0.

In those days, Martin was a tall, lithe athlete who made everything look easy. All the big clubs wanted him when he was a schoolboy, but he was a real East Londoner and Wally St Pier, our scout, talked the same language.

Martin's versatility would have been the answer to any manager's prayer although the fans didn't always appreciate him. I think, too, that he sometimes feared that his ability to play anywhere would, in the end, deny him a regular first-team place in his best position. But just what constituted his best position, no one knew for sure.

Even so, Martin was a regular first-team player until that 8–2 defeat by Blackburn Rovers on Boxing Day 1963. Ron dropped him and brought in Eddie Bovington, a more functional midfield player. Eddie kept Martin out of the side and played in the FA Cup final five months later. When Martin complained that he was being overlooked, Ron told him, 'You'll be back and you'll play at Wembley one day.'

Martin voiced his fears of being considered a general dogsbody. 'What is my best position?' he asked, and Ron said he would work out a solution for the new season. This was, basically, to give Martin a free role, behind the strikers, playing wide when he chose to. It was a job only a player of Martin's quality could do and as a result he became a member of the World Cup-winning team of 1966 and one of the most accomplished players of his era.

Like me, Martin noticed the way in which Bobby dedicated himself to improving his game. After most of the other players had finished working, he was still out on the pitch at our old training ground at Grange Farm in Chigwell. He was usually first to arrive and last to leave. Martin and I followed his example.

Malcolm Allison, who spent eight years in West Ham's first team before beginning his spectacular coaching career, had a considerable influence on Bobby in his early days at Upton Park. Along with Noel Cantwell and John Bond, Malcolm was one of the senior players who used to coach local kids on two evenings a week. I wonder how many of today's Premiership stars would give up two evenings a week to work with youngsters on the training pitch.

Among the East London boys taking advantage of the Allison–Bond–Cantwell teach-in every week was the 12-year-old Moore. Malcolm, himself a central defender, saw in Bobby a youngster of enormous potential and took him under his wing. I remember Bobby telling me that the best piece of advice he ever received came from Malcolm. What he told him was simplicity itself – know where you are going to play the ball before you receive it. Bobby treated this as though it was one of his personal Ten Commandments. Watch film of him playing and you will see that he almost always knew where he was going to play the ball before it arrived at his feet. This ability to think swiftly disguised a lack of natural pace but was also one of the essential components in the making of the greatest defender in the world at that time, and arguably of all-time.

One of his other great qualities was his ability to learn, to store information and recognise what was useful to him and what wasn't. He grasped tactics and strategies quicker than I did. He could read situations on the pitch quicker than I could and, most importantly, he knew how to respond. It was his willingness to accept responsibility that made him a natural leader and captain.

Composure? I think he was born with that. Nothing ruffled him. The bigger the game, the bigger the occasion, the brighter he shone. I can remember him at 16 or 17 dribbling the ball out of his own penalty area without a care in the world.

Remember Wembley in 1966? Only seconds remain of extra time, the Germans are surging forward for an equaliser, and everyone is screaming at him to kick the ball out of the ground. Not Bobby! He dribbled the ball around in the penalty area, waiting for the right moment to carry it upfield before passing to me.

They said that he couldn't run, but he was rarely beaten to the ball. They said that he couldn't jump, but he was rarely beaten in the air. He recognised that he was deficient in some areas and compensated by working hard on the training pitch and focusing on his positional play.

He read the game better than any other defender I've seen and this enabled him to become the master at intercepting the through ball, whether it was in the air or on the ground. He read the flight of the ball, anticipated its destination, intercepted it en route and played a pass to a team-mate while the man he was marking was still stuck at stage one of the process. Trying to sneak the ball past Mooro was as futile as trying to sneak the sunrise past a rooster.

In the years we were together he became a wonderful ambassador for the nation. His behaviour on and off the pitch was impeccable. I think he realised that people looked up to him and, for this reason, he took his responsibilities seriously.

On the pitch he possessed an unobtrusive authority and an immaculate sense of style and timing, qualities that he carried throughout his life to every corner of the world. He was fussy about standards. He was always the tidiest guy in the dressing-room. He folded his clothes neatly. You could imagine him going home to wash and iron his boot laces so that they were spotless for the next match.

I shared a room with him on England trips abroad. Every night, on his side table, he had a glass of water, his loose change and his handkerchief. It never changed. In his wardrobe at home, all his suits, shirts and shoes were colour co-ordinated.

I remember talking to the England and Manchester City winger Mike Summerbee in the players' bar after a match at Maine Road. Bobby walked in. Whenever he walked into a room, voices lowered and people looked. You could hear them whispering, 'Look, it's Bobby Moore.' It was no different on this occasion. Bobby got out a wad of pound notes. They were neatly folded and as he peeled off a couple to pay for the drinks, Summerbee cried, 'Look at Mooro. He's the only player I know who irons his money!'

Dedicated as he was to his profession, Bobby liked to socialise and enjoy himself, but on his terms. There were plenty of people in those days who wanted to be seen in his company, and Bobby was always polite, but he was most at ease with his own people from

London's East End. He liked lively characters, not those who were in awe of him. He roomed with Frank Lampard for eight years and they became firm friends. He also enjoyed the company of other West Ham club-mates – Johnny Byrne, Brian Dear, John Charles, Harry Redknapp and Jimmy Greaves. They all seemed to share his wicked sense of humour.

I remember, on more than one occasion, Bobby as England captain, walking along the line of players before the kick-off at Wembley introducing FA dignitaries and guests to the team. 'And this is Roger Hunt,' he'd say as they came up to Jimmy Greaves. He'd wink as you shook hands with the guest and he always kept a straight face. A lot of the people he was introducing didn't have a clue who we were anyway.

Very few people ever disturbed Bobby's famous cool exterior. An exception was Frank Sinatra. On one of West Ham's trips to America he and I bought $100 tickets, a lot of money at the time, to see one of Frank Sinatra's farewell concerts in Los Angeles. He loved Sinatra, not just his music but the whole demeanour of the man. He was a class act and a great professional, much like Bobby. After the show we were taken backstage and introduced to Sinatra. Bobby was speechless. 'I've never been so nervous,' he said afterwards.

Frank Lampard was only a kid, seven years younger than I was, when Bobby took him under his wing. An outstanding young player, he was unchallenged as West Ham's left-back for 16 seasons. Frank was perhaps as close as anyone to Mooro and still recalls, quite vividly, the day Bobby welcomed him as an official, fully paid-up member of the first-team squad. By then he was 19 and had just played his fourth game for the club – a 4–2 win at Leicester in December 1967. He was sitting alone in the players' carriage as we travelled back to London. Bobby, sitting at a table for four, had a spare seat opposite him. He was an imposing figure in a crisp Savile Row suit with the double shirt cuffs thrust forward to reveal the cufflinks. His arms were resting on the table with a can of lager in one hand. With the other hand he beckoned Frank to join him. Frank sat down and Bobby handed him a can of lager.

'Where d'you come from, Frank?' he asked.

'East Ham,' Frank replied.

'Good,' said Bobby. 'You played well today.'

In a few short sentences Bobby put young Frank at ease and made a friend for life. Even today, nearly nine years after Bobby died, Frank will still walk into a nice restaurant with his wife Pat and say, 'Mooro would've loved this place, wouldn't he?'

Bobby appreciated good food, good clothes, good football, good music and although he had some showbusiness friends he never lost sight of his East London roots. He had one or two favoured pubs where the locals let him sit quietly in a corner. One Christmas he was in just such a pub, sitting on a stool with a turkey on the bar in front of him. It was the turkey West Ham traditionally gave to all their players at Christmas. Bobby had not gone home from training and his wife, Tina, waiting to stuff the turkey, had called our house to see if he was with us. Tina then called Bobby's mum, Dot, who said, 'I bet I know where he is.' Dot went straight to the pub where the captain of England was sitting with the family's Christmas turkey.

'Get home with that turkey now,' she told him, much to the amusement of the locals.

'Leave off, Mum,' said Bobby, sheepishly. 'I'm nearly 30 now you know.'

Tina and Judith remain good friends and talk regularly, although Tina now lives in Florida. She and Bobby divorced in 1986. It was sad because we had spent a lot of time together as a foursome.

As a youngster without a car, struggling to establish myself in the West Ham first team, I was grateful for the kindness he showed Judith and me. He and Tina would sometimes pick us up from the station at Ilford. At the end of the evening he'd take us back to the station in his big Jaguar and we'd get the train home to Chelmsford.

When Judith and I started socialising with the Moores they had a sophisticated circle of friends and we felt a bit like country bumpkins, living out in rural Essex. There were times, I must admit, when I used to say that I was a friend of Bobby Moore's just to get a table in a restaurant. It had a magical effect. I remember going out with Bobby and Kenny Lynch one night to a club in London. Bobby and

I were gestured into the club but Kenny, who was following us later, was stopped at the door.

'Members only,' said the doorman.

'But . . . but,' stuttered Kenny, 'I'm with Bobby Moore.'

'Why didn't you say so?' said the doorman, standing back to let him in.

Any youngster, breaking into the first team, held him in awe. Harry Redknapp always referred to him as 'God'. Even today, as the manager of West Ham, he says, 'God would never have done it like that.'

We all showed him the respect he deserved and I think this may have embarrassed him at times. He didn't like people to think of him as anything special. Martin always addressed him, somewhat tongue in cheek, as 'Robert'.

If we got a pat on the back from him it was a moment to treasure. Compliments were unusual. It was rare, too, to see him waste energy by running to congratulate a goalscorer. As the rest of us jumped up and down he returned to his starting position to await the kick-off.

Professionally, there was a very strong bond between us and while I had a huge respect for him as a person and player, I was never sure that he felt the same way about me – or anyone else for that matter. He never said much about anything so when he did it counted. He never shouted much on the field, but when he did you listened. He rarely said 'well done' but when he did you remembered.

In September 1967 we beat Sunderland 5–1 in front of a 40,000 crowd at Roker Park. It was one of those days when I couldn't put a foot wrong. I scored two and made one for Harry Redknapp and one for Martin Peters. Bobby scored the other. I was in the dressing-room afterwards soaking in the bath, feeling pleased with myself, when Bobby sauntered over. 'You were brilliant today,' he said without breaking his stride. A compliment! From Mooro! I've never forgotten it.

Bobby spent 16 years in West Ham's first team. He was in the side before Martin and I and still there when we left. In total he played 642 first-team games for the club, a record at the time, since surpassed by Frank Lampard and Billy Bonds. During that period, a West

Ham team without Bobby Moore was inconceivable. But the day came when Ron Greenwood decided he could do without him. He had already turned down one cheeky attempt by Brian Clough to sign Bobby and Trevor Brooking but, by the spring of 1974, I knew that the relationship between the manager and his most famous player was strained.

You could trace the beginning of the end back about three years. Ron had felt betrayed and let down by Bobby's role in the notorious Blackpool nightclub affair. Although it had happened in 1971, the ill-feeling between the two lingered. Bobby had left the team hotel for a drink in a Blackpool nightclub with Jimmy Greaves, Brian Dear, Clyde Best and the club physiotherapist Rob Jenkins the night before a third-round FA Cup tie at Bloomfield Road. I was sharing a room with Brian Dear that night and he asked me to go out with them but I declined. The fact that we lost 4–0 the following afternoon upset Ron but he was raging by the Monday morning when the newspapers were telling him that four of his players had been out drinking the night before the game. Ron wanted to sack all four but the board of directors persuaded him that fines and suspensions would be sufficient.

Brian Dear left the club within weeks of the incident and later played for Woodford Town before becoming a publican. Jimmy Greaves retired at the end of the season. Clyde Best was just 19 and, happily, learned from the incident. He spent a further five years at the club, making 218 first-team appearances.

Ron took great pride in and professional satisfaction from Bobby's development. He had worked with him in the England Youth team; he had helped shape his understanding of the game; he had an unshakeable belief in Bobby's ability and would never hear a word said against him. Ron was thrilled when Bobby became the youngest winner of the Footballer of the Year award in 1964 and particularly admired the mature way in which he handled the ridiculous allegation about a stolen bracelet in Bogota just before the 1970 World Cup. In short, Ron Greenwood was Bobby Moore's number one fan. Imagine how let down he must have felt when he learned that his captain, his flag bearer on the pitch, had taken team-mates drinking the night before an FA Cup tie.

Their relationship was never the same again. Ron found Bobby increasingly detached and said years later that he thought he was ignoring him in team-talks. Ron used to say that he could talk about Bobby Moore, the footballer, for hours. 'But ask me about Bobby Moore, the man, and I'll dry up in a minute,' he concluded.

Although I'd left West Ham by 1974, I kept in touch with Bobby and other friends and sensed that it was all coming to an undignified end. Bobby's last game in the first team was against those legendary FA Cup fighters Hereford in a third-round tie at Upton Park in January 1974. Hereford had been in the Football League for just two years but they held West Ham to a 1–1 draw. Bobby wasn't picked for the replay, which was probably a blessing because Hereford won 2–1. A month later West Ham announced that he was for sale.

Alan Mullery, Bobby's former England team-mate, persuaded him to join Fulham where the manager Alec Stock was establishing a retirement home for former international players. Fulham later signed George Best, Rodney Marsh and Peter Storey.

Bobby thought he deserved a free transfer as a reward for his outstanding service, but West Ham wanted a fee. They negotiated a good deal for him. Fulham paid £50,000, a bargain even in those days, with Bobby keeping £25,000 of that for himself. He began repaying them immediately. His Second Division debut for Fulham, against Middlesbrough, attracted an attendance of 18,114. The crowd at the previous home game was 6,731.

Despite his differences with Ron towards the end of his career at West Ham, Bobby was nonetheless the last of us to leave Upton Park. Martin went first, in March 1970. I joined Stoke City in an £80,000 deal in August 1972.

Martin's transfer to Tottenham valued him at £200,000, a record at the time, in an exchange deal that took Jimmy Greaves to West Ham. I think the prospect of playing alongside Bobby appealed enormously to Jimmy. He was a great pal and, at one time, the finest goalscorer in the world. But he scored only 13 goals in 40 appearances for West Ham before deciding to retire, so it's not hard to see who got the best of that exchange deal.

Martin flourished at Spurs as we all knew he would. Although none of us talked about it, there was rivalry among the three of us. Martin was the youngest and, by nature, the quietest and probably felt it most keenly. He felt there was a pecking order, and he knew he wasn't top of it. I don't know if that was the public perception but usually when the three of us are mentioned together it's as 'Moore, Hurst and Peters'.

Born in Plaistow, a Dagenham schoolboy, no one could question Martin's roots. He was perfect material for West Ham's youth academy. It became obvious very quickly that no one could question his football ability either. He was a natural at everything, a good athlete and cricketer, and although softly spoken and unassuming, he was harder than most people thought. Never afraid to put his foot in, I didn't once see him intimidated or pull out of a tackle. Sir Alf Ramsey was reluctant to select him for England at first but, in the end, famously acclaimed him as a player 'ten years ahead of his time'.

Alf's initial reservations were based on what he felt was a serious weakness in Martin's game – an inability to head the ball. I never quite understood why he felt this way because Martin was, without doubt, the best header of the ball at West Ham. Alf became a great judge of a player, but in the case of Martin's heading ability he was woefully off target.

Alf came to appreciate Martin's stealth and persistence. He'd make 19 runs into the penalty box and no one would notice. But when he made the 20th they all noticed because the ball was in the back of the net and no one really understood how it got there.

Ron Greenwood often described him as a continental-style player and always insisted that he would be a sensation playing abroad. In those days few understood what he meant, or what Alf meant when he claimed that Martin was ahead of his time. I think both meant that the man in the street didn't fully appreciate the contribution Martin made during the course of a match. That was probably true. Martin won major trophies with West Ham and Tottenham but I believe that he wasn't truly revered by the fans until he went to Norwich where he spent five happy years.

In his nine years in the West Ham first team, he played 364 games and scored 100 goals, a remarkable ratio for a midfield player.

His international record was equally impressive – 20 goals in 67 England appearances.

We had an uncanny understanding on the pitch and I was sorry when he left to join Tottenham, but I understood his reasoning. I think he felt he needed a change. It wasn't simply a matter of improving his chances of winning the major prizes. He wanted to better himself and, at that time, I think he felt he had more chance of doing that under Bill Nicholson at Tottenham. Some said that he wanted to get out of the shadow of Moore and Hurst. I really don't think that was the case.

He had nothing to prove, certainly not to Bobby and me. We're good friends and long after our playing careers ended we were still working together, for the same insurance company in Harrow, Middlesex. Judith and Kathy Peters have been friends since their teenage years and Martin and I frequently blame our wives for the size of our telephone bills.

It's remarkable that three young players should develop at the same club and together play such a pivotal role in England's only success in the World Cup. We were a unit within a unit. We were family if you like and, as with any family, we had little traditions that were unknown to outsiders. Both Bobby and Martin, for instance, liked to be last to pull on their shorts in the dressing-room before kick-off. In the last minutes in the Wembley dressing-room before walking out for the World Cup final I chuckled to myself as I watched the pair of them desperate to comply with their super-stition on the biggest day of their lives. Martin, having pulled his shorts on, noticed that Bobby slyly took his off so that he could pull them on again. As we left the dressing-room to go into the tunnel, Bobby put his shorts on, and Martin suddenly took his off. Bobby, at the front, kept looking back to make sure Martin hadn't taken his shorts off again. I'm convinced this ritual unsettled the bewildered Germans and therefore contributed to our ultimate victory!

Martin may feel that the spotlight has focused on Bobby and me since 1966 but his place in the history of the game is secure. After all, only two English players have scored goals in the World Cup final and he's one of them.

His after-dinner speaking routine contains an inescapable truth hidden in a moment of wry humour – 'Geoff Hurst is revered all over the world for his three goals in the final. But if I hadn't scored the second we'd have lost 2–1.'

Few people can fully understand how the relationship between Bobby, Martin and me worked and evolved over the years, but most will understand how we felt when Bobby died of bowel cancer in February 1993. It is a disease that claims 20,000 lives a year, the second highest cancer killer in the UK.

Martin and I had known that he had a problem since November 1964 when he went into hospital for a course of treatment that was never fully explained. He missed three months of the season but made a complete recovery and we thought no more of it.

In 1991, he became ill again. I went to visit him in hospital after one particularly bad operation for suspected cancer of the colon, but the doctors wouldn't let me see him. That year, having been divorced from Tina for five years, he married Stephanie.

He still lived life to the full, regularly attending football matches as a commentator for Capital Gold Radio in London. I saw him from time to time and realised he was seriously ill. He knew he was dying and although Tina had told Judith, she didn't tell me.

I was enormously impressed with the way he dealt with his illness. His self-control and dignity in the final months of his life were an example to us all. He attended his last match as a commentator on 17 February 1993. It was at Wembley – England 6 San Marino 0. That result would have pleased him.

He died a week later. There was a profound sense of national loss. Tributes arrived from all over the world, but the loss was felt most at West Ham where his friends, the club's fans and the people of East London left their flowers, scarves and messages piled at the tall iron gates in honour of a legend.

CHAPTER SEVEN

How we won
the Cup

I've been asked many times to explain why Bobby Moore, Martin Peters and I remained loyal to West Ham when, at the height of our fame and earning potential, each of us could have moved to bigger clubs.

I think part of the answer is to be found in the rapport we all had with Sir Alf Ramsey and the commitment we felt to the three lions on the England badge. Representing our country provided each of us with a sense of satisfaction that club football simply couldn't match. Until Martin felt the need to spread his wings and move to Tottenham in 1970, the three of us happily devoted each working day to West Ham. We knew the league title was beyond us and we tailored our club ambitions accordingly. A place in the top six in the old First Division was an achievement. We realised that far greater rewards were available if we moved but, unlike today's England players, Bobby, Martin and I didn't have to move to one of the big glamour clubs to satisfy any hunger for recognition beyond Upton Park. Playing for England fulfilled all our wider ambitions.

In those days wearing an England shirt elevated you to a new status within the game. Almost overnight it raised your public profile, enhanced your value on the transfer market and significantly increased your earning potential. Most players secured a big pay rise once they were established at international level. You were made to feel that you were one of the sport's élite. I don't think it's the same in the modern game. Playing international football today should be just as much an honour, but I suspect that the call to represent England isn't valued as highly as it was years ago. For a professional 30 years ago, winning an England cap was not just an enormous privilege, but also opened the door to richer pastures. Today's players are rich long before they play at international level. Fame, along with fortune, is no longer dependent on achievement.

Some of the modern game's most famous personalities have achieved nothing on the playing field. Notoriety off the field can bring the fame and financial rewards that my generation could earn only by their success on the field. Stan Collymore is a classic example of an underachiever with a big reputation. He had one outstanding season at Nottingham Forest and has scored the occasional spectacular goal, but what else has he done to justify his profile and the huge transfer fees paid for his services? He has a huge reputation based on what? It's certainly not an international career that consisted of three England appearances, two as substitute, in three years.

A lot of players in the modern game will end up as millionaires, even though they may have failed to fulfil their potential, and I'm sure Stan is one of them. A few months ago, when I told Judith than Stan Collymore had just announced his decision to retire she replied, 'Retire? From what?'

In common with most other underachievers, Stan will get little sympathy from the football public. He didn't make the most of the innumerable good opportunities that came his way. How long did he stay at any of his clubs? The amazing thing is that clubs still wanted to sign him after his 60-match sojourn – costing £8.5 million – came to an end at Liverpool. He wasn't a Premiership player in my opinion. He was best suited at Southend.

Collymore was not alone in being ridiculously overvalued. How could Nicolas Anelka possibly be worth the £23 million Real Madrid paid for him? He had one outstanding season at Arsenal thanks chiefly to the creative work of Dennis Bergkamp. How long did he stay at Real before moving on to Paris St Germain?

Duncan Ferguson is another striker who, for me, has never justified a big reputation and there are plenty arriving from foreign fields who are happy to give little and take much. You can't blame the players. It's the clubs that set the agenda.

I was happy playing for England and I was happy to accept the benefits that came with the honour of representing my country. I would have loved a league championship medal, but missing out was no big deal. Only a small percentage are fortunate enough to win one – a much smaller percentage are fortunate enough to win the World Cup.

I'm not demeaning the value of the league championship. Winning that would have been one of the great achievements of my career and had West Ham sold me to Manchester United in 1968 it may have been a reality for me. I never knew about the offer but I had no burning desire to leave West Ham anyway, and they had no desire to sell me. I've never regretted staying at the club for 15 years because, for much of that time, I was involved in football on an altogether higher, more challenging, level than was played by most other clubs.

There is only one World Cup – 'the big one' as Alan Ball has always referred to it – and only one group of players in England has been good enough to win it. I remain inordinately proud to be part of that élite group. Had we not experienced the satisfaction of rising successfully to the sport's greatest challenge, and then lived with the hope of repeating the feat in Mexico four years later, the desire for trophies at club level may have tempted us away from West Ham.

For the best part of a decade I happily served two masters, giving them equal commitment and loyalty, Ron Greenwood with West Ham and Sir Alf Ramsey with England. It wasn't difficult. There was no question of divided loyalties. Playing for West Ham enriched my England career, and playing for England enriched my West Ham career.

I first met Alf at Paddington railway station on a damp autumn afternoon in 1964. He had picked me for the England Under-23 squad. He was travelling to Wrexham with the players for a game against Wales. A stocky, impassive figure, he made an immediate impression on me. Throughout the trip to Wrexham he was asking questions. 'Tell me, Geoff, how d'you find playing against so-and-so?' He noted your answers, listened to your conversations, and you suspected that all this information was being stored for future use.

I'm told that he was a 'thoughtful' full-back with Tottenham and England and that was why, in his playing days, he was known as 'The General'. It was clear to me that he was going to be just as thoughtful as manager of England.

I remember wondering on that train journey to Wales how much thought he had put into his famous prediction a year earlier. His reign as manager had started lamentably with defeats by France (5–2) and Scotland (2–1), but then England beat Czechoslovakia, East Germany and Switzerland on an end-of-season tour in 1963 and Alf proclaimed, 'We will win the World Cup.' He had said this with confidence. There were no conditions. 'We have the players, the ability, the strength, the character and the temperament to win the title in 1966,' he insisted.

It was typical of Alf's patriotism, but in some quarters his statement was considered outrageously optimistic. The championship-winning manager of little Ipswich was, some said, a one-hit wonder whose team was struggling for First Division survival when the Lancaster Gate hierarchy appointed him manager. He wasn't even their first choice. That distinction belonged to the Burnley manager Jimmy Adamson, who turned the job down. Alf accepted on condition that he alone would pick the team. Until this time, team selection was the responsibility of a committee.

Alf wanted the England team to be his creation and not a patchwork gathering of players determined by favouritism, parochialism and a show of hands by the blazered committee men of the FA. It does seem absurd now that the England team was selected by committee in those days. Alf wanted his hands on the tiller. He wanted players he knew and players he could rely on. He wasn't too concerned about their club form. What concerned him was how they played for England. He did make it clear to us, though, that he would pick us only if we were playing first-team football at club level. You knew that if you were injured, dropped by your club because of loss of form or in dispute with your club you were unlikely to be called up by Alf.

By the time I met him that day on Paddington station, Alf's power was absolute. He was a strict disciplinarian with the players, but rarely unreasonable. He had standards and if you failed to observe them, you weren't invited to join the squad a second time.

His bold prediction was thrown in his face whenever England slipped up, although defeats were becoming increasingly rare. His confidence began to seep into every corner of the game and by the time 1966 arrived the nation believed that England had a team good enough to sustain a genuine challenge. No England coach since Alf has had the confidence to repeat his prophecy and, in the modern game, it's difficult to imagine anyone making such a bold declaration of intent. Optimism doesn't exist on that scale today. Alf's optimism was based on a realistic assessment of the resources he had available.

Some of his more recent successors have resorted to tub-thumping and flag-waving but this has produced totally unrealistic levels of expectation among the fans. In a sense, I admire Glenn Hoddle and Kevin Keegan. Whatever they genuinely believed in private, they talked up England's chances in public knowing full well that failure would bring the ridicule of the lord high executioners from the tabloid media.

After previous World Cup disappointments, Alf raised the level of expectancy in the mid-sixties, but in those days we had players capable of responding to the challenge. Alf's belief was unshakeable. He transferred this confidence to his players. He made you believe you were an outstanding player. As a young newcomer, I was enormously impressed by his quiet conviction. He seemed to know something that the rest of the world didn't.

England beat Wales 3–2 in that Under-23 international in Wrexham. Disappointingly, I wasn't selected to play. Martin Chivers, then with Southampton, was picked ahead of me and responded with a goal. Chelsea's Bobby Tambling scored the other two.

I was awarded a total of four Under-23 caps, but I didn't meet Alf again until he called me into the senior squad for the first time early in 1966 for a friendly against Poland. It was a crisp, frosty January morning when I heard the news. It was a moment I've never forgotten.

On this particular morning, because of the icy condition of our normal training pitches, Ron Greenwood took us to work on the indoor roller-skating rink at Forest Gate. We were playing five-a-side football when Ron called me over to join him.

'I've just had a message from the FA,' he said. 'You've been put in the squad for the game against Poland.'

I was flabbergasted. Despite making the Under-23s, I never dreamed that I'd play for England. My West Ham career was progressing nicely but at no time did I believe that I'd be called into Alf's senior squad.

'Remember,' said Ron with an optimistic smile, 'the World Cup is just six months away.'

I felt lucky and privileged to be involved and the fact that I wasn't selected to play didn't dampen my elation. Goodison Park, one of the World Cup stadia, was used as a dress rehearsal for the tournament and I travelled to Liverpool by train with Alf and several London-based players. Bobby Moore, who had been travelling the world with Alf for three years, was on the train with George Cohen of Fulham and Arsenal's Joe Baker and George Eastham. What surprised me slightly was the manner in which the players accepted Alf's authority. The atmosphere was comfortable, but even Bobby seemed on his guard in Alf's presence. This, I came to realise, was how it was in public places. In private, Alf was happier to be considered one of the lads.

This was all part of the learning process for any newcomers to the squad. Initially, it was all a little intimidating. I was in élite company and was careful not to say anything out of place. Although I had played against most of the lads in Alf's squad, Bobby was the only friend. I knew Nobby Stiles from the England Youth side. We'd played in Romania together. I also knew Alan Ball from the Under-23 squad, but otherwise they were all strangers to me. For the well-being of the squad, Alf expected all his players to get along socially.

On the first day of training I remember thinking to myself, 'Am I going to be good enough? Will the others take the mickey? Will I get on with the coaching staff?'

Alf decided to work on set pieces and wanted a couple of players to help him demonstrate a point he was making about free kicks. He looked at the crowd of players around him and began calling out names. I instinctively took a step backwards, anxious not to be selected on my first morning. Alf spotted me. He said nothing at the time but later in the training session, when no other players were near, he said to me quite firmly, 'I've got no use for blushing violets. I've picked you for what I know you can do. It's now up to you.'

It was only a small incident but it did a lot for my confidence. It made me realise that I had to have a positive attitude both on and off the pitch. It also demonstrated to me that Alf had belief in my ability. That, more than anything else, convinced me that I was good enough to play for England. One of Alf's secrets was his ability to make players believe in themselves.

I later learned that Alf chose his moment to preach the same message to all the youngsters he selected. We were all given much the same lecture – 'You are here for one reason only. That is because you are a good player and I believe you are good enough to play for your country. You are not here to prove anything to anyone. You will not be asked to do anything for me that you don't do every week for your club.'

The gospel according to Alf set the tone and laid the ground rules for the squad of players he was gathering around him for the World Cup. It was plain to see in the 1–1 draw with Poland – Bobby Moore's goal was his first for England – that he already had the hard core in place. The back four had been in place for at least a year.

Gordon Banks, George Cohen, Ray Wilson, Jack Charlton, Bobby Moore, Nobby Stiles, Alan Ball and Roger Hunt all played that day. Bobby Charlton, normally the first name on the teamsheet, was absent because of injury.

A month later I was called up again. West Germany were the opposition, Wembley the venue. This time I was in Alf's starting line-up, unaware of course that the Germans would play such a significant role in my international career.

The World Cup tournament was less than five months away when I made my senior debut for England. I needed no one to tell me that it was my big moment. I had to make a positive impression. As it turned out, of the 11 Alf selected against the Germans that night only Keith Newton and Norman Hunter did not play in the World Cup.

My own contribution was nothing special. The best I can say is that I made no serious mistakes. It was a match of indifferent quality with Nobby Stiles, curiously wearing the No. 9 shirt, scoring the only goal. The Wembley fans were clearly unhappy with us at the end but I remember Alf saying in the dressing-room afterwards, 'That lot will be cheering their heads off if we get the same result against the Germans in the final.'

But had I done enough? I felt a bit like a bandsman who had been given the music for last week's concert. I did all the things I had been doing for West Ham – just as Alf insisted – but either the ball came too late or it didn't come at all. I covered miles of that turf, but I was out of step with the rest of them, or were they out of step with me?

Would I get another chance? The answer came a month later when I was in the squad to play Scotland at Hampden Park. Alf kept me in the team and when I scored England's opening goal with a right-foot shot from the edge of the penalty area, I learned for the first time what it felt like to silence 134,000 screaming Scots. Wonderful!

This time I was calling for the ball, demanding it, in fact, and getting it early which is what I was used to at West Ham. It was a thrilling match that we eventually won 4–3. Nobby Stiles, the goalscorer against the Germans a few weeks earlier, produced heroics at the other end of the field this time. His header off the line in the dying moments of the game denied the Scots an equaliser.

I think my goal and my whole performance registered positively with Alf. He liked solid, undemonstrative characters who would not be intimidated by a hostile atmosphere. Being a good player was not, in itself, enough for Alf. He also looked for the personalities who would maintain dressing-room harmony and enhance team spirit. Disruptive individuals were quickly weeded out.

To be fair, though, most of the players who fell by the wayside in those early months of 1966 were left out simply because Alf couldn't accommodate them all in his final squad of 22. He had an enormously talented pool of players from whom to choose and originally named a provisional World Cup party of 40. This was reduced to 27 by the time we went to our World Cup training headquarters at Lilleshall. Here the intention of every player was to ensure that they were one of the 22 Alf would name as his squad for World Cup duty. Every time a new tactic was introduced in training you could sense everyone trying to judge whether this increased or decreased their chances of a place in the squad. I convinced myself at least six times that I was in the squad. Just as often I went to bed depressed because I was certain that I was out.

Eventually, when the time came, after the friendly against Yugoslavia in May, Alf took the five unlucky players aside, one at a time, and explained to them why they would not be in his squad. It was desperately disappointing for the five who were so close – Johnny Byrne, Bobby Tambling, Keith Newton, Gordon Milne and Peter Thompson.

Throughout the build-up period, and into the tournament itself, Alf mixed and matched his tactics and personnel. The backbone of the side had been in place for nearly a year but he remained unconvinced about the use of wingers.

In his days at Ipswich he had shown remarkable tactical skill in leading a club from the obscurity of the Third Division to the league title in five years by organising limited resources well. He was about to show the same resourcefulness as England manager. Although no one questioned the quality of England's players at the time, Alf realised that in one area we were lacking high-class performers. He believed that the wingers in his squad might not be good enough for the challenge ahead. Thus he created his radical 'wingless wonders'. Although committed originally to wingers, he abandoned this traditional concept in favour of a 4–3–3 system which, ultimately, was modified to a 4–4–2. The point was that both systems functioned efficiently without two orthodox wingers, relying instead on sound team play and hard work.

Alf played the Southampton winger Terry Paine in the next warm-up match against Yugoslavia at Wembley in May and, significantly, introduced Martin Peters for the first time. Martin could play anywhere but it was his ability to control the left flank and cross the ball early that was to prove so critical in the weeks ahead.

We beat Yugoslavia 2–0. I played at the front alongside Jimmy Greaves. Jimmy and Bobby Charlton scored the goals. I still wasn't sure whether I'd get a place in the World Cup squad, but what helped my case was the growing realisation among the back players that it helped them to have me at the front as an outlet. When under pressure, defenders could resort to the high ball forward and my ability to win the ball in the air gave them this option. I always remember Ray Wilson saying that, as a full-back, he appreciated it when I played because he could use the long ball and know that there was a good chance England would retain possession. He felt less confident about the long ball forward when Jimmy and Roger played together.

When Alf finally named his squad of 22, I'd played three games for England and scored just that one goal at Hampden Park. I was honoured to be involved, and relieved. We reported for training at Lilleshall, the vast, imposing country estate in Shropshire that had once been the home of the Duke of Sutherland. It was a wonderful place to prepare for the World Cup.

Over a period of 18 days of intensive training, we were allowed a drink on just one evening. There were plenty of 'Stalag Lilleshall' jokes, but when a whisper reached Alf of the formation of an 'escape committee' he wasn't happy. He called us together one morning and said, 'I just want you to know that if anyone even thinks about popping out for a pint they'll be finished with me and this squad.' That was the end of the 'breaking out' jokes. We were together for nearly two months – the period at Lilleshall, a two-week European tour and the tournament itself – and we were allowed just one other evening off the leash, after a 6–1 win over Norway in Oslo.

The competition for places in the team was so intense that when

Nobby's pregnant wife Kay suggested he come home for the birth he replied, 'Pardon? Are you joking?' Nobby knew that if he left, even with Alf's blessing, he could have returned to find that his place in the pecking order had gone to another player.

We may have joked about it, but no one abused Alf's trust. We had some strong characters in the squad, none stronger than Jack Charlton. He wanted to be part of any 'escape committee' if it carried the promise of a drink at the end of the tunnel. But even Jack, later to become the successful manager of the Republic of Ireland, observed the rules. He tried Alf's patience from time to time. It was a battle of wills between two strong men. There was mutual respect, but they didn't speak to each other often and any time Jack addressed Alf the answer was invariably the same, 'No.'

This suggests to me that Alf didn't need to like a player to work with him. What was important was that they respected each other. I remember the legendary Jock Stein once saying of his great Celtic side, 'There's half in my team I wouldn't have dinner with, but I wouldn't drop any of them.'

At 10.30 each evening Alf walked into the TV lounge where the players spent most of their time after dinner. 'Good night, gentlemen,' he used to say. That was enough. Very often we'd be at the critical stage of a movie, but everyone got up and went to their rooms. I missed the ending of *Butch Cassidy and the Sundance Kid* three times during Alf's reign as England manager. It wasn't until 1990 that I realised they got shot!

Occasionally you'd hear Alf, his assistant Les Cocker or the physiotherapist Harold Shepherdson walking along the corridors outside the players' bedrooms. Sometimes they'd knock and ask if you wanted any plasters or bandages for the morning training session, or they'd ask if you wanted a sleeping pill. We knew that the real reason for the nightly tour was to check that we were all in our rooms.

Alf's staff was meagre compared with the huge entourage that accompanies the England squad today. He and Les took the training sessions, assisted at Lilleshall by the former Manchester United and England half-back Wilf McGuinness, who briefly followed Sir Matt Busby as manager at Old Trafford. Apart from 'Shep', the physio, the only other member of staff with whom we had regular contact was Dr Alan Bass, an immensely likeable Harley Street consultant and Arsenal's team doctor. He was known as 'Alfie' after a TV actor of the time.

Alf Ramsey was the common denominator, the cement that bound us all together. He was all-powerful and one of the things that made his job possible was the willingness with which we all accepted his authority. I'm not sure that the national coach today could wield the same, unquestioned authority.

Consider this. One day shortly before the tournament, each player was issued with the official England suit, in heavy, grey flannel, totally unsuitable for the time of year. Had we asked for a lightweight suit Alf would almost certainly have refused. Along with each suit we were given the FA's enamel badge which we were to attach to the lapel. The suit was just about acceptable, but with the badge in the lapel you looked like a school prefect.

On formal occasions, Alf would say to the players, 'Suits, if you please, gentlemen.' The first time that we had to wear the suit I decided not to wear my badge. The first person I should meet would have to be Alf.

'Geoffrey, where's your badge?' he asked. 'You're improperly dressed.'

'Sorry, Alf,' I said. 'I think I've lost it.'

'Not to worry, Geoffrey,' he said. Without a flicker of expression, he reached into his pocket, pulled out a handful of badges and pinned one to my lapel. 'Now don't lose that one,' he said.

So, suited, booted and fully badged, we flew to Helsinki for the first of four warm-up internationals. I partnered Roger Hunt, his Liverpool team-mate Ian Callaghan played as a single winger and, surprisingly, Leeds United defender Norman Hunter was preferred to Bobby Moore. There had been some speculation that Bobby's place was under threat from the less talented but far more aggressive Hunter. Norman was a good player, with an outstanding left foot, but I couldn't envisage Alf starting the World Cup without his captain.

England beat Finland 3–0 and three days later faced Norway in

Oslo. Alf left me out of the side and played Jimmy Greaves and Roger Hunt together. He had 22 players in his squad and I understood, as did everyone else, that the manager wanted to explore all his tactical options. Jimmy scored four goals in a 6–1 win. Bobby Moore was back in the side, too, scoring a rare goal in response to the speculation.

I returned alongside Jimmy for the game against Denmark in Copenhagen. We won 2–0 but I knew I hadn't played well. It was no surprise when I was left out of the side for the final dress rehearsal against Poland in the coal-mining city of Katowice.

England won a tough game 1–0 with Roger scoring the goal. He and Jimmy led the attack and I guessed that they'd probably be in the starting line-up for the opening World Cup game against Uruguay. I wasn't complaining. I was still a novice at this level, just happy to be part of it all.

We returned to London in buoyant good humour. I don't think we quite shared Alf's conviction about the outcome of the tournament, but we all knew that at the very least England would be difficult to beat. We were conceding few goals at the time and our away record suggested that we had one of the best-organised defences in the world.

In the 14 away games prior to the World Cup we had lost just once – to Argentina – which to my way of thinking renders ridiculous the theory that England won the World Cup only because we played at Wembley. The truth of the matter was that we were a far better team in away matches.

Alf allowed us to return to our families for two days before reassembling on the Friday to prepare for the opening game on Monday, 11 July. He said later that his decision to let the players rest and relax for two days was one of the most important he made during England's preparations.

It was a relief to unwind for a couple of days at home with Judith because as soon as we returned we were thrust straight back into a boot-camp routine. This time we were staying at the Hendon Hall Hotel in North London, not too far from Wembley Stadium. My room-mate was Martin Peters. In the build-up period, Alf had insisted that players change rooms frequently to (a) get to know your team-mates and (b) avoid the creation of cliques. I think some England coaches have had problems with cliques in recent years but there was no evidence of this during my seven years with the England squad.

As hosts, England were highly fancied to do well. We were considered efficient rather than inspired. Brazil, winners in Sweden in 1958 and Chile in 1962, were inevitably ranked among the favourites along with Argentina and West Germany.

The great players? Well, you would have to include Pele, Tostao, Gerson and Garrincha of Brazil, even though they failed to get past the group stage; Portugal's Eusebio, Coluna and Torres; Hungary's Albert and Bene; Germany's Emmerich, Overath and Seeler; and the legendary Russian goalkeeper Lev Yashin.

You couldn't ignore the quality of some of England's players. We had, in my opinion, five world-class performers in that 22-man squad – Gordon Banks, Bobby Moore, Ray Wilson, Bobby Charlton and Jimmy Greaves. How long is it since England have had five world-class players in the same side?

All the indications in the build-up were that Greaves and Hunt would start the opening match together, and that is what happened. I wasn't disappointed to be left out. I sat behind Alf at Wembley in my grey flannel suit, proud and happy to be involved. I'd have laughed six months earlier had someone suggested that I'd be sitting behind Alf Ramsey as part of the England squad when the World Cup kicked off. I tried to keep the whole experience in perspective and was quite content to sit and watch and hope that I might get a chance to play.

It was a typical opening game – dour, unimaginative with few risks taken by either side. Tension gnawed at all the players. England, as the host nation, were under pressure. The Uruguayans were determined not to be beaten. They defended in depth, marking Greaves and Bobby Charlton out of the match. It wasn't much of a spectacle and, not surprisingly, a difficult match ended 0–0.

Next day, rather than allow us to fret over the newspaper criticism,

Alf took us all in our grey uniforms to Pinewood Studios where we met Sean Connery and Yul Brynner. I always thought this was a clever move by Alf. He didn't want any sense of disappointment taking root in the camp after the opening game. He wanted to keep the mood light.

At the studios we watched them shoot a scene from the latest James Bond movie. During the course of filming, Connery came into view. Alf, who wasn't the brightest bulb in the chandelier when it came to naming pop singers and movie stars, said in a hushed voice, 'Look, lads, it's Sean Connery!' He pronounced Sean as 'seen'. Typical of his mischievous nature, Bobby Moore put his arm around Alf and with his eyes raised towards heaven said, 'Now I've shorn everything.'

For the next four days I worked hard in training in the hope that I might get into the team to play Mexico. I didn't. Alf stayed loyal to Jimmy and Roger, but I was delighted for Martin Peters. He was called into the side wide on the left with a solitary winger, Terry Paine, on the right flank. Terry replaced John Connelly, the Manchester United winger who had played against Uruguay. England looked a more cohesive force in this game, winning 2–0, thanks largely to a stupendous performance from Bobby Charlton.

Bobby scored a spectacular goal, picking the ball up in his own half and running forward with it before shooting from 30 yards. It was the moment that set the World Cup alight. It lifted everyone and made us believe that we were going to have a real say in the outcome of the tournament. He set up the second goal with a through ball to Greaves whose shot rebounded for Roger Hunt to score from close range.

Bobby was one of the game's great two-footed players. No one seemed to know for sure which was his stronger foot. I think he was best with his right foot, but his brother Jack believed his left foot was his best. In the end, it didn't really matter. I wish England had a player of his quality today.

France, who had drawn with Mexico and lost to Uruguay, needed to beat England in the final group game to reach the quarter-finals. But they lost their most influential player, Robert Herbin, with an early injury and were furious when Roger Hunt scored in the 37th minute from what looked like an offside position.

As we all celebrated Roger's opening goal, Jacques Simon lay dazed by an ugly challenge from Nobby Stiles. He later admitted it was a bad tackle, but claimed he had timed it wrongly. I was again left out of the side and so was not among those castigated by Alf when we returned to the Hendon Hall Hotel that night.

He accused the lads of being complacent, excusing only the hard-working Hunt who had scored both goals in a 2–0 win. The match was significant, too, for the injury to Jimmy Greaves and the last appearance in an England shirt in that tournament of an orthodox winger. Talented Liverpool winger Ian Callaghan made way for the return of Alan Ball. Alf knew we would need Alan's competitive spirit and work rate against Argentina in the quarter-finals. He particularly wanted him to block the forward runs of the Argentine left-back Silvio Marzolini.

In the opening three games, Alf had used three different line-ups. In the first game against Uruguay he played Ball on the right side of midfield with the winger Connelly on the left; against Mexico he played Martin Peters on the left side of midfield with another winger, Terry Paine, on the right flank; and against the French he introduced a third winger, Callaghan, on the right flank with Martin retaining his place on the left side of midfield.

What next? Alf had tried three wingers but none of them featured when he named his side to play Argentina. For the first time he played two midfield players in the wide positions – Ball on the right and Peters on the left. The wingers were abandoned.

In a sense, he felt he had the best of both worlds with Martin and Alan. They were competitive, worked hard, defended diligently and when the time was right Martin, particularly, could cross the ball as well as any winger. What's more, he could cross the ball early, as he'd been taught at West Ham.

This may have been in the back of Alf's mind when he told me I would be in the side against Argentina because Jimmy's gashed leg wouldn't heal in time. It was desperately bad news for Jim but when I telephoned Judith with the news I couldn't conceal my delight.

Undoubtedly talented, Argentina had a reputation as a cynical and provocative team. The quarter-final was potentially an explosive affair but that, in my opinion, didn't excuse the FA's intervention in Alf's selection policy.

The day before the match the FA asked Alf to drop Nobby Stiles from the team because of his tackle on Simon. They thought he would be a liability in what was likely to be a turbulent clash with Argentina. Alf had already questioned Nobby about the tackle on the Frenchman. 'Did you mean it?' he asked. Nobby said, 'No. It was an accident.' Loyal to his players as always, Alf accepted Nobby's version and refused to withdraw him from the team. 'If Stiles goes, I go,' he said. The FA backed down and Nobby remained in the team.

That wasn't quite the end of the episode. The next day, Les Cocker and Harold Shepherdson pinned Nobby to a wall in the dressing-room. 'Alf's stuck his neck out for you,' they said. 'Don't let him down.'

As it happened, Nobby did a great job man-marking Ermindo Onega, but from the opening series of fouls it was clear that Argentina intended to kick their way to the semi-finals. The German referee Rudolf Kreitlein tried to impose some order and at one time, according to the distinguished football writer Brian Glanville, was 'inscribing names in his notebook with the zeal of a schoolboy collecting engine numbers'.

Nine minutes before half-time the Argentine captain Antonio Rattin, objecting to the booking of a team-mate, was sent off for 'violence of the tongue'. He had a formidable reputation and Ray Wilson called him 'The Rat'.

The 6ft 3in Rattin, towering over Kreitlein, refused to go. For eight minutes he argued with the referee, FIFA officials, policemen and the chief of the World Cup referees Ken Aston, a tall, distinguished schoolmaster from Ilford. Finally, with great reluctance, Rattin left the pitch. The remaining ten Argentinians held out remarkably well until 12 minutes from time when a goal straight from the West Ham coaching manual ended their resistance.

Peters, out on the left, collected a pass from Ray Wilson. His cross curled in early to the near post. I knew where it would go and was running to meet it before the Argentine defence could react. I met the ball with a glancing header. It was a classic West Ham goal, my second for England, and it secured a place in the semi-finals of the World Cup.

It was chaotic at the end. The police had to protect the referee from angry Argentinian players and Alf tried to stop us exchanging shirts with them. They all wanted to fight afterwards and threw a chair through our dressing-room door.

'Send them in,' cried Jack Charlton. 'Send them in! I'll fight them all!' Nobby and Ballie were standing behind Jack echoing his words. 'Yes, let them in.'

Alf, so angered by Argentina's tactics and tackling, described them afterwards as 'animals', a remark that was to haunt him for years. It was sad that such a sporting event should provoke a furious row between the European and South American nations. At one point the South American countries threatened to pull out of FIFA because of what they claimed was a European conspiracy. On the day we beat Argentina, Uruguay were beaten 4–0 by West Germany and had two players sent off by Jim Finney, an English referee.

Three days after the unedifying spectacle against Argentina, England faced Portugal at Wembley in what turned out to be one of the finest games in the tournament. The Portuguese had a brilliant team, built around the incomparable Eusebio, who had been their saviour against North Korea in the quarter-final at Goodison Park. Astonishingly three goals down to the unknown North Koreans, Eusebio inspired the Portuguese fight-back, scoring four goals in their eventual 5–3 win. Alf chose Nobby to shadow him and that turned out to be a tactical masterstroke because Nobby had a great game.

Alf, in fact, retained the team that had beaten Argentina. This meant I lined up again alongside Roger Hunt. It was a wonderful game, played in a generous spirit with plenty of open, attacking football and good sportsmanship from both teams. No foul was committed until the 23rd minute.

Having knocked out Brazil, Portugal were considered the new

favourites, and played like potential champions, until Bobby Charlton struck – twice. It was one of his best performances in an England shirt and I'm pleased to say that I had a hand in his second goal. I collected a pass from George Cohen, turned in the box and rolled the ball into Bobby's path. He did the rest with his usual clinical efficiency. From a personal point of view, it was a relief to leave the field feeling satisfied with my contribution over the 90 minutes. I had not played well on the pre-World Cup tour but felt that my form returned against Portugal.

Near the end of the match, as Portugal bombarded our goal, Jack Charlton was forced to punch away a header from Torres that had beaten Gordon Banks. Eusebio scored from the penalty spot but we survived a tense final few minutes. As I walked off at the end, I remember looking up at the great scoreboard above the Wembley terraces showing the scoreline England 2 Portugal 1.

As you can imagine, I felt quite pleased with myself. Having struggled to get in the side initially, I scored the winning goal against Argentina and set up the winner for Bobby Charlton against Portugal. Life couldn't get much better for a footballer.

England had reached the final of the World Cup. It was an emotional moment. One or two of the lads shed a tear. When we got back to the dressing-room an ecstatic Jack Charlton cried out in a loud voice, 'We can have a drink tonight, Alf, can't we?'

Alf said, 'No.'

He was close to fulfilling his prophecy. He would allow nothing to get in the way.

CHAPTER EIGHT

A winning team

THE IMAGE OF BOBBY MOORE HOLDING ALOFT THE WORLD CUP at Wembley is etched indelibly in the minds of generations of football fans. At the end of England's epic win, Bobby climbed the 39 steps to the royal box to accept the golden Jules Rimet Trophy from the Queen. She was wearing white gloves and, typically, he wiped the mud from his hands on the velvet drapes of the balustrade before greeting her. I followed him up the steps and over the years I've seen the same piece of film dozens of times. It's part of the folklore of the game and the TV record of that memorable day safeguards for future generations Bobby's role in one of the greatest moments in English sport. The photograph of him carried aloft on the shoulders of jubilant team-mates as he clutches the trophy is perhaps the most enduring, and certainly the most poignant, image of England's finest hour.

History could have recorded a very different chapter in the Bobby Moore story. None of us at the time realised just how close he was to losing his place in the team. Bobby was England's greatest captain, much admired by Sir Alf Ramsey, but it now seems that at one point the manager contemplated the unthinkable – dropping his captain from the World Cup final team.

I wasn't aware that Alf had thought this way until many years later when a group of the 1966 team met at a reunion party some time after Bobby had died. We were talking about old times and how Alf preferred to keep his cards close to his chest in matters of team selection. George Cohen recalled an incident in the cloistered seclusion of the Hendon Hall Hotel in the immediate aftermath of the semi-final win over Portugal. Purely by chance, he overheard snatches of a conversation between Alf and the only two men he confided in – his coach Les Cocker and his physiotherapist Harold Shepherdson. They were discussing Bobby Moore generally and, specifically, his contribution in the matches against Portugal and Argentina. George quite clearly remembers Alf saying that he was not sure whether to play Bobby against the Germans. 'How d'you think Norman would do?' he asked Les Cocker. Les knew as much about Norman Hunter as anyone on the England staff because he was Don Revie's coach at Leeds, where Norman played.

The rest of the lads were as astonished as me by George's recollection of Alf's conversation. No one doubted the authenticity of George's claim, but we all agreed that to have left Mooro out of the final would have been unthinkable. During the rest of our evening together the conversation kept returning to the same subject. That was hardly surprising as it was the first time that most of us had ever given such a scenario any thought. Looking back, we felt it significant, for instance, that when we played the Germans at Wembley in February 1966 – my debut game – Norman had played, and played well, though not at centre-back.

We also thought it significant that during the build-up to the tournament, Bobby had been troubled by a contract dispute with West Ham. As is often the case with contract negotiations, Bobby and the club were involved in a game of brinkmanship. Alf didn't like it when his players were in dispute with their clubs.

Bobby was content at West Ham although, after a disappointing season that included a semi-final exit in the European Cup-Winners' Cup and defeat by West Bromwich Albion in the League Cup final, there had been talk of Tottenham wanting to sign him. Tottenham were the glamour club in London at the time. Their manager Bill

Nicholson and Ron Greenwood were great friends. It was hard to envisage Bill trying to lure Bobby away from Upton Park without Ron's agreement.

Bobby's contract with West Ham expired on 30 June 1966, just 11 days before England's first World Cup match against Uruguay. After that date, technically he was no longer a registered player with any Football League club and could therefore not play for England in the World Cup. Alf asked Bobby to solve the problem quickly and one afternoon, just before the Uruguay match, Ron Greenwood arrived secretly at Hendon Hall. Alf ushered him and Bobby into a quiet side room and within minutes a new contract had been signed.

As I recall the events of that summer, I remember Bobby feeling concerned not so much about finishing West Ham's season empty-handed but how that might affect his place in the England set-up. He had taken great pride in leading England for the two-year period before the World Cup. Alf gave him the captaincy against Uruguay at Wembley in May 1964. George Cohen made his international debut at right-back that day, replacing Blackpool's Jimmy Armfield who had been the regular skipper in the previous three years.

The prospect of losing his grip on the captaincy would have worried Bobby, especially as the emergence of a rival threatened his place in the England side. Norman, two years younger than Bobby, won the Second Division title with Leeds in 1964 and reached the FA Cup final the following season. That year he made his England debut in a 2–0 win over Spain and the fact that Alf selected him against the Germans in February 1966 and used him in two more warm-up matches against Yugoslavia and Finland clearly concerned Bobby.

Previously considered untouchable in the heart of the England defence, Bobby went into the 1966 World Cup knowing that he had a rival, who, pertinently, was Jack Charlton's defensive partner at Leeds. If Bobby hadn't been around, Norman would have won far more than 28 England caps. He was quicker and more aggressive, but he didn't have Bobby's timing, composure, distribution or experience. He was also prone to occasional lapses of concentration as we were to see in the decisive World Cup qualifying tie against Poland at Wembley seven years later.

Whatever Alf's feelings on the subject at the time, he made the right selection decision when he finally announced his team for the final. None of us had any doubt about that. Bobby played magnificently in the final and, afterwards, was voted Player of the Tournament. It was another seven years before he finally relinquished his place in the England side. He was captain in all but 17 of his 108 games for his country, a record that is unlikely to be equalled by an outfield player.

So, whose image would have flashed round the world that day in 1966 had Bobby not played – and assuming we would still have won without him? Which of us would have accepted the Jules Rimet Trophy from the Queen? Having discussed it with the team, none of us is sure who Alf would have made captain. He tended to favour captains in defensive positions and that would probably have made either George Cohen or Ray Wilson favourite. But Bobby Charlton was the most experienced player and one of only three men to have deputised for Bobby as captain on the rare occasions he was absent before the 1966 World Cup. The others were Jimmy Armfield and Ron Flowers.

Years after the event George Cohen's revelation about Bobby shocked us all but, when we gave it some deeper thought, we realised that Alf wouldn't have considered such radical upheaval unless he thought it was right for the team. We realised, too, that for all Bobby's status in the game, none of us would have questioned Alf's decision. We respected his judgement, acknowledged his insight into the strengths and weaknesses of his players and accepted that his word was final.

I don't know whether Bobby ever suspected he might be left out of the team for the final. He was told he was playing after our last training session the day before the match. Alf told ten of us individually that we would be playing, and stressed that we weren't to say anything to anyone. So, who was the 11th player, the one who was not told he would play the next day? It wasn't until years later that we discovered that Alan Ball went to bed that night uncertain of his place in the team. Alf had said nothing to him during the course of Friday. It was late morning on Saturday, 30 July when Alan was told by Alf that he would face the Germans. Why did he leave it so late before telling him? We have discussed it among ourselves over the years. I think most of my team-mates that day believed that I was the player most likely to be left out if Jimmy Greaves recovered from the gashed shin he received against the French. But Alan Ball's theory is different. He believes that he was the most vulnerable. He believes that he would have been left out had Jimmy recovered in time. Alan was the only one who wasn't told that he was in the team because Alf wanted to give Jimmy as long as possible to prove his fitness.

Alan thinks that, had Jim played, Alf would have reverted to a 4–3–3 formation to confuse the Germans. Had this been true, Alan would have been sacrificed, England's midfield strength would have dropped to three men, but the striking strength would have increased to three – Roger Hunt, Jimmy and myself.

It's strange now to speculate about such things because, for me, Bobby Moore and Alan Ball were our two best players against Germany that day. Martin Peters and I might have scored the goals and stolen the headlines but Mooro and Ballie laid the foundations for a famous victory that changed all our lives.

Alan Ball, the baby of the team, was my man of the match in the final. He blossomed as others wilted. At the end, Alf said to him, 'Young man, you'll never play a better game in your life.' Alan ran the legs off Karl-Heinz Schnellinger. I thought his stamina and prickly determination were critical elements in our victory. Just 20 and full of boyish enthusiasm, he demonstrated the self-belief that took root five years earlier when Bolton Wanderers cruelly told him that he wasn't big enough to be a professional footballer. He didn't give up. Having learned the nuts and bolts of the game from his father, himself a player and manager, he eventually served his apprenticeship with Blackpool before satisfying all his ambitions with Everton, Arsenal, Southampton and England.

In the final he forced, and then took, the corner that led to England's second goal and set up the third with his cross to me from the right flank. His energy in the 30 minutes of extra time gave us the edge over the Germans.

As I struck England's fourth goal at the end, I looked across to see if I had any support. I did. It was Alan Ball. Even today, he's as provocative and opinionated off the field as he was on it. I sometimes think his greatest pleasure in life is annoying Jack Charlton. When we were playing together he would have the dressing-room in stitches at Jack's expense. He used to take Jack's jackets off the peg, hold them up in the middle of the dressing-room and say, 'Do they still wear these in Yorkshire, Jack? How long have you had this one?'

If Jack writes or leaves a telephone message these days, Alan never replies. 'It annoys him,' says Alan with a grin.

He doesn't get away with everything because Jack teases Alan, too. They're great mates, but they just like to wind each other up. I think they have come to realise that it's what the rest of us expect when we're all together.

For me, Jack's achievements make him a unique figure in the game. I don't think anyone would argue with the fact that, of the team of 1966, he enjoyed the most successful managerial career. I thought what he did for the Republic of Ireland was quite remarkable.

One of the things I most admired about Jack was his honesty. He wouldn't kid himself or anyone else about his own ability. He happily admitted that he'd never been in Bobby Moore's class as a footballer, but he could stop others playing. That was his forte. He was a genuinely tough guy in a tough Leeds United team and I played against him many times. He wasn't vicious but he had a long memory. When the chance came, he would seek revenge with those long, awkward legs on those who hurt or upset him.

I think Alf considered him to be the perfect defensive partner for Bobby. One half of the combination was a skilful technician who read the game magnificently. The other half was an uncompromising, mobile stopper, as hard as nails and an intimidating opponent in the air. I think this defensive combination clearly revealed Alf's obsession with creating a perfectly balanced team. He thought it vital to get the balance right when picking his 11 men. This was one of the secrets of his success as a manager.

I remember Jack asking Alf to explain why he continued to pick him for the England team. Bear in mind that Jack was 30 when he made his England debut against Scotland in 1965.

'I don't always pick the best players, Jack,' he explained. 'I have a pattern in my mind and you fit the pattern. I pick you because you won't trust Bobby Moore.'

Alf particularly valued the way Jack was always around to cover for Bobby. He was magnificent at this. I know statistics can be used to prove anything but in Jack's 35 matches for his country he finished on the losing side just twice. That tells you all you need to know about his role alongside Bobby Moore in that England side.

George Cohen, on the right, and Ray Wilson, on the left, provided the balance in Alf's full-back equation. They had a natural affinity on the field despite their backgrounds and personalities being very different. George was a west London boy who spent his entire career with Fulham. At the time, they were a bit of a music-hall joke, thanks largely to the irreverence of their chairman Tommy Trinder, but they were nonetheless one of the best-loved clubs in the entire Football League. A solid, powerful defender, George used to make thunderous forays along the right flank for both Fulham and England. His crossing wasn't so good, though, and the locals at Craven Cottage claimed that, with the wind in the right direction, he could easily put one of his long passes into the Thames.

He was great fun and often the butt of jokes. He had a very high step when he ran and sometimes when we were watching a videotape of England playing, one of the lads would run the film backwards knowing that we'd all fall about laughing at George's running action. Physically, George was perhaps the strongest of all of us and I'm sure this helped him in his successful fight against cancer. He has now retired from the property business he built up after his playing days ended. He still takes an interest in the game and talks a lot of sense about the standards of defensive play.

A laconic northerner from Derbyshire with a wicked sense of humour, Ray Wilson was the oldest of the World Cup team. He was 31, six months older than Jack, in the summer of 1966, and together they used to love taking the mickey out of the southern boys. He was the complete full-back, a man who could attack and defend with equal competence. His tackling was precise and his distribution accurate and I'll always be grateful to him for beginning the move that led to my winning goal against Argentina.

What pleased Alf was the understanding Ray had with George. When George ventured upfield, Ray stayed back, and when Ray attacked on the left, George stayed back. It was the perfect partnership.

One of the most experienced players in the team, Ray had made his England debut in 1960. In total he played 63 times for his country in a career that embraced Huddersfield, Everton and Oldham. When he retired, he concentrated on his undertaker's business. I went to visit him once at his funeral parlour, but he was out burying somebody. He's very good company and spends his spare time these days walking. I've promised that I'll join him one day for a long trek through Yorkshire.

When we were playing, he used to room with Bobby Charlton which was appropriate considering they were both world-class players. Bobby of course was one of the world's great players at the time and England were fortunate to have such a versatile talent in the team. The two Bobbys – Charlton and Moore – were arguably England's most famous players.

Bob had survived the Munich air disaster in 1958 and played in the Manchester United team that won the European Cup in 1968. He won the first of his 106 England caps against Scotland in 1958, at a time when Tom Finney, Billy Wright and Nat Lofthouse were still pulling on the white shirt. What Bobby could do better than anyone was score goals. Others may have scored more, but few scored more spectacular goals. I remember particularly the run and shot of stunning simplicity and beauty against Mexico and his second against Portugal, driven home with awesome power.

He scored on his debut at Hampden Park, hit another two in his next match against Portugal at Wembley in 1958 and just went on scoring. A total of 49 goals in a 12-year international career gave him a record he still holds as England's top marksman.

But Bob was far more than simply a goalscorer. He was comfortable as a winger, a striker or midfield player and it was here, in the heart of the game, that I always felt he was most effective. I think that it was as an organiser, full of power, running and spontaneity, that Alf considered him most valuable.

He graced the game in an era different from today and, like Bobby Moore, his sportsmanship and sense of fair play provided parents and schoolteachers with an example to set before children. His standards were high, his values deep and he was loved throughout the football world. He remains a wonderful ambassador for the nation, a man full of gentle dignity. We worked closely together during the Football Association's attempts to secure for England the right to host the 2006 World Cup and it was plain to see the affection in which he is still held around the globe.

Even at the height of his considerable fame, he had a modest, unaffected demeanour and, because of his status among the players, was often chosen as the mouthpiece for the England squad, especially when we felt we needed to approach the manager. We all knew that Alf would never drop Bobby.

When we were issued with our grey flannel suits in 1966, Bobby was chosen to ask Alf if, on less formal occasions, we could dress casually. 'No,' said Alf firmly.

During the final tournament, we were travelling regularly from the team hotel in north London to the Bank of England ground at Roehampton in south-west London for training. Some days we would spend three hours travelling by coach to and from the training ground. We asked Bobby to suggest to Alf that we should train at a ground closer to the hotel. Bobby waited for his moment and one day, when the team bus was stuck in traffic on the way to Roehampton, Bobby went to the front of the coach and put the suggestion to Alf.

'Bobby, I'll give it some consideration,' said Alf. Before Bobby had returned to his seat, Alf turned and called down the bus, 'I've considered it and we'll stay as we are.'

Although he wasn't a great tackler, Bobby wasn't a player you could take lightly. He was hard and competitive and together with Jack played a big part in creating the defiant spirit in Alf's team. At the time, they were probably the most famous brothers in the country and although you hear lots of stories about family rivalry, when they're with the rest of us they get on together like a house on fire.

In the final analysis, when Alf had the team the way he wanted it, Bobby had the central midfield role that allowed him to create and push forward to support the strikers. He was able to do this as often as he did because of the discipline and diligence of his Manchester United club-mate Nobby Stiles.

Alf gave Nobby the holding job in midfield, just in front of the back four, with Alan Ball wide on the right and Martin Peters wide on the left. Martin, the most versatile player in Alf's squad, played just three games for England before the World Cup started, but he adapted to that role on the left flank with remarkable ease and confidence. Along with the two Charltons, Nobby and Alan were responsible for ensuring that we chased every lost cause. In many ways, Nobby and Alan were the heart and soul of the team. They wouldn't let you get away with anything.

Alf was fond of both of them because he admired their attitude and the way they could follow his instructions. They came together in the side for the first time in the 1–1 draw with Yugoslavia in May 1965 and by the time I was involved the following spring they looked as though they had been in tandem for years. Aggressive, functional, hugely confident, it was easy to see why no one would take liberties with these two. There wasn't much of either of them but what there was of Nobby and Alan was all muscle, determination and resilience. In playing to their strengths, they made it look an easy game. Many professionals never realise the value of doing the simple things well.

One day after training, as we all sauntered off the pitch, Alf called them both to one side. 'Have either of you got a dog?' he asked. Alan said that he had. 'You know how when you throw a ball your dog chases after it?' continued Alf. 'Well, that's what I want you both to do for Bobby. Win the ball and give it to him.'

No player won the ball as efficiently as Nobby Stiles. His tackling was just the legal side of murderous – but it was legal. I remember some years ago watching a film of Manchester United's victory over Benfica in the European Cup final of 1968. I'd forgotten how many times Nobby tackled Eusebio in that match. But what a man, that Eusebio! Each time Nobby chopped his legs from under him, he came back for more of the same. A few weeks after watching the film, I saw Nobby at a function in London. 'D'you see some of those tackles?' he said. 'I couldn't believe how bad I was!'

Nobby was terrifically competitive, didn't slack and didn't appreciate slackers. If he thought I wasn't pulling my weight he would scream unrepeatable abuse at me. He put his heart and soul into it, and expected the same level of commitment from everyone else. He hated losing.

When we played the French, his tackle on Simon had repercussions but Alf refused to drop him because he knew his value to the team. He was a tough little guy and his reputation went before him. In the semi-final against Portugal, Antonio Simoes hit him hard in a tackle. As Nobby retells the story these days in his after-dinner speeches, when he climbed back to his feet, Simoes said to him, 'If you don't stop kicking Eusebio, I'll kick your teeth in.' Nobby says he replied with that famous toothless grin, 'You've got a problem then, pal, because my teeth are in the dressing-room.'

I suppose if you didn't know him he was a fearsome figure. At a dinner not so long ago, Jack Charlton talked warmly of Nobby, who was in the audience. 'How could people all over the world be so frightened of him?' he asked. 'Look at him now – such a pathetic little figure!'

Nobby was a far better player than people thought. He used the ball intelligently and he and Alan had a great understanding on and off the field. It was all part of the balance Alf was seeking. They roomed together throughout the World Cup and each morning Nobby got up at seven to go to church. Alf never knew and Alan told no one.

For me, one of the most important figures in the team was my strike partner Roger Hunt. When I was put into the team for the quarter-final against Argentina we had played just three matches together. He was vastly more experienced than I was, having made his England debut in 1962. Four years later he was already a goalscoring legend on Merseyside and in 11 years with Liverpool scored an incredible total of 245 league goals. There was nothing spectacular about his game but he was a prodigious worker. We were both sturdily built and I felt we were battering rams, forcing gaps in the opposing defence for others to exploit.

Roger was typical of the players who appealed to the legendary Liverpool manager Bill Shankly. As he laid the foundations for decades of Liverpool domination, Shankly successfully combined the creative skills of the Scots with the strength and determination of the English – qualities admirably demonstrated by Roger. He was fast, hard and possessed a terrific right-foot shot. I think I was probably a bit better in the air but I would never have scored the goals I did without his support and running.

Roger was originally an inside-right and spent most of his career at Liverpool playing with wingers. When he pulled on an England shirt, he had to adapt to an entirely different system of play.

He had a wonderfully dry sense of humour that he demonstrated to perfection when I asked him for his memories of that day in 1966. I was involved in the preparation of a book to commemorate the thirtieth anniversary of England's World Cup victory and in his letter to me Roger wrote: 'When the fourth goal went in I remember helping out in defence, enabling you to stand upfield waiting for the ball!'

There are some players whom you appreciate fully only when you begin to train with them on a regular basis. Roger was one, Gordon Banks was another. Gordon was a brilliant goalkeeper but I didn't know just how good he was until I joined the England squad and started shooting at him. His positional sense was fantastic. In fact, in training exercises I found myself trying to out-think Gordon because most of the shots I hit instinctively, he saved.

He was a master of angles, position and distance and his judgement was rarely found wanting. Courage he had by the bucketful and, unlike some of his contemporaries, his shot-stopping style was coldly efficient rather than spectacularly eccentric.

I cannot recall a serious mistake by him in all the games we played together for England. His save from Pele in Mexico in 1970 is still widely regarded as a classic example of the goalkeeper's art. His

Showing an early gift for posing – aged one!

Top: Family holidays were invariably spent on the beach at Rhyl, north Wales. Here I am, in the early 1950s, with my younger brother Robert and, left to right, my favourite uncle and aunt Jack and Frances Senior, Dad and Mum.

The earliest photo of me in football kit. My best friend John Parry and I played for the King's Road Primary school team. I refused to wear my new boots, which are on the ground behind us, until the first match.

I also played for the King's Road Primary school cricket team. I'm in the middle of the centre row. I can still name most of these boys!

I used to watch my dad play for Chelmsford City. Here he is, back row, fifth from left, in the late 1940s.

Opposite above: My first trip abroad and a sign of West Ham's success to come. I also established myself in the team, ending the tour as top goalscorer.

Opposite below: Happy day! Judith and I married on 13 October 1964 at Chelmsford Cathedral. My four team-mates facing the camera are: (left to right) Ken Brown, best man Eddie Presland, John Sissons and Roger Hugo.

RANDALL. ISLAND. STADIUM
N.Y.C. 1963.

My first big test, scoring against Manchester United in the 1964 FA Cup semi-final at Hillsborough. I don't think they'd allow us to play in conditions like this today!

Learning the trade in Cassettari's café round the corner from West Ham where Ronnie Boyce (centre), Eddie Bovington and I used sauce bottles to demonstrate tactics.

On the train home following our semi-final win at Hillsborough. Our reserved dining car was overrun by jubilant West Ham fans.

The 1964 Cup final, West Ham United v Preston North End. We were trailing 2–1 when my diving header hit the bar, bounced on the line and went in – as usual!

My first taste of glory. I join my fellow goalscorers Johnny Sissons (left) and Ronnie Boyce in the dressing-room at Wembley.

ARDEN PHOTOGRAPHIC

The great Johnny Byrne salutes the crowds on our triumphant bus journey through East London as Bobby Moore lifts the FA Cup, the first of three trophies he was to win at Wembley in consecutive years.

Opposite above: Bobby Moore lifts his second trophy – the European Cup Winners' Cup, May 1965. Our two-goal hero, the late Alan Sealey, is second from the left.

Opposite below: I joined Sir Alf's squad for training at Lilleshall just before our pre-World Cup tour. Five in this picture were left out of the final party – Bobby Tambling, Johnny Byrne, Gordon Milne, Peter Thompson and Keith Newton.

Top: A classic West Ham goal and my first in the 1966 World Cup, against Argentina at Wembley. I was at the near post to meet an early cross from club mate Martin Peters (just visible in the background).

Above: Another typical West Ham goal. Me scoring England's first against West Germany in the final from Bobby Moore's free kick.

sudden absence, because of food poisoning, from the quarter-final against West Germany perfectly illustrated his value to the team.

For my own part, his save from my penalty in the League Cup in 1972 cost West Ham a place in the final. He was playing for Stoke that day, and by then an illustrious career that began at Chesterfield and blossomed at Leicester City was about to be ended by an eye injury sustained in a car crash.

A solid, unflappable, light-hearted character, he was known to us all as Fernandel because he looked very much like a soulful French comedian of that name. I always enjoyed his company and, as he reminds me from time to time, he was very nearly a team-mate at Upton Park. Moore, Hurst, Peters and Banks – all West Ham men! What a prospect!

Ron Greenwood tried to sign Gordon from Leicester City before the 1966 World Cup. He wasn't available so Ron made a record bid of £65,000 for Bobby Ferguson of Kilmarnock. The deal was agreed but Kilmarnock asked Ron to delay finalising the transfer until after Kilmarnock were knocked out of the European Fairs Cup. While Ron was waiting, Leicester decided to sell Gordon and, remembering West Ham's interest, informed the club that he was available. Ron was in a dilemma but it says much for his integrity that he remained faithful to his agreement with Kilmarnock. Gordon joined Stoke City.

Gordon was an integral part of England's success in 1966. In six games he kept four clean sheets so he was doing something right. But our success wasn't just down to shot-stopping or goalscoring. What we had as a team was something special. We shared a dream and when we get together today it's just like it was all those years ago. We are a team again, a single unit, with a common aim. It's as if nothing has changed.

We had some tremendous individual players and we all had one thing in common – Sir Alf Ramsey. He brought us together and turned a bunch of good lads into world beaters. The credit for that must go to him.

It's easy to spot players who have ability. What's not so straight-forward is identifying attitudes and realising which personalities will combine well to form a strong team. That was Alf's strength. The fact that we still enjoy each others' company and still wind each other up as if we were back in the dressing-room merely confirms what Alf realised all those years ago. He believed we were unbeatable in 1966 and although we might all be grumpy old men now, we still believe we're unbeatable. That's what team spirit does for you.

CHAPTER NINE

Better to be faithful

It was Theodore Roosevelt who claimed that it was better to be faithful than famous. I guess it was a vote-catching statement for an American president but over the years I've had many opportunities to test his theory and, on balance, I have to agree with him.

Fame, when it arrived in the Hurst household in the immediate aftermath of the 1966 World Cup, burst upon us like a whirlwind. Obviously I was known locally as a West Ham United footballer, and the 1964 FA Cup final, followed by the European Cup-Winners' Cup in 1965, had elevated my status nationally. But I wasn't famous until I scored the hat-trick against West Germany in the World Cup final. Without asking for it, without even wishing it, I was suddenly a global name, overnight. On the morning of Saturday, 30 July 1966 I was Geoff Hurst, the West Ham and England footballer. On the morning of Sunday, 31 July I was Geoff Hurst, the only man in history to score three goals in the World Cup final.

It was a new feeling. I quickly came to realise that many elements of personal fame are enjoyable and beneficial, but I also learned that there is a price to pay.

On balance, the good outweighs the bad. Being recognised can be amusing and uplifting and it has provided me with a lifetime of happy memories although one or two embarrassing moments don't bear repeating. I learned early on not to take a big-name reputation too seriously. Judith is of much the same opinion. When she is asked, 'What does your husband do?' she replies, 'He's in insurance.'

Her insistence that our three daughters enjoyed the privacy of a normal childhood meant that the youngest, Charlotte, wasn't fully aware of her father's background until she was about ten when a schoolfriend told her that 'my dad saw your dad on television'. As Judith drove Charlotte home from school one day, she said, 'Mummy, is Daddy famous?'

Some people thrust themselves at you, others are quite literally speechless. Some, when they recognise you, have the good grace not to interrupt or interfere and others say, 'I'm sorry to trouble you, but would you mind signing this for me?' I'm one of those. Many years ago I met one of my heroes, Ronnie Barker, in the foyer of a West End theatre.

'Excuse me,' I said. 'I've always been a big fan. Could I have your autograph?'

'It would be a pleasure,' he replied. 'So long as I can have yours too!'

Some people, and perhaps I'm not one of these, are simply too polite to ask for an autograph. Years ago, Judith and I were having dinner in a restaurant while on holiday in Portugal. On the other side of the restaurant sat a man on his own. When he finished eating he left and at no time gave any indication that he'd recognised me. When we asked for the bill, the waiter explained that the man eating on his own had paid for our wine and left a note. It said, 'Having no wish to intrude on your privacy, please accept the wine as a token of appreciation for the pleasure and memories you gave me in 1966.'

That, I thought, was a very gracious and stylish deed, one that I've never forgotten. The note was unsigned, so I don't know the man's name, but I would like to meet him one day. The restaurant owner knew him as a regular visitor so I wrote him a note of thanks in the hope that he would collect it one day.

I realise now, as I enter my sixties, that for many people meeting a famous person is a source of enormous pleasure. It's not meant to sound conceited but for me it's a source of satisfaction, too. There's nothing wrong with making people happy. Ask Tim Jacobs. You won't have heard of him and nor had I until Judith and I joined our good friend Terry Hopley at his home in Australia for the 2000 Christmas holiday. Terry used to ghost write my column in one of the East London weekly newspapers when I was at West Ham and he later became a very successful business entrepreneur. One of his most recent ventures involves a share of The Glades golf course, just south of Brisbane. It's a beautiful course, designed by Greg Norman. Another of the shareholders is Ian Baker-Finch, the 1991 British Open champion.

One glorious morning I was playing with Terry and a friend of his when Tim Jacobs, Portsmouth fan, seven handicap golfer and father of two, arrived at the course. He was on holiday with his family, but had left them on the beach for the day to look for a round of golf. They told him at the clubhouse that a three ball had just started and he was taken out in the buggy to the second tee. I was already in the rough when I saw this figure climb from the buggy and start walking towards me.

He was transfixed. He didn't take his eyes off me, which I found very disconcerting as I tried to play out of the rough. He walked past me once, turned round and walked past me again before finally realising that I was part of the three ball he was looking for.

We had a great time together. At the end of the day he met Ian Baker-Finch. As he left the clubhouse that evening he said, 'This has been the greatest day of my life.' I'm sure that was an exaggeration but, even so, he'd clearly had a memorable day and I was happy to have played a small part in that. Sadly, celebrity status doesn't always produce such a happy ending. When fame is suddenly thrust upon you, it inevitably influences the way others view you. In that sense, it becomes a burden, especially if close friends and family believe that your new status has in some way altered the nature of your relationships. My relationship with my mum and dad was profoundly changed by England's World Cup victory. They found my new fame hard to handle. I don't know why. Their change of attitude towards me and my family became a source of great sadness. I had a wonderful, loving childhood and a normal son–parent relationship with them until 1966. After the World Cup that summer, they increasingly treated me more as a celebrity than a son.

They had taken a while to accept Judith as my girlfriend and then as my wife but eventually they looked upon her as part of the family. We never lived far from my mum and dad and when Claire was born in 1965 they were doting grandparents. Even now, I can see my father sitting by her cot at our house in Hornchurch, transfixed by his new granddaughter.

Before the World Cup we visited them and they came to us regularly. After the World Cup it was soon noticeable that their visits to us were becoming infrequent. Eventually they stopped altogether. I regret now not sitting down with them at the time. Perhaps we could have healed the rift.

What caused it? I don't know. I can only suppose that they felt Judith and I had outgrown them and the kind of lifestyle we had been used to. This was not true. We had not changed, but their perception of us had. It became increasingly sad for us because our three daughters barely knew their grandparents on the Hurst side of the family. Now that I'm a granddad myself I can't understand how my parents could let those years slip by without seeing their grandchildren.

In 1987, more than 20 years after the World Cup, they refused our invitation to Claire's wedding. They were divorced by this time but I heard through other members of the family that they both thought it was going to be a showbiz occasion and they would be uncomfortable with all the famous guests. They also persuaded my sister Diane not to attend. There were no showbusiness people at the wedding. My parents just thought we lived that kind of life. The truth of the matter is that I went out of my way to avoid it.

I still saw my father from time to time and in 1998, when I received my knighthood at Buckingham Palace, I invited him to the investiture. By then he was with his second wife, Joyce, but he refused to attend.

I still find their attitude inexplicable. Had I been a social climber and nightclubber who mixed with all the pop singers and movie stars I could perhaps have understood their reservations. But that wasn't the case.

It's true that the sixties was a lively decade and that Moore, Hurst and Peters were suddenly elevated to the forefront of the new personality cult. This was the era of the youth revolution, of the Beatles and Rolling Stones, Mary Quant and mini skirts, Carnaby Street and mini cars. The country was struggling economically, and England's World Cup triumph caught the mood of a nation that was seeking heroes, good news and something to celebrate. Bobby Moore was a wonderful figurehead at the time but, for pure unadulterated glamour, George Best was football's biggest box-office star.

In the months following the World Cup final I had a decision to make. Did I want to embrace this glamorous world or did I want to concentrate on my career as a professional sportsman?

I decided on the latter course of action. I tried to avoid the pitfalls that have trapped so many young footballers suddenly handed wealth and fame, especially in recent years. I studied Bobby Moore and how he handled himself in public. He was used to it and therefore better equipped to handle the adulation. I admired his style. He believed in doing things properly. He was a great professional and was always careful in public not to discredit himself or his profession. He was an enormous help to me as I came to grips with my new status.

I didn't have an agent at any stage during my playing career and have never regretted that. I have been told that, with professional help, I could have made myself a fortune from advertising, sponsorships and marketing, but the thought of capitalising on my fame off the field of play didn't appeal to me. Nonetheless, I was flattered when the well-known American agent Mark McCormack approached me shortly after the World Cup.

Curiosity aroused, I met representatives of his organisation in a London hotel one morning and they explained that they wanted to act on my behalf and exploit my name for commercial purposes. At the time, McCormack was well established in the golf world and football was something relatively new to him. Signing me would have been a breakthrough into big-time football for his company.

My earnings from outside the game were insignificant because I wasn't interested in doing other things and the opportunities were a fraction of what they are today. Nevertheless, in the end I turned them down. Not only did they want to take 20 per cent of the fee for the work they found me, they also wanted 20 per cent of my annual salary with West Ham. Had I joined McCormack things may have turned out differently, but at the time I was happy with my life. I'd been earning £45 a week – more than twice the average national wage – when Alf Ramsey first picked me to play for England in February 1966. As a result of that call-up West Ham doubled my wage. Then, immediately after the World Cup, West Ham realised that they would have to pay me much the same as Bobby Moore. I negotiated a six-year contract with the club that was worth £140 a week – a fortune in those days. My salary had risen threefold within six months and I became one of the highest paid players in the First Division. Even so, I soon realised that I had been naïve to commit myself to a six-year contract with no pay rise. Money held its value then but I should still have had an annual pay increase written into the contract.

There were other financial benefits. Each player received a £1,000 bonus from the Football Association for winning the World Cup on top of the £60 match fee we received each time we played for England. The other source of income was the £300 I received from adidas each time I wore their boots in an England international game.

For me, at least, there were few other financial spin-offs. I appeared in a television advert for a deodorant, helped market a pair of green football boots, not very successfully, and later had a weekly column in the *Evening Standard* in London.

None of this was going to make me rich, but nevertheless my earnings from West Ham were now such that I had to look at some form of long-term investment. For the first time in our married life we had some spare cash and I felt we were wasting it. I remember splashing out £100 on a watch for Judith. It was a lot of money in those days. Football was a short-term career and we both realised that we would be better putting our money to work for the future. It was Bobby Moore's financial adviser, Jack Turner, who told me that I should invest in property.

At the time, Judith and I were living with our first daughter in the semi-detached chalet bungalow we bought when we married. Jack Turner advised us to invest in something bigger and more expensive. So we moved upmarket, to Chigwell, where we paid £12,750 for a large, detached house owned by a Tory MP. It was a big jump up the housing ladder but it taught me a lesson that has stood me in good stead for years – property is the best investment.

The new house needed refurbishing, and Judith quickly turned it into a home. It is something she has done successfully whenever we have moved. She just has a knack for this sort of thing – selecting furniture, fabrics and wallpapers – and I hope she's enjoyed it because we've moved house often enough over the years!

The real worry for us concerned the new neighbours – or rather one neighbour in particular. The West Ham vice chairman Len Cearns, later to become the club chairman, lived in the same road in Chigwell. Should a player move into the same road as his club's vice chairman? Was this a little above my station in life?

It seems ridiculous now, but it was a consideration in those days. Several people pointed out to me that Mr Cearns lived in the same road. These days a chairman is lucky if he can afford to live in the same road as his players.

I suspect that one or two of the neighbours we left behind in Hornchurch felt that we no longer considered them friends, but that was their mistake. As with my parents, it was a matter of perception. We hadn't changed. We moved to a bigger house because we wanted to invest the money I was earning. It saddened me, though, to find Judith in tears one day because the wives of one or two of the West Ham players, girls she considered friends, were mocking our decision to move into what they described as a 'fancy neighbourhood'. They'd been really bitchy behind her back, and that upset her. I suppose some jealousy was inevitable. It was one of the downsides of the whole thing.

I'll never forget the curious glances from behind shifting curtains when a royal blue Rolls-Royce pulled up outside our semi-detached in Hornchurch just 48 hours after the World Cup final. I remember Judith saying 'My God! What will the neighbours think?' as we climbed into the back of our chauffeur-driven limousine.

Radox, who had awarded a £250 prize to England's top goalscorer, had sent the car to take us to the lunch at a London hotel where I was to receive my cheque. Bobby Moore was also to get a prize as the Player of the Tournament.

It was my first ride in a Rolls-Royce. The driver couldn't stop talking and chatted away about the film stars he'd ferried around and King Hussein, who had been in his car the week before. Whenever the car stopped at traffic lights or a junction, people peered in. You could see them saying to each other, 'Look! It's Geoff Hurst.'

You have to learn to handle celebrity and that takes time and patience. You face new situations each day and learn from them. I was a quiet, undemonstrative child and remained that way. I was never entirely comfortable with the fame that accompanied those three goals. I didn't like promoting myself, and still don't. I have been known, though, to refer to myself, tongue in cheek, as a 'superstar' among the office staff where, years after I retired from the football field, I worked in the insurance business. It was all part of the banter of office life. I could never have seriously referred to myself in that manner.

Without realising it at the time, I became public property. For months after the World Cup I received invitations to functions that would have occupied every evening of the week for about two years had I accepted them all. Had I wanted to become a social lion this was my chance. I turned down most of the invitations.

I also received thousands of letters, most congratulating me, some asking for photographs or autographs, some pleading to borrow my World Cup winners' medal, some asking for advice. One mother asked me to write to her young son, telling him that he would never be a professional footballer if he didn't eat his cabbage. I wrote to the lad telling him the secret of my success was cabbage, which was untrue. I've never liked cabbage.

I also agreed to a request from a local hospital to borrow the No. 10 shirt I wore in the final. I didn't find out why they wanted it until sometime later when a photograph arrived in the post of Matron wearing the shirt at the hospital's fancy-dress party.

I received a lot of letters asking why I puffed out my cheeks whenever I struck the ball. Some asked why I didn't wear false teeth if my own were falling out. This came about because I had been frequently photographed in matches with one front tooth missing. It was knocked out when I was playing club cricket for Chelmsford. I was batting and the ball flew off the top edge and caught me in the mouth, knocking one of my front teeth about 15 yards to point! It was painful, but I went back and scored 50!

I did have a false tooth on a plate, which I left in the dressing-room whenever I played. I decided not to have any dentistry during my football career because of the risk of further damage. There were occasions in the weeks immediately following the World Cup when I feared I might get one or two more teeth knocked out. I remember taking Judith shopping in Romford a few days after the final. It was a mistake. We were followed by a crowd that grew in size and excitement until it finally exploded in pandemonium in a super-market. Judith was swept away and bundled into the bacon counter before the staff finally rescued us from the crowd.

Recognition for a footballer in those days was a 'hands on' experience. You went out into the street and you handled it for yourself. If you didn't like it, you had to lock yourself away at home and close the curtains.

Around Christmas time in 1966 I went into a famous department store in Ilford to buy a fountain pen. As I was talking to the young lady sales assistant it quickly became obvious that I'd been spotted. Word spread through the store and within a few minutes an orderly queue of shoppers had formed around me. I patiently signed all the autographs and discovered that some were returning with a football book or magazine for a second signature. At this point I still hadn't bought the pen. Finally, as the queue subsided, I said to the young lady sales assistant, 'Sorry about that. I'll take this Parker please. Can I give you a cheque?'

'Only if you have some form of identification, sir,' she replied.

By and large, I found the public response to me ranged from heart-warming to overwhelming, but London's East Enders never let it go to my head. One cinema in Ilford asked me to present a mini car to a competition winner. I agreed and arrived at the cinema as arranged. As I stood in the wings waiting to make my entrance on the stage, the MC gave me a huge build-up. Finally, he announced, 'And so ladies and gentlemen, a big hand please for our very own World Cup hero – George Hurst! Come out here, George, and show yourself!'

There were other embarrassments but, on the whole, I found fame a fascinating experience that still throws up moments of unexpected amusement. I don't think I could ever be accused of taking it too seriously. When I collect my granddaughter from school she enjoys the interest I sometimes generate among the other parents. Some of them know me, and some don't. When someone who is clearly unsure asks, 'Are you Geoff Hurst?' I reply, 'No, I'm Brian Ward.' I don't know why I picked that name. On one occasion when I was asked, 'Are you Geoff Hurst?' my granddaughter piped up, 'No he's not. He's Brian Ward.'

I like to put people at their ease when they approach me. It makes me feel uncomfortable if I know my presence is making someone else feel awkward. I particularly dislike the moment I'm spotted in an enclosed area, a railway carriage or an aeroplane, for example. It's happened so often. A fellow-traveller whispers to the man next to him, 'Is that Geoff Hurst?' Then others start asking, 'Who is it?' I don't enjoy that kind of attention. I feel very uncomfortable. I'd rather pass by unnoticed.

You can't win with some people, the envious types. You'll never satisfy them. I used to spend a lot of time listening patiently, trying to cope with an embarrassing situation. I don't waste my time now. You learn through experience. I can usually tell within seconds those who are jealous, resentful, bitter or just want an argument. I just say, 'Excuse me, but I have to go.'

Generally, though, people are wonderful to talk to. Some years after the World Cup, when I was playing for Stoke City, I bumped into three vagrants on Euston Station. The first one said to me, 'You're what's his name, the golfer, aren't you?'

'No he ain't,' said the second one. 'You're that footballer, ain't you?'

'Yeah,' said the third man. 'You're that Geoff Hurst. Yeah, we've got you, haven't we? You're Geoff Hurst. I remember, 'cos when you got those three goals I was away at the time.'

'Somewhere nice?' I asked, thinking he would say Portugal or the Costa Brava.

'Yeah!' he replied. 'Pentonville. I'll never forget it 'cos when your third went in we had a great celebration and smashed up the cell.'

Another man I met in the street one day told me that, as referee Gottfried Dienst blew the final whistle his excitement was such that he threw his new-born baby into the air so hard that she banged her head on the ceiling. I've often wondered whatever happened to that poor child!

Within a week of the World Cup finishing, Bobby, Martin and I were back at West Ham in pre-season training – no complaining about too many matches and not enough rest in those days. On 20 August, just three weeks after the final, we kicked off the new season against Chelsea at Upton Park. The three of us went out on to the pitch early and the crowd – more than 36,000 had squeezed into the ground – gave us the kind of prolonged standing ovation that brought tears to your eyes. It was a great feeling to walk out in front of our own fans as conquering heroes.

Unfortunately the atmosphere that day did more to lift Chelsea than us. West Ham didn't play well. Bobby, Martin and I probably needed a longer break. We had each played between 70 and 80 games for club and country over the previous 12 months, but that is not an excuse for our defeat. Chelsea beat us 2–1 with Charlie Cooke scoring the winner. Our goalkeeper Jim Standen was out of position, leaving him an empty net.

It turned out to be a disastrous start to the new campaign. We had approached it with such optimism but we didn't pick up our first point until the fourth game – a 2–2 draw at home with Arsenal – and we struggled all season.

However, I managed to pick up where I left off the previous season. In 1965–66 I scored 40 goals in 59 first-team games for West Ham – 17 in Cup ties – and the season following the World Cup produced 41 in 49 games for the club. When asked by reporters at the time how I felt, I remember saying, 'Ten feet tall!' A couple of days later one of the newspapers sent a photographer to our training ground at Chadwell Heath. He lay on his back and took a photograph of me from ground level upwards. It made me look ten feet tall. I still have the photograph in my collection of memorabilia.

I suppose when you're scoring goals at that rate it's inevitable that one of the bigger clubs should show an interest in you. In my case the bigger club was the biggest of them all – Manchester United. I didn't know it at the time because West Ham didn't tell me, but Matt Busby wanted me to join United. His interest had been sparked off by a note Ron Greenwood sent to other First Division clubs stating that West Ham had players available for transfer. When the Manchester United manager telephoned to ask if the players for sale included Hurst, Ron told him, 'Of course, if you include Charlton, Law, Best and your grandstand!'

Some time later, just before United left Manchester to play Gornik Zabrze in Poland in the European Cup, Busby called Upton Park again. Ron was out this time and the club secretary Eddie Chapman took the call. When Ron returned, Eddie told him that Matt Busby had just offered £200,000 for Geoff Hurst. It apparently angered Ron that Busby had misunderstood the initial conversation about me. Ron sent a terse telegram to Busby in Poland. It read: 'No. Regards. Greenwood.'

I found out about this later when the story eventually found its way into the newspapers. At no point had West Ham consulted me, but that wasn't unusual at the time. Some clubs still had a rather traditional attitude to their players.

Of course, I was enormously flattered by United's offer. The record fee at the time was the £115,000 they had paid Torino for the Scotland striker Denis Law. I was valued at nearly double that. It was a huge fee, but it didn't disturb me when I found out about it.

I have often wondered what it would have been like to play for

Manchester United. Busby, a great manager at Old Trafford, was a legendary figure and his work laid many of the foundations for United's later successes. Had Ron Greenwood sold me I would probably have played in the United side that beat Benfica 4–1 at Wembley in the 1968 European Cup final.

As it turned out, I stayed at West Ham for another four years and I'm pleased I did. I'm not a person who thinks that the grass is greener on the other side of the hill. I stayed faithful to them and, in my book, that was as good as being famous.

CHAPTER TEN

'We're going to bring back the pot!'

ALF RAMSEY, KNIGHTED IN THE 1967 NEW YEAR'S HONOURS, had set a new standard for English football. Some even claimed that winning the World Cup was the worst thing that could have happened to the English game because it established a high benchmark against which all future campaigns would be judged. In other words, anything short of winning the World Cup again would be regarded as failure.

How prophetic! That, of course, is exactly how it's turned out. How many England managers have tried to emulate Ramsey? It was a sad day when the Football Association decided they could no longer remain faithful to Alf. In the years since then, they have regularly scoured the directory of English coaches, hiring and firing in the hope that they would eventually find a worthy successor. They tried Don Revie, Ron Greenwood, Bobby Robson, Graham Taylor, Terry Venables, Glenn Hoddle and Kevin Keegan before turning in desperation to Sven-Goran Eriksson. When I was a player, a foreigner would have had about as much chance of becoming the national coach of England as I had of knocking out Muhammad Ali and winning the world heavyweight boxing championship. There was a time when we would have had at least six top-quality English coaches jostling for the job. That's no longer the case. The most suitable candidates, and these are very few, are not available; the others are either not good enough or don't want the job anyway.

I would still prefer the national coach to be English. It doesn't say much for the standard of coaching in England if the FA, the guardians of the sport and as such the body responsible for coaching development, couldn't find a suitably qualified English-born national team manager.

I suppose that once the big English clubs started employing foreign players in significant numbers it was just a matter of time before they started employing foreign coaches. Just as foreign players have restricted the development of English-born youngsters, so the increasing number of foreign coaches means fewer job opportunities for English coaches and therefore fewer candidates for the top job with the national team.

In my day, you could count the foreign players on one hand. At West Ham we had Clyde Best from Bermuda, Ipswich had Colin Viljoen from South Africa, and there were a couple of Danes with Newcastle and Crystal Palace. Otherwise, the dressing-rooms of the First Division clubs were the domain of English, Irish, Welsh and Scots players.

The Scots were enormously influential in shaping the game in England and many of football's most successful managers during my career – Matt Busby and Bill Shankly for instance – were from north of the border. Sir Alex Ferguson and George Graham have maintained that trend in the modern game.

One of the annual highlights of the domestic season was always the England–Scotland clash in what was known as the Home International Championship and later the British Championship. It saddened me when this, the oldest international fixture in the world, was finally abandoned in 1989 because of the hooligan problem.

Although the two nations met in a play-off for a place in the 2000 European Championship, none of today's players will have experienced the noise, emotion, colour or sense of menace that accompanied England's regular visits to the old Hampden Park. It was no place for the faint-hearted. I'll never forget playing there. In those days, the surface was never remotely as good as the Wembley pitch, which was billiard-table smooth until they staged the Horse of the Year Show on it. Hampden Park had a greater capacity. They could squeeze 134,000 on to the dark, towering terraces. The stadium was considered the finest in the world when it opened in 1903. I played for England all over the world and can say quite emphatically that the Scots generated an atmosphere that I didn't experience anywhere else.

We always wanted to beat the Scots and they always wanted to beat us. If we lost, none of our lads cherished the prospect of returning to their clubs where the Scotsmen among the dressing-room cynics would make life hellish for a few weeks. Fortunately, we gave Bobby Ferguson and John Cushley few opportunities in our dressing-room at Upton Park. I felt that the Scots relished their victories more than we did, probably because a Scottish victory was rare. When they beat us they really wanted to make the most of it.

The England–Scotland fixture provoked tribal passions in First Division dressing-rooms. Some clubs had almost as many Scottish players as English ones. Tottenham's Bill Nicholson, one of the most successful club managers of the sixties, insisted that at least two Scottish players were essential components in all of his teams. During his time at White Hart Lane he had some of the great Scotsmen of that era – Bill Brown, Dave Mackay, Alan Gilzean and John White, who was so tragically killed by lightning at the peak of his career. It was Bill who first recognised the potential in an Edinburgh youngster called Graeme Souness.

I sometimes wonder why we have so few Scottish players in the English game today. Without doubt, the influx of foreigners has damaged the development of local boys north of the border far more than it has done in England. In my time I played against some great Scotsmen both at club and international level – Paddy Crerand, Billy Bremner, Peter Lorimer, Eddie Gray, Frank McLintock, George Graham, Ian St John, Charlie Cooke and Denis Law were as important to their First Division clubs as any of their English team-mates.

Denis Law was my favourite. His reaction when England won the World Cup demonstrated the traditional rivalry between the two nations. He avoided the television that day, choosing instead to play golf. Finally, of course, he heard that the 'auld enemy' had beaten West Germany 4–2. It was, he said, a horrible shock, one he would never get over!

I idolised him in those days and to have a drink with him in Manchester was to understand what hero-worship meant to the United fans. I still see him from time to time and he's great company. He says what he thinks. He never sat on the fence as a player either. If you kicked him, he kicked you back, with interest, but I suspect that it was his volatile temperament that helped make him such a great striker.

I remember watching him for the first time on a frosty day in January 1960. I sat in the stand at Upton Park as this pale, lightweight figure skipped across an icy pitch. His goal at Leeds Road had earned Huddersfield an FA Cup third-round replay at Upton Park. Although he didn't score in the replay, Huddersfield, then in the Second Division, beat us 5–1.

He'd joined them as a 15-year-old and apparently arrived at the ground wearing steel-rimmed glasses. Some at Huddersfield thought he had been recommended to them as a practical joke. Some joke!

There were more prolific goalscorers, but Denis did more than simply score goals. He gave a theatrical performance in which, over the course of 90 minutes, he managed to be both villain and hero. He scored goals with an unmistakable flourish that sent a tremor through the opposition and then stood, with a single arm raised above a distinctive mop of blond hair, to salute the crowd. I remember him scoring goals of quite matchless virtuosity. His bicycle kick was a speciality as was his ability to outjump taller defenders and head spectacular goals. He was, quite simply, unique among his contemporaries and, not surprisingly, is one of the few British players to have been voted European Footballer of the Year.

In a sense, I suppose, it was quite fitting that he should play such a significant role in one of Scotland's few victories at Wembley. Out of the six games I played against Scotland, this was the solitary defeat, but it was the one that mattered, particularly to the Scots. England were the undisputed world champions, unbeaten in 19 matches. Denis revealed outrageously quick reactions to score the opening goal against England that day in March 1967.

With 12 minutes remaining it looked as though Denis's goal would be enough to win the match but, incredibly, four goals arrived in the last minutes. Bobby Lennox drove home a second for Scotland and, five minutes from time, Jack Charlton scored off a post for England. Jimmy McCalliog made it 3–1 before, in the final seconds, I met a cross from Bobby Charlton with a powerful header.

So Scotland won 3–2 and became the first nation to defeat the new world champions. It was hugely disappointing, especially as our conquerors were the Scots. Typically, Denis and his team-mates claimed that Scotland should now be declared world champions! They even claimed that Alf Ramsey's decision to replace Roger Hunt with Jimmy Greaves, the first team change he'd made in seven games, strengthened the England side and therefore enhanced the value of the Scottish victory.

I can't dispute that the Scots deserved their win but I've always felt it was something of a hollow victory. These were the days before substitutes were allowed in the Home Internationals and for much of the game England were forced to carry three injured players.

Jack Charlton broke a toe in a challenge with Bobby Lennox after 15 minutes. He went off for treatment and returned in the 30th minute but spent the rest of the match hobbling around painfully at centre-forward. I was told that he just edged me out of first place for the football writers' 1967 Footballer of the Year award, and I think the part he played that day at Wembley had a lot to do with it.

He was a stoical, uncomplaining character throughout his England career, one of those Alf knew he could rely upon. We clearly missed his presence in the heart of the defence against Scotland and later injuries to Ray Wilson and Jimmy Greaves accentuated our problems. We ended the game with Bobby Charlton playing at left-back.

What added to the significance of the Scottish victory was the fact that the result had a bearing far beyond the Home Championship. It had been decided that the next two annual competitions between the home nations would serve as the qualifying programme for the 1968 European Championship – then known as the Nations' Cup – in Italy. Scotland's win at Wembley gave them the 1967 Home International Championship title and also put them at the head of the qualifying group for the European finals the following year. When we met ten months later, the Scots, having dropped a point against Wales, needed to win to reach the finals. A draw would be sufficient for England to qualify.

Another seething crowd of 134,000 greeted us noisily in Glasgow but Martin Peters silenced them, scoring the goal that gave England a 1–1 draw and a place against Spain. The Scots were distraught. Our dressing-room was jubilant.

As we drove away in the England team bus afterwards, the Glasgow hordes hurled abuse with one or two drunks lifting their kilts to reveal – well, nothing very much at all! So, I felt, the natural order of things was restored with the minimum of fuss. England were back on top in the gloating stakes!

We played Spain over two legs, winning 1–0 at Wembley with a Bobby Charlton goal, and 2–1 in Madrid with goals from Martin, again, and Norman Hunter. I missed the Wembley game with a poisoned toe and couldn't win my place back for the second leg. That poisoned toe probably cost me a career-total of 50 England caps. I finished my international career one cap short of half a century.

For the first time, then, England had reached the last four of the European Championship – an achievement repeated by Terry Venables and his England side in 1996. England were drawn to meet Yugoslavia in Florence in June. Italy were playing Russia in the other semi-final. En route Alf took us to Hanover to play West Germany in a warm-up match. It was a pretty meaningless affair. Only Gordon Banks, Bobby Moore, Alan Ball and myself of the World Cup-winning team were chosen to play. It was a hot day and a hard pitch and adidas had persuaded us to wear their new boots, which didn't help. A Franz Beckenbauer shot hit Brian Labone and ricocheted past Banks to give the Germans a 1–0 win. I was disappointed. I hated losing, whatever the circumstances.

The Germans, of course, were ecstatic. They'd never beaten us before in 38 years of trying, which tells you something about how the balance of power in European football has switched in more recent years. It was Alf's first defeat on the Continent since his opening game as manager – a 5–2 defeat by France in Paris in 1963.

Perhaps he could have chosen a less demanding warm-up match because I think we felt under pressure four days later when we faced Yugoslavia in front of a 30,000 crowd. As world champions, we were the team everyone wanted to beat. Yugoslavia made that clear from the kick-off.

It was a brutal, ill-tempered match. Alan Mullery, who had by now succeeded Nobby Stiles as England's midfield ball winner, was clubbed down within a minute of the start. This was just a taste of what was to come. It was one of the most violent games I can remember, and the Italian crowd loved every minute of it, screaming their delight every time an England player was fouled.

They were jubilant when Dragan Dzajic, Yugoslavia's outstanding winger, scored the only goal late in the game. Another disappointment, another England defeat, but that is not why we remember this game. This is the match in which an England player was sent off for the first time. Mullery, sent crashing for the umpteenth time when Miljan Trivic caught him with his studs, lashed out instinctively with his right boot, catching the Yugoslav across the legs. Trivic fell as though he had been hit by a missile and began a series of rolls, twists and somersaults that would have earned prolonged applause in Billy Smart's circus. As soon as it was clear that the Spanish referee had decided to send off 'Mullers', the little Yugoslav jumped to his feet and began running round in circles waving his arms in the air. We all shared Alan's sense of frustration.

As he walked off the field he was pelted with rubbish by the crowd and was steered down the tunnel by Nobby Stiles, the man he had replaced in the team. In the dressing-room afterwards Alf put his arm around Alan and said, 'I don't think anybody, if they were any sort of man, could have stood for much more of what you had to put up with.'

The atmosphere immediately after the match was anything but

friendly. The England party went by coach to a reception but it was such a shambles that Alf ordered us back to the hotel. There was a lot of friction and ill feeling at official level.

The following day, after a visit to the Vatican in Rome, Alan received a telephone call from his wife in his hotel room. She'd been reading the newspapers at home. She wasn't happy with him.

England were not blameless in that match, but nor did Mullers deserve his ignominious place in the history books. He was a terrific addition to the England squad at the time, enormously powerful and enthusiastic.

As a result of his sending off he missed the third-place play-off match against Russia in Rome. The Russians had held Italy to a goalless draw but the Italians were deemed winners on the toss of a coin!

Bobby Charlton and I scored the goals that beat Russia 2–0 and installed England officially as the third best team in Europe. Judith flew out to watch the match and we spent a romantic evening in the Eternal City. Nine months later our second daughter, Joanne, was born.

The final went to a replay after a 1–1 draw and Italy, inspired by Luigi Riva, beat Yugoslavia 2–0. It was disappointing not to add the European title to our world title but, nonetheless, I have no doubt that the England team between 1966 and 1970 was easily the best in the nation's football history.

Between winning the World Cup in 1966 and beginning our defence of the title four years later, England were beaten just four times – by Scotland at Wembley, Germany in Hanover, Yugoslavia in Florence and Brazil in Rio.

By the time we met Brazil on the World Cup warm-up tour to Central and South America in the summer of 1969, we had good reason to believe that we could win the Jules Rimet Trophy for a second time. Many observers felt that the squad Alf was building for the defence of the title was stronger than the one that won it in the first place.

Alf had phased out Ray Wilson, George Cohen, Roger Hunt and Nobby Stiles, and although Jimmy Greaves was still an outstanding goalscorer and just 29 at the time of the 1969 tour, the rift between himself and the manager had never healed. He played just three more games for England, the last against Austria in 1967, following Alf's decision to give his place to me for the Argentina match in 1966.

Others were challenging for regular places in the team. Alan Mullery had already established himself as an energetic and resourceful midfield successor to Nobby Stiles. Terry Cooper, of Leeds United, was widely considered to be the best attacking left-back in the world. Everton's Brian Labone was the outstanding candidate to inherit Jack Charlton's defensive duties, and in Francis Lee of Manchester City Alf had unearthed a striker of pace and aggression. 'Franny' could play anywhere across the front line and I felt his presence gave us a little more variety in attack.

Competition for places had never been fiercer. Everyone wanted to play for England. Everyone wanted to catch Alf's attention. We were the world champions. We were about to defend the title in Mexico. There was no better time to be an England footballer.

The survivors from 1966 couldn't be sure of their places. My goals for West Ham at least kept me in the squad. In season 1968–69 I scored 31 goals in 48 first-team matches and won the Hammer of the Year award for the third time. That was the season when I scored six in one match against Sunderland. It was also my most prolific scoring period for England – eight goals in seven matches including a hat-trick in a 5–0 win over France at Wembley in March 1969.

Two months after that match I flew out of Heathrow with Alf and the rest of the lads for the tour to Mexico, Uruguay and Brazil. Alf had picked the opposition with a view to preparing us for the conditions we could expect when we returned to defend the trophy in Mexico the following summer. As we settled into the plane for the long flight to Mexico City, the lads asked Alf if they could have a drink. It had been a long season and he wanted them to relax. He agreed to their request. The stewardess went around the squad taking their drink orders.

When it was Bobby Moore's turn, he ordered an orange juice. I was surprised – and impressed. Bobby liked a drink but, for him, this was a business trip. He wanted to be sure that he was on the plane the following year when Alf took the squad to Mexico. He wanted to be at his physical best for the warm-up games. He wanted to leave Alf no room for doubts. The defence of the title was still a year away but Bobby was already preparing himself for the challenge. It was typical of the man. Even he, with around 80 England caps and approaching his third World Cup tournament, took nothing for granted.

Bobby played in all four matches on the tour. He was immaculate alongside Brian Labone in the first game in the high altitude of Mexico City's Azteca Stadium. A crowd of more than 105,000 watched the locals hold the world champions to a goalless draw. The Mexicans were happy and, from our point of view, the experience gained from playing at 7,000 feet would prove invaluable the following summer.

Three days later an England XI met a Mexican XI in front of a 45,000 crowd in Guadalajara in a match that was not given the status of a full international. Nonetheless, Bobby wanted to play – and did. He, Alan Ball and Martin Peters were the only members of Alf's squad to start both games in Mexico. With what was basically the second team, England won 4–0, Jeff Astle and Allan Clarke each scoring two goals.

But perhaps the most significant episodes of England's visit to Mexico involved Alf's confrontations with the local media. He wasn't the most diplomatic of people and his abrasive attitude towards the local press succeeded only in stirring up animosity. He claimed that we had been promised a motor-cycle escort to the Azteca Stadium. It didn't arrive. He complained that his players had been jeered and abused by fans. Without realising it, 'Señor Alf' was brewing trouble for our return the following summer.

From the heat and clamour of Mexico, we flew south, over Amazonia to Montevideo, the genteel, old-fashioned capital of Uruguay at the mouth of the Rio de la Plata. This was a city that appeared to be caught in a time warp. I remember just one traffic light and streets full of very old American limousines. Here, on the

South Atlantic, it was much cooler. We beat Uruguay 2–1, Francis Lee and I scoring the goals.

Then it was north again to Rio de Janeiro where we met Brazil in front of a 160,000 crowd in the vast Maracana Stadium. The two Bobs – Moore and Charlton – had played in the same stadium five years earlier when Brazil won 5–1, just three days after England had beaten the United States 10–0 in New York.

Charlton, who had missed the game in Uruguay due to injury, was now fit and returned to face Brazil. He replaced Francis Lee but played in midfield, which meant that I was to be a lone striker. England were the World Cup holders but Brazil, then as now, were top dogs in the global glamour stakes. World Cup winners in 1958 and 1962, they paid us the compliment of fielding a full-strength team that included some of the great names of football – Pele, Gerson, Tostao, Jairzinho, Clodoaldo and Carlos Alberto among them. Their game was slick and sophisticated and when they had the ball it was difficult to win it back. We knew we had to make the most of any opportunity. When a chance presented itself to Colin Bell, he carefully drove his shot beyond the veteran goalkeeper Gylmar, who played in the first international between the two nations in 1956 and, of course, kept goal when Brazil triumphed over Sweden in the World Cup final two years later.

Gordon Banks saved a penalty from Carlos Alberto, enabling England to hold the lead until the 80th minute. By then the heat and travel fatigue were beginning to take a toll. Alf could have put on substitutes, but he didn't, a lesson he may have called upon the following year against the Germans in the heat of Leon. He was strongly criticised for substituting Bobby Charlton and Martin Peters when victory looked certain against West Germany. It should be remembered that he had used substitutes regularly in the build-up period and had realised that the conditions in Mexico meant that recovery time for players between games would be significantly longer.

But on this occasion, it was the Brazilians who took advantage of tiring limbs. With ten minutes remaining, Tostao equalised from Jairzinho's cross. Two minutes later Tostao returned the favour. He swept past the exhausted Keith Newton and pulled the ball back to Jairzinho to score the winning goal.

There was no disgrace in this defeat. England were worth a draw at least. It had been a wonderful contest. Alan Mullery particularly had contributed hugely. He had kept a tight rein on Pele, the best player in the world at the time, and in that game convinced Alf that he would have a critical role to play in the World Cup the following summer.

We had been away a fortnight, travelled halfway round the world and some of us had played four games in that time. We had seen nothing to dampen our enthusiasm or dilute the belief that England could win the World Cup for a second time. Among the lads on the long flight home the general view was that England and Brazil would be favourites to meet in the final in Mexico City the following summer.

During the flight Bobby Charlton happened to mention to Alf how exhausted he felt after a long, hard season. 'I'll be glad to get home, put my feet up and spend a few days with my wife,' he said.

Alf's reply was typical. 'Had I known you felt like that, Bobby, I wouldn't have selected you,' he said.

Alf's preparations for the 1970 World Cup were painstaking. On that flight home from Brazil he made it clear to all of us that nothing would be allowed to detract from the business of successfully defending the title.

If he had any doubts in the months that followed he kept them to himself. That must have been difficult at times because, although England remained unbeaten throughout 1969–70, we played poorly twice against Holland and could only draw with Wales and Scotland.

Only against Belgium in February 1970 did we truly look like potential champions. It was a cold night in Brussels with snow in the air. Chelsea's talented striker Peter Osgood made his England debut alongside me and I think that night convinced Alf that he would be worth a place in the World Cup squad. We played well, beating Belgium 3–1 with two goals from Alan Ball and a header from me.

Judith had travelled independently to Brussels to watch the match. The following morning she joined me briefly at the team hotel. We bumped into Alf in the lobby and I asked if I could take Judith back to her hotel.

'Yes, Geoffrey,' he replied. 'But don't be long.' Then he turned to Judith, and poking her in the chest with a finger, said, 'I hear you're going to watch us in Mexico in the summer. I want you to know that we're not going there for your enjoyment, and we're not going there for my enjoyment. We're going there to bring back the pot and I don't want any interference from you or anyone else.'

Tact was not high among Alf's list of qualities. He didn't want any meddling or intrusion from players' wives in Mexico. He could have broached the subject more tactfully, but I have no doubt that his attitude was absolutely right. Events a year later proved that to be so.

CHAPTER ELEVEN

'¿Dónde está el brazalete, Señor Moore?'

ON A SUNNY MORNING EARLY IN MAY 1970 I PUT ON MY NEW FA suit, kissed Judith goodbye and set off to win the World Cup again. Looking back, I like to think that it was just another day at the office. It was more than that, of course, but most of us believed that England had a realistic chance of becoming the first European team to win the World Cup in Latin America. Alf Ramsey had correctly predicted that we'd win in 1966 and now claimed that his latest England team was stronger and more experienced than four years earlier. I was happy to be part of it still.

The squad, 28 strong, met at White's Hotel, near the FA's offices in Lancaster Gate, and flew from Heathrow, via Bermuda, to Mexico City where we were due to spend most of the next month preparing for the opening match of our World Cup defence. We left London on 4 May. The first game, against Romania in Guadalajara, was on 2 June.

The decision to award the World Cup to Mexico had been taken by FIFA in 1964, since when debate had raged about the effects of heat and altitude. The intense heat of a Mexican summer and the breathing difficulties experienced at heights above 7,000 feet had prompted Alf to take advice from the London School of Tropical Medicine and the Medical Research Council. He had also visited Mexico twice himself and studied reports from the British Olympic Association who had, of course, the experience of the Mexico Olympics in 1968.

As part of the preparation programme Alf persuaded the FA to organise two full international matches, against Colombia in Bogota (8,500 feet) and Ecuador in Quito (9,300 feet). Although medical opinion was divided on the best means, there was no doubt that some form of acclimatisation was essential if players from lowland countries were not to be at a disadvantage.

High-altitude training for many athletes before the Mexico Olympics led to an increased oxygen supply to the muscles and greatly enhanced performances. Alf had read all the necessary data. The 1968 Olympic soccer tournament, for instance, demonstrated quite clearly that teams could adapt to the conditions in Mexico. The three medal-winning nations were Hungary (gold), Bulgaria (silver) and Japan (bronze) with the Mexican hopefuls eliminated at an early stage.

Alf wanted us to be the best prepared of the 16 competing nations. Not everyone shared his views on the optimum acclimatisation period. The West German team, for example, arrived in Mexico nearly three weeks after England.

Initially we were based in Mexico City where we trained daily at The Reforma Club, a large, leafy, British-owned recreation and leisure club. Each day we became more accustomed to the thin air. We had blood tests, heart tests, lung-capacity tests, swallowed slow sodium tablets, played cricket and even, at Alf's suggestion, organised a football match against the travelling English media. Because they were short of players, Alf agreed to reinforce the media team with his own presence in their defensive ranks. Most of the reporters had been advised by the amiable England doctor Neil Phillips, the Middlesbrough club physician, not to move any faster than walking pace during the match. This came naturally to the majority of them! Even so, one or two required treatment for heat exhaustion.

On 18 May, still a fortnight before the opening game, we flew to

Colombia's mountain capital, Bogota, nearly 1,500 feet higher than Mexico City. It was here that, quite unwittingly, Alf's best-laid plans began to unravel. A drama was about to engulf the England squad and dominate the critical days immediately before our defence of the World Cup.

We had been warned of the perils of low-life Bogota and told specifically to buy presents and souvenirs only in reputable shops. So, once we'd checked into the best hotel in the city, El Tequendama, it was no surprise that Bobby Moore and Bobby Charlton chose to browse among the glass showcases in the Green Fire jewellery store in the hotel lobby. Bobby Charlton was looking for a present for his wife, Norma. Other hotel guests, including some of the players, wandered idly through the shop. After a few minutes England's two most famous footballing sons left the shop and sat in the lobby. Both were astonished when they were approached by the shop proprietor and asked to explain the alleged disappearance of a bracelet. Neither was aware of the Colombian pastime of levelling false charges at visiting dignitaries.

The police were called and, in the presence of Alf Ramsey and other FA officials, Moore and Charlton made formal statements. That, we thought, was the end of the matter. But Alf, always fearful of some foreign conspiracy, was a worried man. Several of the players knew what had happened and there was a theory that one of us might find a bracelet planted in our room.

Not a word about the incident was whispered to any outsider. It said much for the camaraderie and sense of loyalty within the squad that no mention of the alleged theft leaked to the media. I'm pretty sure that a similar story today would be front-page news within 24 hours.

Three days later, when the England party flew from Bogota to Quito after beating Colombia 4–0, the small party of travelling Fleet Street journalists, about ten in all, still had no idea of what had happened in the lobby of El Tequendama hotel. The mood among the players as we left Bogota was a mix of relief and optimism. The win over Colombia had been a fairly emphatic statement of intent.

Martin Peters performed brilliantly against a talented Colombian team, strengthening the growing conviction that he was rediscovering his 1966 form at just the right moment. He scored England's first two goals, each time drifting unmarked into the danger zone, and hit a superb pass to create the opening for Bobby Charlton's goal. The craft of Peters and the work-rate of Alan Ball, England's other goalscorer, helped create the impression that England were ready for the real business and would cope successfully with the conditions in Mexico.

On the same day as the full international in Bogota, England's second 11 beat Colombia 1–0 in a B game with a goal from Jeff Astle, who scored just five minutes after coming on as substitute. Other significant figures in that team included Peter Bonetti, Norman Hunter, Jack Charlton, Nobby Stiles, Emlyn Hughes, Allan Clarke, Peter Osgood and Colin Bell – and this was the reserve team. They all knew that within a few days Alf would have to trim his squad from 28 to 22, so six disappointed players would be sent home. We were all playing for our places but I have little doubt that no England manager since Alf has had a squad of such quality *and* quantity.

Almost every member of the squad played at some stage in one or other of the two games in Colombia, gaining vital match experience in unfamiliar conditions. At 8,500 feet, Bogota was some 3,000 feet higher than Guadalajara's Jalisco Stadium where the World Cup defence would begin. I can't honestly say that the rarefied atmosphere caused us too much concern. Perhaps that was because we were adapting to the conditions.

On 24 May we played in the mountain stronghold of Quito, a beautiful, ancient Indian city in a high valley in the Andes. At 9,300 feet breathing is a little harder but the speed and movement of the ball in the thin air was really noticeable. England played well again, winning 2–0 with goals from Francis Lee and Brian Kidd, while the B team beat the champions of Ecuador, Liga University, 4–1.

Jeff Astle, the West Bromwich Albion striker who was challenging me for a first-team place, scored a hat-trick in that game, with Emlyn Hughes, then a mere stripling at Liverpool, adding a fourth. I played in both senior internationals and although I didn't score I made sure that my contribution in each was significant. I never took my place in the England team for granted and I think the same could be said of all the World Cup winners of 1966. That's what made them special individuals, a fact acknowledged graciously at the end of the senior team's victory by Ernesto Guerra, the manager of Ecuador. He said, 'England have a real team of great character and will be better than most of the other nations in Mexico.'

I remember the praise he lavished on Bobby Moore, who retained an icy, impregnable calm and seemed quite unconcerned by the fact that the following day when we were due to return to Mexico City we would have to change planes in Bogota.

The next morning, eight days before our opening game, we boarded a plane for the first leg of the flight back to Mexico City. We had a five-hour stopover in Bogota and Alf, with typical diligence, arranged for us to fill the time by watching a James Stewart western called *Shenandoah* – his favourite type of movie – back at El Tequendama hotel in the city.

As we waited in the airport terminal to be taken to our coaches, I noticed Alf and other FA officials in deep conversation with a man I later learned was Keith Morris, the British Chargé d'Affaires in Bogota. I thought no more of it until I noticed, a couple of hours later, Bobby Moore was not with the rest of us watching the movie. We were back in the air en route to Mexico via a refuelling stop in Panama City before most of us realised that the England captain wasn't on board. By the time we landed in an electric storm at Panama City, the travelling media knew what had happened a few days earlier in Bogota.

We spent an hour in the transit lounge at the airport. I remember Alf pacing up and down while the desperate reporters tried to make contact with their offices back in London. These were the days before mobile telephones.

When we finally arrived in Mexico City it was about nine o'clock at night. It was a hot, humid evening and bedlam reigned in the airport terminal. We were greeted by another electric storm – this time the flashbulbs of cameras. During the time we were in the air the world had woken up to the fact that Bobby Moore, the captain of the defending champions, had been accused of theft. Mexico City airport was heaving with reporters, photographers, television news teams, FIFA officials, British Embassy people and the curious onlookers who always seem to gather at these moments.

Jeff Astle, a nervous passenger at the best of times, hadn't enjoyed the turbulent flight. Having had a few drinks to calm his nerves, he arrived in a state of spectacular disarray. In the mayhem, the airport cameramen focused on him and one headline in *El Heraldo* the following morning welcomed England as 'a team of thieves and drunks'. We were, I suspected at the time, about to pay the price for Alf's indifferent attitude to the Mexican media the previous summer.

Back in Bogota, Mooro was under house arrest because a highly strung shop assistant, Señorita Clara Padilla, claimed to have seen him lingering over the glass cabinet that contained the gold bracelet, worth £625, that had allegedly been stolen. From the original FA party, Dr Andrew Stephen, the chairman, and Denis Follows, the secretary, had stayed behind in Colombia to protect Bobby's interests.

Soon after we arrived back in Mexico City, Judith called me at our hotel. Earlier that day, she said, a tearful Tina Moore had asked if she could help with the children. Back home in Chigwell, the media were camped outside Bobby's house. The police helped to smuggle Tina and the children out of the Moore house in Manor Road and for the next few days they stayed at our house. Roberta had just started school, and Dean was a baby.

On 29 May, four days after his arrest and four days before the opening game, Bobby was released. We all knew it was a farce. We all knew he was the innocent victim of a fabricated charge. I remember Alan Mullery saying, 'With his money, Bob could afford to buy the whole shop!' The inevitable lack of evidence, glaring flaws in the shopgirl's statement, global outrage, diplomatic pressure and the growing realisation that Bobby was simply the latest hapless victim of a frame-up, secured a conditional release for the captain of England. The following day he was on his way to join the squad in Guadalajara, but it was five years before the Colombian authorities officially closed the case.

So, who stole the bracelet? Did a bracelet go missing at all? In the months immediately after the 1970 World Cup there were mischievous suggestions that a third player was viewing the same jewellery with the two Bobs, but no one has ever been named. The only other person I know to have been in the jewellery store at the time in question was Monte Fresco, the *Daily Mirror* photographer who covered most of the big sporting events in his long career and was a friend of many of the players. Although he was aware of the accusations made against Bobby, he kept that information to himself and, like the rest of us, could not have known that the story would develop so dramatically.

Monte and I have been pals for years. He was probably the best known and most respected of all the Fleet Street cameramen of that era and was often seen sitting in airport terminals playing cards with the players.

If anyone was in need of a few pesos that day it was him – though, of course, he was no more guilty than either of the Bobs. Somewhere on the journey from Mexico City to Bogota he had lost his wallet. This included his passport, the travellers cheques supplied by his office and his personal cash. When Alf heard about this he told Monte that he would organise a whip-round among the players. Although Alf retained an aloofness when in the presence of the media, the relationships between him, his players and most of the travelling press corps were probably better than those of their counterparts today.

By the time Bobby was released, the rest of the squad had departed the heaving capital of Mexico and moved north west to the more refined cathedral city of Guadalajara where, amid parks, fountains and horse-drawn carriages, England were due to begin the defence of the World Cup.

To have lost Bobby Moore at that stage would have been a terrible blow but I don't think any of us believed that we would defend the World Cup without him. The whole affair had a Monty Python aspect to it, although at the time I don't suppose Bobby saw it quite like that. When he finally flew out of Bogota he was mobbed at the airport by well-wishers who had elevated him, almost overnight, from small-time jewel thief to global superhero.

Bobby had retained his calm, his sense of perspective and his dignity throughout the entire squalid affair. Alf, who had handled the whole business in a stern, businesslike manner, greeted him at Guadalajara airport and took him straight to training. He hadn't trained, or slept properly, for four days, but it spoke volumes for his character that he slipped straight back into World Cup mode with a minimum of fuss.

That night Alf deviated from his own unwritten law that forbade his players and their wives to mix on foreign trips. He told Bobby to take a taxi across the city to see Tina, who had arrived with Judith earlier that day. Bobby took Judith a bouquet of flowers. 'That's for looking after Tina and the kids,' he told her.

Months earlier, Judith and Tina had made plans to travel to the World Cup in a foursome with Kathy Peters and Frances Bonetti. For Bobby, Tina's presence provided significant support at a difficult time. The restoration of Bobby had an immediate effect on morale and the mood of the players at the training ground. The squad was complete once again. The lads were buzzing. Bob had lost some weight but that was the only visible sign of his ordeal.

Joao Saldanha, the previous manager of Brazil, visited us at the training ground one day and told Bobby that he'd had exactly the same experience in the same hotel in Bogota. We were due to play the Brazilians in the second of our group games and Joao, like practically everyone else in Mexico, was already calling it the 'real' final.

Unlike England, the Brazilians had won all the public-relations victories in Mexico. Their charm offensive had included visits to schools and hospitals, gifts to the poor and compliments to the rich. Alf's first move on arriving in Guadalajara was to ban the players from talking to the local press. We were not allowed to leave the hotel under any circumstances. We withdrew into our bunker. The FA flew in English frozen food. We even had our own bus and driver flown to Mexico. Our charm offensive could not have upset more people had it been devised by Attila the Hun.

In such circumstances we inevitably became the team everyone wanted to beat. Alf was a public-relations disaster. Some, of course, might view his aversion to the press as a strength, arguing that it meant he focused solely on one thing – winning football matches. He certainly never allowed anything to deflect him from his chosen course of action. It was quite obvious to me, though, that his past history – dating back to 1966 when he called the Argentine players 'animals' – weighed heavily against him among the Latin nations. Not only were we the team everyone wanted to beat, we were also the team the Mexicans loved to hate.

We had to accept, of course, that the locals felt an affinity with Brazil. But I was angered by the animosity towards us and it was clear that Alf did nothing to discourage the belief among the lads that Mooro had been picked upon in the hope that it might disturb England's preparations and loosen our grip on the World Cup. More than once, in Alf's company, I heard the phrase 'Latin plot'.

It was hardly a surprise then that, two days before the opening game against Romania, we were very nearly embroiled in another scandalous accusation, involving the theft of a watch. This time a jeweller arrived at our hotel and displayed his goods on tables in the foyer. During the course of the day some of the players mingled with other guests to look at the watches, rings, necklaces and gemstones. The jeweller was packing up at the end of the day when Alf came to the players who were drifting into the restaurant for dinner.

'There's been a theft,' he said discreetly, with his eyes raised to heaven. 'A watch is missing. No one is being accused at the moment, but you won't be surprised to learn that we're high among the list of suspects.'

Alf then suggested that rather than risk further allegations and another frenzy of anti-English publicity we club together and pay for the watch. I think we put in about ten dollars each and the jeweller went away happy. Not a word of this incident ever appeared in any newspaper. The accusation was as nonsensical as the one against Bobby, but Alf asked the players to confide in no one. I tell the story now to demonstrate how values have changed. In those days there was a far greater sense of loyalty among the players. They rarely betrayed their manager or team-mates.

Alf had absolute power. He was the boss, his authority was never questioned and his word was law. If he said, 'Don't talk to the press,' no one talked to them. He dealt with some strong characters – think of Jack Charlton and Nobby Stiles – and you might have expected, in such circumstances, some players to break ranks. None did. I have the impression that in today's game, football management is more a matter of consensus and compromise. England coaches now have nothing like the authority that Alf enjoyed, and I think they need it even more than he did. I was invited by Kevin Keegan to stay with the England squad in their hotel in Spa, Belgium, during Euro 2000 and I was immediately struck by how times have changed. The players travelled with their mobile telephones and mobile fax machines and seemed to be in constant touch with their agents. All the agents have contracts or an understanding of some sort with the tabloids. Anything newsworthy appears in the newspapers straight away. Alf would not have tolerated such intrusion.

He kept a tight rein on everything that affected his squad and, by and large, the players responded positively and responsibly. Even the six he finally axed from his squad of 28 accepted their fate with good grace. Compare that to Paul Gascoigne's lamentable behaviour at England's training base in La Manga when Glenn Hoddle, the manager at the time, told him that he wouldn't be in the squad for the World Cup in France.

The unlucky six dropped from the 1970 squad were Ralph Coates (Burnley), Brian Kidd (Manchester United), Peter Shilton (Leicester City), Bob McNab (Arsenal), David Sadler (Manchester United) and Peter Thompson (Liverpool). I had a bit of sympathy with all of them, particularly the older ones. Kidd and Shilton were only 21 at the time and Shilton, of course, went on to become a goalkeeping legend, winning a record 125 caps for England between 1970–90.

McNab, who won the league and FA Cup double with Arsenal the following season, flew home immediately to sit on one of the first television panels. All were invited by the FA to stay, but only Sadler and Thompson decided to do so. The rest went home. Me? I was delighted to be one of eight members of the World Cup-winning team of 1966 still in the squad.

The 1970 World Cup kicked off in Mexico City's Azteca Stadium in blazing heat on Sunday, 31 May. We watched on television at our hotel in Guadalajara. The Mexican kids representing England at the opening parade – they even had a blond Bobby Moore lookalike – were loudly booed and jeered by a crowd of 112,000. Otherwise, it was a brilliant and colourful ceremony, deserving of a more entertaining opening match than the ponderous goalless draw between Mexico and Russia.

The following day Alf finalised his line-up for England's opening match against Romania. There were no surprises. It was his first choice 11 – Banks, Newton, Labone, Moore, Cooper, Charlton, Ball, Mullery, Peters, Lee, Hurst. It was a very good team in my opinion. Terry Cooper was a fantastic left-back, more accomplished than Ray Wilson in the attacking half of the field. Francis Lee, a competitive, 20 goals a season striker, gave us a bit more flair at the front than Roger Hunt and, despite a stocky build, had boundless energy. Brian Labone was a commanding central defender who worked well alongside Bobby and was probably a better passer than Jack Charlton. But Alan Mullery was the real bonus in the heart of midfield. Although he made his debut against Holland in 1964, he missed the World Cup two years later. After that, Alf quickly realised that he was a better long-term bet than Nobby Stiles. Nobby was still in the squad, along with Jack, but in 1970 Mullery was a player at the peak of his prowess. It was impossible for Alf to ignore him. Strong and mobile, he demonstrated against Pele when England played Brazil that he ranked among the most diligent markers in the world.

Mullers was impressive in the opening game against Romania. They were a physical side and kicked everyone especially Keith Newton who was forced to hobble off. He was replaced by Tommy Wright and he, too, was kicked as soon as he touched the ball.

England, though, were clearly superior. I had a header saved and Francis Lee hit the crossbar before I ran on to a pass from Franny and drove a left-foot shot into the goal. It was enough to give us a 1–0 victory.

The following day, Brazil beat Czechoslovakia 4–1 in the same stadium. The crowd, at 30,000, was 20,000 less than watched our match against Romania. They loved to hate us, the locals, but they loved to watch us too it seemed. We saw the match on television. Brazil's defence didn't look remotely equal to their attack but it didn't really matter when you had an offensive line-up that included players of the calibre of Pele, Gerson, Rivelino, Tostao and Jairzinho.

The day before we were due to face Brazil, I committed the cardinal sin of leaving the England hotel without permission. We were living on the ninth floor of the Hilton in the middle of town and I needed to get out of the hotel. At times it was a bit like living in a prison. There was a settee by the lifts on our floor and for most of each day either Harold Shepherdson or Les Cocker sat there checking our movements.

I hadn't been sleeping well and arranged to meet Judith early in the morning for a cup of coffee. We were walking hand in hand through central Guadalajara when suddenly she spotted Les Cocker on the opposite side of the road. Before she said anything I'd ducked into a shop. Judith walked on and returned a few minutes later to find me cowering at the back of the shop. I was lucky. Had I been spotted I suspect my World Cup would have been over.

That night, the eve of the big match against Brazil, I wasn't the only member of the England party who didn't sleep. The Brazilian fans joined forces with the Mexicans to import the Rio carnival to the front door of the Hilton Hotel. The Samba bands played all night. Cars circled the hotel with horns honking. The players eventually all moved into a few back rooms, but it made very little difference. All night we could hear the chant 'BRA-sil, BRA-sil'.

At breakfast the following morning, the world champions looked as though they had been up all night, which most of us had. To make matters worse the demands of television meant that FIFA had agreed to a noon kick-off when the temperature would be close to 100°F.

Judith was among a record crowd of 71,000 squeezed into the baking Jalisco Stadium. We lost 1–0 but could so easily have won.

Alf was forced to make one change to the team, Tommy Wright replacing Keith Newton, the victim of the Romanian brutality in the previous game. Brazil were without Gerson, injured in the win over the Czechs. Paulo Cesar replaced him on the left and the speed with which he ran at Wright in the opening minutes gave us an idea of what to expect. The Brazilians swarmed all over us but they couldn't break down our organisation.

Bobby Moore played one of his finest games for England – he timed his tackling to perfection – but Alan Mullery challenged him for the man of the match award. Mullers pinned Pele in his own half, forcing him deeper and deeper to get the ball.

Pele was easily the greatest player of my generation, and probably the best of all time. I really couldn't understand how Maradona had the gall to complain when FIFA voted Pele 'The Player of the Century'. I played against him for England and for West Ham when we met Santos in a friendly match. He could play anywhere on the field. He was as strong as a bull and for a man of about 5ft 9in could leap into the air like a salmon. No one, before or since, could match his ball control. Vision, shooting ability, pace, courage – he had an abundance of everything required by a great footballer. Just to round it all off, he scored goals at a greater rate than anyone else in the world game. Having met him several times, I can confirm that he's a lovely chap, a wonderful ambassador for Brazil and the entire football family.

That might help you assess the true worth of Alan Mullery's contribution against Pele that afternoon in Guadalajara. The temperature reached 98°F and Alan, like most of us, lost about 10lb in weight.

Only once that afternoon did Pele seriously get the better of Alan and, on that occasion, he couldn't quite outwit the last line of England's defence – Gordon Banks. Most football fans will have seen on TV or at least heard about Gordon's remarkable save from Pele in what developed into a classic encounter between the two great football powers of the time.

The Brazilians still held the early initiative when, after just ten minutes, Jairzinho brushed past the England left-back, Terry Cooper, and centred perfectly to the back post. Pele climbed to meet the ball, heading it down crisply inside the post. As the ball bounced just inches away from the line the crowd were spontaneously greeting a goal when Banksie came from nowhere, swooping with incredible agility across the goal to scoop the ball over the bar. Pele was stunned, as we all were.

I was privileged to witness some of Gordon's finest saves, but nothing matched that one from Pele. In time, the film of that save became one of the most enduring images in World Cup history.

From that moment we grew in confidence. We had good scoring opportunities in each half. I remember bursting through the Brazil defence and then hesitating, believing myself to be in an offside position. Francis Lee had a chance but headed straight at their goalkeeper, Felix, and Alan Ball clipped the bar with a shot.

Perhaps our best chance fell to Jeff Astle, who came on late in the game for Lee. By then, sadly, we were a goal down, Jairzinho having capitalised on the groundwork of Tostao and Pele. Astle should have equalised. A panic-stricken defender headed the ball to his feet with only minutes remaining. Jeff was inside the penalty area with Felix out of his goal and no one else to beat. Somehow he contrived to miss the target altogether.

Looking back, it was extraordinary that England resisted as well as we did in those conditions. I lost nearly a stone in weight. In the dressing-room afterwards Dr Phillips pointed out to us that the American army-training manual forbade exercise when the thermometer exceeded 85°F.

We were bitterly disappointed because we deserved at least a draw, but we knew we had played a full part in a magnificent match. It was perhaps the most enthralling game of the entire tournament and at no time in my six-year international career did England play better than they did that day. There was no need for despair. We knew we could still qualify for the quarter-finals. Indeed, we could still face Brazil in the final. First, though, we needed to draw our final group game with Czechoslovakia.

That night we reflected on our performance at a cocktail party. 'If only Jeff had put that one away,' was a phrase I heard more than once that evening. Alf seemed content enough and was happy to see his lads relaxing. He even allowed the four wives to attend the party.

At the end of the evening I asked him for permission to escort Judith back to her hotel.

'Yes, Geoffrey,' he answered. 'But you know you have to be back by midnight, don't you? You do know what time midnight is, don't you Geoffrey?' Judith gave him one of her withering looks.

'Yes, Alf,' she said. 'We know. It's when both hands are pointing upwards!'

The Czechs had lost to both Brazil and Romania, so Alf believed this was an ideal opportunity to give one or two of the squad players a match. He made three changes, bringing in Jack Charlton, for what was to be his final game for England, Allan Clarke and Jeff Astle. I was rested.

To be honest, we struggled and, as in the games with Romania and Brazil, Alf sent on two second-half substitutes to reinforce flagging limbs. Alan Ball was one of them and probably had our best scoring chance in open play, shooting against the bar. The only goal of an indifferent, sterile game came when a Czech defender, Kuna, was unluckily penalised for handball as he fell in the penalty area. Clarke, the Leeds United striker making his England debut, scored from the spot, pitching us into a quarter-final clash with, yes, them again – West Germany.

We had three days to rest before the quarter-final and in that time we had to move to Leon, where the Germans had played their group games. At some stage during those three days Gordon Banks drank a bottle of beer and the consequences of that brief, innocent pleasure were dire.

I remember lying by the pool in Leon, going through the sunbathing routine that Alf insisted we follow, wondering whether I would be as fortunate this time against the Germans. They still hadn't forgiven me for the goal they claimed hadn't crossed the line at Wembley.

The match in prospect was a fascinating one. The Germans had outscored every other nation in the three qualifying matches, Gerd Muller scoring seven of their ten goals. But England had conceded just one goal in three matches and were generally acknowledged to possess the best defence in the world. A key component of that defence was Banks, probably the best goalkeeper in the world.

Alf took every precaution to ensure that his squad remained free of illness. He had a lifelong suspicion of foreign food. The only player in the squad who'd had a hint of sickness was Chelsea's Peter Osgood, who missed training one day with an upset stomach.

Our daily sunbathing routine, devised by Alf and his medical advisers, provides an idea of just how painstakingly he worked and planned to avoid the kind of illnesses that befall so many unsuspecting visitors to hot, humid climates. We spent most of each day in a light blue FA-issued leisure suit that looked like a boiler suit. We must have looked ridiculous but not as ridiculous as we looked when we all trooped out to the pool together for synchronised sunbathing.

Alf tried to keep us out of the sun but agreed reluctantly to a short period each day provided we were smothered in sun protection cream and supervised by a member of the coaching staff with a whistle and a stopwatch. First we were allowed five minutes on our backs. Then the whistle blew and we had to turn over and have five minutes on our fronts. The next whistle meant we could have five minutes in the pool. Then the whole routine would start again.

We had to strip down to our shorts for the daily weigh-in ritual and this gave Alf the chance to see how much sun we were getting. I think it was his way of checking on us, rather like going round the hotel rooms at night asking if we wanted sleeping pills. It was good management I thought at the time, discreet management.

It must have been particularly galling for Alf and Dr Phillips, having got this far with no more to worry them than Osgood's tummy bug, suddenly to face the prospect of losing a player as important as Gordon Banks just hours before the quarter-final against the Germans. Gordon first complained that he felt unwell the night before the match. He thought he'd be fine the following morning, but that wasn't the case. I remember watching him, that bright Sunday morning, walking across the lawn of our hotel on the arm of Dr Phillips. It was quite clear to me that he wouldn't be in the team that afternoon.

Did Gordon's absence cost us the game that day? It's a sweeping oversimplification to say that it did, but there is no doubt in my mind that his understudy, Peter Bonetti, should have saved one, if not two, of the goals that beat him. A goalkeeper of feline grace and spectacular agility – hence his nickname 'The Cat' – Peter had deputised for Gordon on six previous occasions and, in that time, had conceded just one goal. He was no slouch between the posts, but he had never played in a match as remotely important as the one now facing him.

My own feeling at the time, and nothing has altered my opinion down the years, was that Peter's mind was not wholly on the job. It was elsewhere, across the city, with his wife Frances. Peter was a man who took his family responsibilities seriously. It was clear to several members of the squad that he was struggling to concentrate on the challenge ahead when he was suddenly drafted into the team that day. Banks was a difficult enough act for Bonetti to follow if fully focused. In the circumstances at the time, I think it was almost impossible for him.

I understood then why Alf was so reluctant for the players' wives to travel to Mexico. We kept them away from the team hotel but, in a sense, that made us worry about them even more. It was precisely the scenario Alf had hoped to avoid.

As we approached the stadium in the team bus, flanked by Mexican police outriders, the mood among the players was confident. We knew the Germans had nothing we couldn't handle. They had five survivors from the 1966 final, as had we, and the early stages of another thrilling match seemed to suggest that the end result would be the same again.

For an hour we played brilliantly, with strength and invention, our solid 4–4–2 relentlessly disciplined with the full-backs Terry Cooper and Keith Newton overlapping regularly to compensate for the lack of wingers. The first goal, after 30 minutes, belonged exclusively to Alan Mullery. Having exchanged passes with Francis Lee, he hit a superb ball out to Newton on the right. The full-back carried the ball forward before crossing to Mullery who arrived like an express train in the German area. His shot, from about ten yards, was unstoppable; his first goal for England in his 31st international match. It had taken him nearly six years to score that goal – a long wait but at that moment well worth it!

The German response was immediate and only a wonderfully timed tackle by Bobby Moore prevented Franz Beckenbauer scoring an equaliser. Basically, though, England were so dominant that at half-time the German manager Helmut Schoen made a defensive change bringing on Willi Schulz in place of Horst Hottges. Before Willi could get his bearings, we scored again. The second half was just five minutes old when Mooro robbed Uwe Seeler and passed out of defence to Alan Ball. He passed to me, and I set Keith Newton away again on the right. Once more he finished his run with an excellent cross and Martin Peters appeared from nowhere to score in his usual style.

To this point, Peter Bonetti had enjoyed a trouble-free afternoon. England led 2–0, about 20 minutes remained and those of us who had been with Alf for some time knew that no team of his had ever surrendered a two-goal lead.

But there's a first time for everything. Schoen, the wily German coach, sent on fresh legs in the 57th minute. Jurgen Grabowski replaced Reinhard Libuda and clearly had instructions to wear down Terry Cooper. Exhausted by the killing heat, Cooper slowly faded from the game and should have been substituted. Instead, Alf took off Bobby Charlton and Grabowski, full of running, was allowed to grow in influence.

Bobby, playing his 106th game for England, hobbled off seconds after Beckenbauer had handed the Germans a lifeline. His initial shot was blocked by Lee, but he picked up the rebound and, although Mullery was forcing him away from the goal, managed a second shot. It was an unexceptional drive, but it seemed to surprise Peter Bonetti. He dived late and the ball squirmed under his body and into the net.

Alf immediately sent on Colin Bell for Charlton and, soon after that, tried to reinforce the defence by replacing Martin Peters with Norman Hunter. Whatever his thinking, at a stroke he had radically altered the shape of England's midfield. Beckenbauer had greater freedom to dictate the rhythm of the game but we were still creating

Top: Elation! Gottfried Dienst, the Swiss referee, has just awarded England's third goal despite German protests.

Above: The Germans suffered defensively for much of the game because they had no one to match me in the air.

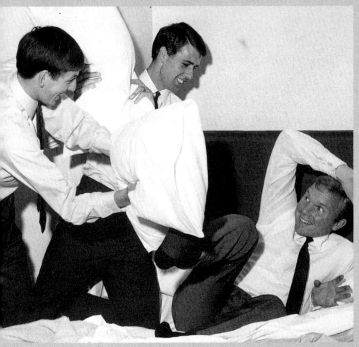

It just got better and better: following Bobby up the Wembley steps for the third time in three years.

Suddenly the world had changed for the three of us and, the morning after the final, everyone wanted to photograph us – even in the hotel bedroom.

Opposite above: Judith and I bask in the acclaim at the Royal Garden Hotel the following morning. Note my black eye – the result of a collision with the German goalie Hans Tilkowski.

Opposite below: You wouldn't believe it but this was Sunday lunch the day after our World Cup final victory, hosted by ATV at Boreham Wood. The Jules Rimet trophy occupies place of honour.

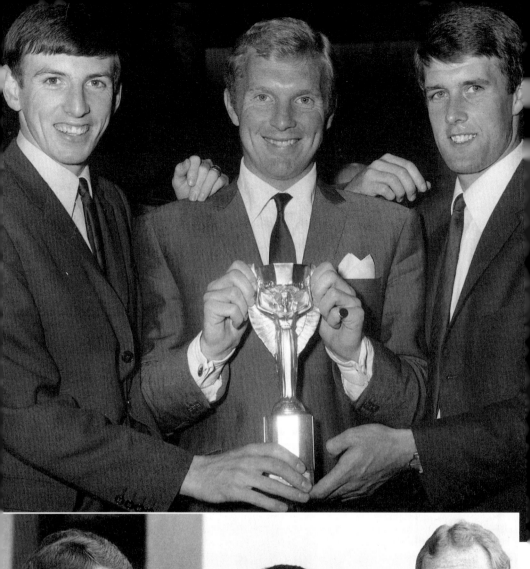

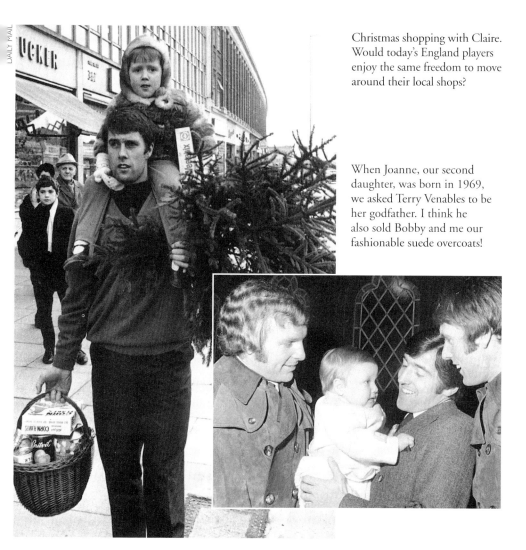

Christmas shopping with Claire. Would today's England players enjoy the same freedom to move around their local shops?

When Joanne, our second daughter, was born in 1969, we asked Terry Venables to be her godfather. I think he also sold Bobby and me our fashionable suede overcoats!

Opposite above: Sad to remember the way it was – Bobby Moore, who died in 1993, was a great friend to Martin and myself.

Opposite below: It was always a privilege to talk football with two of the greatest players in history. If you don't recognise them, then you're reading the wrong book!

At home with the Hursts, 1968. Most of the silverware on the table has since been stolen by burglars.

What a back four! Kathy Peters, Judith, Tina Moore and Frances Bonetti watched all England's matches during the 1970 World Cup in Mexico.

I love to be in the thick of the action. Billy Bonds and I challenge for a high ball against Stoke's Mike Pejic and Stuart Jump (no. 11).

Left: I took his place in the 1966 World Cup but there's no doubt in my mind that Jimmy Greaves was the greatest goalscorer of my era. It was a privilege to have him alongside me at West Ham for the last year of his top-class career.

Alan Hudson, who revived Stoke's fortunes in the 1970s, stayed with us for a few months and Judith introduced him to the mysteries of the kitchen. She, though, retained control of the rolling pin!

Right: Ronnie Harris was one of my most fearsome opponents but when I joined him at Chelsea I was able to view his talent from a different perspective.

A smiling Brian Mears (centre), the Chelsea chairman, introduces his new management team of Hurst and Gould in 1979.

Top: Back in the World Cup routine, this time as a coach in the dugout with, left to right, Don Howe, Ron Greenwood and Dr Vernon Edwards. We drew 0–0 with Spain and, although unbeaten, we still went out.

Above: Helmut Haller left the field with the 1966 match ball and later explained that 'if you score the first goal in a World Cup final you get to keep the ball...'

chances and when I got my head to a near-post cross from Colin Bell I thought I'd scored. The ball ran inches wide of the post.

It was a costly miss. With eight minutes remaining a weary Brian Labone mishit a clearance to Karl-Heinz Schnellinger. The German sweeper drove the ball back into the middle and our defence failed to move forward quickly enough to catch Uwe Seeler offside. With his back to goal, the little striker catapulted himself high enough to head the ball backwards over the stranded Peter Bonetti.

It was a freakish goal, I thought, but it meant extra time again. Having fought back from two goals behind, the initiative was with the Germans. Early in extra time I headed another cross from Colin Bell over the bar. I also met a good cross from Francis Lee which, this time, I drove into the net. For no obvious reason, the referee Angel Coerezza disallowed it. No player was offside and none had committed a foul.

That was our last chance. Ten minutes into extra time Grabowski's mastery of the shattered Cooper proved decisive. Grabowski crossed, Johannes Loehr headed the ball back into the middle and Muller met it with a thunderous volley past Bonetti who was rooted to his goalline.

That was it. England, the holders, were out of the World Cup. The dressing-room was like a field hospital at the end of a battle. Players were speechless, shell-shocked, numb with fatigue. Alan Ball was in tears. Bobby Charlton sat with his head in his hands. It was his last match for his country. Others would never play for England again – Labone, Newton and Bonetti.

I felt sorry for Peter but his role in our downfall was beyond argument. Some blamed Alf's tactics, his decision to replace Martin and Bobby with Colin Bell and Norman Hunter. But it was impossible not to wonder what would have happened had Gordon Banks played.

England hadn't conceded three goals in a match since the Scots beat us at Wembley in 1967. I felt that we hadn't been overthrown. We'd abdicated. For me, the sense of togetherness wasn't quite what it had been in 1966. Those in the squad who don't play regularly are as important as those who do and we had a tight unit in 1966. I'm not sure we had the same cohesive force in Mexico.

Football historians could probably trace England's decline as a football power to that hot day in June 1970. What none of us knew then was that it would be 12 years before England even kicked another ball in the finals of the World Cup.

It was one of the lowest points of my life. The following day, as the official party prepared to return to England, Judith and I flew to Acapulco with Bobby and Tina for a short holiday. I watched the rest of the tournament from the poolside.

Italy beat the Germans 4–3 in the Mexico City semi-final. I fancied the Germans to win, but they had clearly suffered physically from their long, hard game with us. Much as expected, the fabulous Brazilians beat Uruguay in the Guadalajara semi-final and then overwhelmed Italy 4–1 in the final. I couldn't help thinking as I watched that game that it should have been us playing Brazil in the Azteca Stadium that day.

CHAPTER TWELVE

Not them again!

I WAS HAPPY NOT TO BE ON THE OFFICIAL FLIGHT HOME FROM Mexico. It was, in a sense, the sad closing chapter to the most memorable and successful period in English football.

It certainly marked the end of the 1966 team. Bobby Charlton, Jack Charlton and Nobby Stiles, all in the squad in Mexico, were about to follow the examples of Ray Wilson, George Cohen and Roger Hunt and retire from the international game.

Jack told me later that he noticed Alf sitting alone during the flight home. He thought it was time they had a heart-to-heart chat so he walked down the plane and sat next to Alf. Jack was 35 and for five years had epitomised the resilience and bulldog spirit of the Ramsey era. But he'd played just once in Mexico and suspected that his international career was over.

'I've had a great run in the team, Alf, and I owe it all to you,' he said as he eased himself into the seat next to the England manager. 'I'll never forget what you've done for me. It's been a big part of my life and I've enjoyed every minute of it. I've had some great times. But life moves on, Alf, doesn't it? I think it's time for younger men to have a turn. What I'm trying to say is . . . well, to be honest, Alf, I think I've had enough.'

'I totally agree,' Alf replied with his usual candour.

Five of the 1966 team remained to play on beyond that 1970 defeat by West Germany – Gordon Banks, Martin Peters, Bobby Moore, Alan Ball and me. I was 28 and felt that I still had a lot to offer England. The reality was to prove somewhat different. I had just eight games left to play in the white shirt.

For Mooro and me, refreshed after our break in Acapulco, the sense of anti-climax continued deep into West Ham's domestic season. Martin Peters had been sold to Tottenham Hotspur in March 1970 and, for the first time in nine years, the three of us were not together in the dressing-room at the start of a season.

There was none of the pomp that had greeted our return to club football in 1966. England's failure to retain the World Cup provoked the inevitable gnashing of teeth and soul searching. Most fingers pointed at Alf and blamed the loss to West Germany on his decision to substitute Martin and Bobby Charlton. It was a tactical decision by Alf at the time. With England leading 2–0, Alf substituted two of his most industrious midfield men because it took the players much longer than usual to recover from matches in the climatic conditions in Mexico. The winners were due to play in the semi-finals just three days later.

Perhaps the substitutions had a role to play in our defeat but the loss of Gordon Banks was, without question, the key element. Alf wouldn't use that as an excuse. He remained steadfastly loyal to his players and would criticise none of them. Loyalty ranked high in the gospel according to Alf. We took it for granted and, to my knowledge, he never betrayed any of us at any stage of his 11 years as England manager. He could quite justifiably have used the absence of Banks as an excuse but this would have implied criticism of Peter Bonetti, his understudy that day. Peter received a lot of criticism in the press but none of any significance that could be attributed to the manager.

Typically, Alf didn't help his cause by stating on his return home that England had nothing to learn from the Brazilians, who in 1970 had one of the best teams, if not the best, I've ever seen. It was a ridiculous statement and he later tried to claim that he had been misunderstood.

The Brazilians had won the World Cup for the third time, so earning the right to keep the Jules Rimet Trophy. Their enterprise, artistry and attacking play captivated everyone. England, on the other hand, were remembered for less attractive qualities like 'work rate' and 'defensive organisation'. The cynics, and there were plenty of them, celebrated the triumph of the artist over the labourer.

'Total' football, as played by Holland and the mighty Ajax team that won three consecutive European Cups from 1971–73, was about to sweep impressively across the European scene. The belief that players were interchangeable, that defenders could attack as effectively as forwards, was largely alien to the English game where the great 'method' teams like Arsenal and Leeds were the trendsetters.

This then was the backcloth against which Sir Alf Ramsey and England's overthrown champions began the rebuilding process in August 1970. At West Ham, we started the season against Tottenham at White Hart Lane, Bobby and I facing Martin and Alan Mullery just eight weeks after we had all been united in our bid to retain the World Cup.

We twice came from behind to draw 2–2 in a thrilling match watched by 53,640. Jimmy Greaves scored one of our goals, as if to remind Alf of the talent he abandoned prematurely. Even in those days Jimmy was still impishly humming the tune 'What's it all about, Alfie?' I don't think he ever forgave Alf for the way he discarded him.

Jimmy joined West Ham in the part-exchange deal that took Martin to Spurs. My admiration for his technique remained undiminished although the qualities that had made him such a waspish penalty-box predator were fading. We didn't see the best of him at West Ham. He had suffered with hepatitis, a debilitating illness, late in his career at Spurs and, of course, had a developing drink problem. Today Jimmy claims that if you ask Chelsea fans which were his best years, they will say those at Chelsea. If you ask Spurs supporters they will say those at Spurs. But if you ask West Ham supporters they will say those at either Chelsea or Spurs.

Initially, though, the signs were encouraging. Jim made a sensational debut for West Ham, scoring twice in a 5–1 win over Manchester City at Maine Road in the spring of 1970. He always scored on his debut for a new club. I scored twice that day and Ronnie Boyce hit the other, one of the most extraordinary goals I've seen. Joe Corrigan, the City goalkeeper, kicked the ball clear from the edge of the penalty area and turned to walk back towards his goal. The ball landed in the centre circle and Ronnie volleyed it straight back. Joe heard the reaction of the crowd and turned to see the ball sail over his head into the net. Some years later Joe told me, 'Just for a second that day, I thought we were playing with two balls!'

Jimmy, still only 30, scored four goals in his next six appearances to the end of season 1969–70, and Ron Greenwood, not unreasonably, felt that his signing might prove to be a masterstroke. Sadly, that wasn't the case. The goals were drying up. Ron tried him briefly in a midfield role, but that didn't work either. Jim scored nine goals in 32 First Division games in 1970–71 and announced his retirement at the end of the season. He threw away one or two useful years of his career in my opinion and after dabbling in the insurance business for a while became an enormously popular figure on TV.

West Ham really needed a significant contribution from him that season but it wasn't forthcoming. We struggled to score goals. We didn't win our first match until I scored a hat-trick against Burnley at Upton Park in October. The little winger Johnny Ayris made his debut that day, creating one of my goals.

We lost five consecutive games over the Christmas and New Year period, slumped to 20th in the table and suddenly relegation looked a real possibility. The sombre mood at Upton Park wasn't helped by our FA Cup exit in the third round at Blackpool. Blackpool's early season form had been as bad as our own. They were bottom of the First Division and had won one of their previous 18 games. Although the Bloomfield Road pitch was icy, that was no excuse for our 4–0 defeat.

This was the occasion of the Blackpool nightclub affair and

Jimmy's involvement in it marked the beginning of the end of his brief spell at West Ham.

It turned out to be a disastrous season, perhaps the most miserable of my time at Upton Park. We finished 20th in the First Division table, just avoiding the two relegation places. These were filled by Blackpool and Burnley who, hard though it is to believe, had played even worse than us during the previous nine months.

I was still scoring at the rate of a goal every other game and, despite West Ham's poor form, was determined to retain my place in the England side. Five months after the disappointment in Mexico, Alf had us back together for a friendly match against East Germany at Wembley.

It was a big game largely because Alf wanted to convince those who had questioned his management that England remained a major force in world football. He discarded the 4–4–2 system and played Francis Lee and Allan Clarke up front with me. He also gave a first cap to Leicester's brilliant young goalkeeper Peter Shilton and recalled Emlyn Hughes and David Sadler, both relatively inexperienced at international level.

It proved to be a winning combination. I was delighted to set up goals for Franny Lee and Martin Peters and midway through the second half Allan Clarke also scored a well-executed goal. England won 3–1, giving Alf just the performance he wanted before England began negotiating the qualifying programme for the 1972 European Championship.

In all that season, England won six and drew one of seven games. So, from a morale point of view, the World Cup exit hadn't been disastrous. We were no longer world champions, but we were still buzzing. We beat Greece and Malta (twice) in the European Championship and finished the season with a heart-warming 3–1 win over Scotland at Wembley.

Somewhat surprisingly, Alf dropped Bobby Moore from the team that played Malta in Valletta. He gave the captaincy to Alan Mullery for the first time and introduced Martin Chivers (Tottenham), Roy McFarland (Derby County), Colin Harvey (Everton) and Joe Royle

(Everton) to the side, and left out several established players including me.

It was one of those nightmare trips. We arrived on the island to discover most of the squad's baggage had been mislaid and then we had to train in the dark in the little Gzira Stadium in Valletta. Everyone expected a massacre but in the end we scraped through 1–0 with a goal from Martin Peters.

Martin's wife Kathy had travelled with Judith to the match and quite inadvertently the two girls had booked into the same hotel as the players. When Martin and I realised this we told the girls to keep out of the way but Alf soon discovered they were there. Just before we returned home, he pulled Martin and I to one side and said quite plainly, 'Neither of you will be selected again if your wives ever book into the same hotel as the team in the future.'

At least at that stage, in February 1971, it appeared that I still had a future with England. The reality was somewhat different. Time was running out. Just as the West Germans had ushered me on to the international stage in 1966 so they would bring down the curtain on my six years of international football.

First, last, worst, best – the Germans had figured at every significant turn in my career. Even my one European triumph at club level had been against a German team – TSV Munich in the Cup-Winners' Cup final of 1965. I played my first game for England against West Germany at Wembley in February 1966. The best moment of my career came against the same team in the World Cup final five months later. The worst moment? West Germany again in the quarter-final defeat in Leon in 1970.

Somehow it was quite appropriate that Franz Beckenbauer and his countrymen should provide the opposition when I pulled on an England shirt for the last time in April 1972. I didn't know, of course, that I'd never be back in the Wembley dressing-rooms as a player. A back condition that troubled me occasionally was becoming more of a problem but I'd still scored 16 goals in first-team matches for West Ham that season and felt that I had another year or two to offer at the highest level. Because of the way I played, with my back to goal for much of the time, I took a lot of buffeting from unsympathetic defenders over the years. The legacy was lower back pain and muscle spasms. This didn't, in itself, stop me playing, but it was beginning to affect my ability to run and jump for high crosses. I was no longer as powerful as I had been. I had a lot of physiotherapy and manipulative treatment and I was once encased in a cast to immobilise my back. All these things helped but, as many professional footballers find, there is often a price to pay for the physical demands you make on your body during your career.

I was lucky enough to avoid serious injuries during my playing career and, apart from the odd twinge in my back, I don't have any health or fitness problems today. I've become a disciple of power walking and find that helps to keep me supple, enabling me to play golf regularly with no back pain.

Thirty years ago, though, when I was in my early thirties, Alf must have believed that my days as the England centre-forward were over. I think he was wrong but I would say that, wouldn't I?

England had qualified for the two legs of the European Championship quarter-finals and I had played my part, scoring in wins over Switzerland in Basle and Greece in Athens. The goal against the Greeks in December 1971 was my 24th and last for my country.

The two quarter-final matches against West Germany were arranged for the following April and May. Alf tried to organise friendly matches in the spring but had to admit defeat when the Football League clubs refused to release their players. This meant that when we faced the Germans in the first leg at Wembley on 29 April, the England team had not played for five months.

When Alf named his squad he was unable to call upon Derby County's Roy McFarland, who had established himself as England's new centre-half, because he was injured. Alf decided to give Bobby Moore an unfamiliar marking role in the middle of the defence. This was not his strength.

The fact that Alf chose a midfield trio of Martin Peters, Colin Bell and Alan Ball encouraged the Germans to believe that they could attack us when they came to Wembley for the first leg. Sure enough, the Germans exploited Bobby's indecision in his new role and took a first-half lead through Uli Hoeness, his shot deflected into the net by Norman Hunter.

Midway through the second half, Francis Lee equalised and at that stage Alf would probably have settled for 1–1. It was not to be. Six minutes from time Bobby upended Siggi Held in the box and Gunther Netzer scored from the penalty spot. With two minutes remaining, the predatory Gerd Muller scored a magnificent third goal.

By this time I was sitting on the substitutes' bench, having been replaced by Rodney Marsh of Queens Park Rangers. It was the first time Alf had substituted me and I remember thinking that perhaps I would have to get used to the feeling. As we sat disconsolately in the dressing-room afterwards, discussing the degree of difficulty involved in overturning a 3–1 deficit, it didn't occur to me that I might not even be in the squad for the second leg in West Berlin. I hadn't played badly. In fact, I thought that none of the other five attacking players in the starting line-up that day – Lee, Chivers, Peters, Ball, Bell – could claim to have played any better than me. Alf's decision to take me off 20 minutes from the end was a mystery. Even Helmut Schoen, the West German manager, said afterwards that he thought I was England's best player.

This defeat was nearly as upsetting as the one in Leon. We were not used to losing at Wembley. Before the Germans, only three other continental teams had beaten us at Wembley – Hungary, Sweden and Austria. In reality, though, it was no disgrace to lose to the Germans at that time. Helmut Schoen had built what I have always regarded as their best team. Everything revolved around Beckenbauer, by then vastly experienced at international level. Schoen had the pick of the Bayern Munich team that was to dominate the European Cup in the mid seventies before the arrival of Liverpool. Sepp Maier, Georg Schwarzenbeck, Paul Breitner, Gerd Muller, Uli Hoeness, Karl-Heinz Rummenigge and Beckenbauer were all club-mates and many figured in West Germany's eventual successes in the 1972 European Championship and the 1974 World Cup.

I assumed I would have a role to play in the second leg on 13 May, a week after Leeds had beaten Arsenal 1–0 in the Centenary FA Cup final and a fortnight after West Ham's season finished with a 1–0 win over Southampton. Ron Greenwood had left Bobby and I out of the team for the Southampton match specifically so that we would be fresh for England's return date with the Germans.

I had no good reason to believe that Alf wouldn't pick me. Judith, as she did so often in those days, made plans to fly out to watch the match with Tina. By the time Alf had named his squad, without me and Alan Mullery, it was too late for them to change their plans. The girls wanted to go ahead with the trip and I decided I would go, too, as a spectator.

As a result of his omission, Mullers wrote to Alf saying that he no longer wanted to play for England. 'I'm thirty years old and have no chance of making the 1974 World Cup,' he wrote. 'I want to spend more time with my family.'

Alf named his squad on 3 May. Six days later, having come to terms with the fact that my England career was probably over, Allan Clarke and Francis Lee pulled out of the squad because of injuries. I was reinstated. The following morning I joined the squad for training and hurt my back. They were due to travel later that day and it was clear that I had no chance of responding to treatment in time for the match. I had to withdraw from the squad, and that was the end of my career with England.

I travelled to West Berlin as a spectator as planned but, because of a room shortage, couldn't book into Judith's hotel. We watched the match together and England restored some pride and honour with a resolute goalless draw. But it was the Germans who progressed to the semi-finals. Alf had adopted a defensive strategy with Peter Storey and Norman Hunter in midfield and afterwards the German manager complained, 'England confused the jungle with a football pitch.'

West Berlin in the days of the Iron Curtain was a vibrant city and, suspecting that such opportunities would be few in the future, Judith and I went out for the evening with Bobby and Tina, and Franz Beckenbauer and his wife. We didn't get back to Judith's hotel until the early hours of the morning. Because all the big hotels in the city were full, she was sharing a room and king-sized bed with Tina Moore. I made my way back to my own hotel.

The next morning I learned that, sometime after my departure, Mr and Mrs Moore let themselves into Judith's room, where she was asleep in the king-sized bed. Mr Moore was so spectacularly relaxed that Mrs Moore realised he was incapable of returning to the England team hotel. So when she eventually climbed into bed next to Judith, Bobby fell into the same bed next to Tina. In the morning, Judith curled up at one end of the bed, was woken by the telephone ringing. Bobby answered. It was a member of the Football Association staff. They'd been looking for him. He was about to miss the charter flight back to London. Tina, bleary-eyed, sat up in the middle of the bed.

'Oh! Judith,' she said. 'Good morning. Bobby, it's Judith. Say good morning to Judith.'

'Good morning, Jude,' he said with as much dignity as he could muster in the circumstances.

Later, after Bobby had rejoined the England squad, Judith inadvertently picked up some of Tina's perfume in the bathroom, as they were preparing to check out.

'D'you mind? Pinching my perfume,' said Tina.

'You've got to be kidding,' said Judith. 'I've just shared my bed with you and your husband.'

I returned from West Berlin still unsure of my international future, but I was never picked again. Only four of the 1966 World Cup winners remained in the team – Gordon Banks, Bobby Moore, Martin Peters and Alan Ball. Gordon played just two more games, winning his 73rd and last cap in a 1–0 win over Scotland a fortnight after returning from West Berlin.

Alf kept faith with Bobby for a further 18 months. He played his 108th and last game for England in a 1–0 defeat by Italy at Wembley in November 1973. Martin played his 67th and last game for England in May 1974 and Alan played on for another year, until May 1975 when he was awarded his 72nd cap in a 5–1 win over Scotland.

By this time, the Football Association had disgracefully sacked Alf. I thought they treated him appallingly. If you consider some of the England performances in recent years and compare those with the single game that cost Alf his job, you begin to realise how unjustly he was treated.

The beginning of the end came at Wembley in October 1973 when England needed to beat Poland to qualify for the finals of the World Cup. The Poles had already beaten England in Chorzow and knew that a draw would be sufficient for them to qualify.

Three weeks before the second leg, England had demolished Austria 7–0 at Wembley, the biggest win against a foreign side since 1961, so I was optimistic when I took my seat in the stand for the Polish game. Brian Clough, one of the biggest names in club football at the time, had no fears either. With words that would haunt him for years, Clough described the Polish goalkeeper Jan Tomaszewski as a 'clown'.

England bombarded the Polish penalty area from the kick-off but found Clough's 'clown' in truly outstanding form. We were guilty of some spectacular misses but Tomaszewski saved anything on target. A film montage of Tomaszewski's contribution that night shows that England created more chances in that one game than they have done in entire seasons in more recent years. Poland had one chance to score, and did so, 12 minutes into the second half. Norman Hunter, the defensive fixture alongside Roy McFarland following Bobby's retirement from international football, made the uncharacteristic error that would have such dire consequences for Alf. Rashly attempting to dribble round Gregorz Lato, he lost possession to the Polish winger whose cross from the right was driven into the net by Jan Domarski. His shot went through the legs of Emlyn Hughes, unsighting Peter Shilton in England's goal.

England equalised six minutes later with a penalty from Allan Clarke and had further chances denied them by Tomaszewski. In desperation, Alf sent on Derby County's Kevin Hector with two minutes remaining. He nearly headed the winning goal but, in truth, had little chance to influence the game at that late stage.

The corner count that night reflected England's domination –

26–2 – but it was little consolation for Alf. England had failed to qualify for the finals of the World Cup for the first time and, to rub salt into the wound, the Scots had already secured their place in West Germany.

The pressure, much of it generated by a cynical media, mounted and finally on 1 May 1974, the FA sacked the man who had won the World Cup for England. I always thought it significant that about ten years later the FA secretary at the time, Ted Croker, apologised and admitted that they had got it wrong. The FA have spent much of the last 40 years trying to find a coach good enough to replace Alf. Apart from Bobby Robson, whose England team reached the 1990 semi-finals, no one has even come close to his achievements.

I was proud to be part of his team. He played a major role in my life. Like Ron Greenwood, he showed faith and loyalty. Some said he was too loyal to his established players and should have introduced youngsters earlier. I think that was rubbish, much of it provoked by an ill-informed press, but I suppose it's par for the course. It happens today. I discussed this once with Alan Shearer when we met while on holiday. He, too, suffered constant sniping from some quarters of the media once he'd established himself in the team.

When Alf left me out of his squad my own feeling was one of enormous disappointment. I felt I could still justify my place. I thought that I could have played for England for another one or two seasons. It was a sad and unsatisfying way to end an international career. But that's the way it was in those days, and I think it's probably much the same today. Many big name players, before and since, have complained that they were left out without a letter of explanation or even a consoling word from the coach.

I had six great years in an England shirt and played in two World Cups so it was always going to be disappointing when the end came. Playing for my country had been a big part of my life and I would have been just as upset had Alf written me a personal letter of explanation.

I had no bitterness towards him. I was grateful that he selected me in the first place. His decision made an enormous difference to my life. On all the occasions we met in the years before he died he never explained to me why I was left out. He was always the same – friendly but slightly aloof. The player–manager relationship remained intact. 'How are you, Geoffrey?' he would ask as if I was still reporting for one of his training sessions. 'Fit and well, I trust.'

When Alf died in April 1999 English football lost one of the century's most significant sporting figures. I went to his funeral but was disappointed not to see more representatives from the game's establishment paying their last respects to a great Englishman.

CHAPTER THIRTEEN

Pottering about

THE TWO GREAT PILLARS OF MY CAREER EACH COLLAPSED FROM under me within a fortnight in the spring of 1972. My whole life had revolved around playing for West Ham and England and, suddenly, I was no longer wanted by either. It was tough to accept at the time and one of the lowest periods in my professional life.

My career at West Ham ended, without me realising it, on a damp April afternoon, just a fortnight before I played my last game for England against West Germany in the quarter-finals of the European Championship.

A crowd of 32,660 watched me play my 499th and last game for West Ham against Liverpool at Upton Park. No one in the ground that day knew that it was my farewell appearance after 13 seasons of first-team football. So, sadly, I never had the chance to say a proper goodbye to a crowd of East Londoners who had initially shown so much patience with me and, ultimately, provided such fun, support and encouragement. The West Ham fans were, and still are, special people in my life.

At the time, Liverpool were chasing Derby County for the First Division title. They beat us 2–0, and finished the season one point behind Derby. But they were emerging as one of the greatest European club sides of all time and had, in their ranks, an ebullient youngster called Kevin Keegan who, six months later, would make his debut for England against Wales.

I sensed a new era on the horizon, not just for England and Kevin but for West Ham and me. Although I was at the end of the contract I'd signed in 1966, I had no burning desire to leave Upton Park. So I was disappointed to learn that the club was willing to release me. When Manchester United had tried to sign me five years earlier, Ron Greenwood told me nothing about the deal. This time Ron came to me and said that Stoke City had asked whether I was available. When United wanted me, I wasn't told. When Stoke wanted me, I was told. It was quite obvious to me that the club didn't intend to offer me a new contract. In the circumstances I felt there was no point in staying at Upton Park. Perhaps rashly, I told myself, 'If they don't want me, I don't want them.'

There was no question of pleading to stay at West Ham. My view has always been that as one door closes another opens. I'm not an emotional person. I was not the sort to pour out my heart to the newspapers. I'd always kept a tight rein on my feelings. I was a bit miffed when Alf left me out of the opening World Cup match against Uruguay in 1966, but I said nothing. Had I made a fuss he might have discarded me as a troublemaker. I sat tight and my turn came. It was a lesson I never forgot.

With hindsight, I shouldn't have jumped so quickly. I should have given it a bit more thought. Had I done that I would probably have come to the conclusion that, although it was time to move from West Ham, it would be beneficial for the family to stay in the London area.

What disappointed me as much as anything else was that, having decided my time was up, the club insisted on asking for a transfer fee. I'd been in the first team for 13 years and felt they could at least have given me a free transfer after that kind of service. I'd cost them all of £20 – the signing-on fee all groundstaff boys received when they were offered their first contract as full professionals. Now they wanted £80,000 for me. That wasn't a fortune, even in those days, but I felt it was mean. I shouldn't have allowed it to happen, but I did, and Stoke were willing to pay the money. It was a wrench to leave the club that I'd grown to love. I was proud of my achievements at Upton Park.

What made an impression on me at the time was the acknowledgement by the vastly experienced Stoke City manager Tony Waddington that, in his opinion, I remained among the most prolific goalscorers in the First Division. I left West Ham with a total of 248 goals in 499 first-team games. It was an average of one every two games and is still a post-war record for the club. Only Vic Watson with 326 goals in 505 first-team games between 1920–35 has scored more for West Ham.

I would have had an extra goal to embellish my record had it not been for the spectacular agility of my new Stoke City team-mate Gordon Banks in my last season at West Ham. Stoke provided the highlights of my final season at Upton Park with a series of matches that must be engraved indelibly on the minds of all West Ham fans of that period.

Anyone who claims an allegiance to West Ham will know the significance of Stoke City in 1971–72. We played them twice in the First Division, winning 2–1 at Upton Park and drawing 0–0 at Stoke, and four times in the League Cup, which was the forerunner of the Worthington Cup. For a while it looked as though the League Cup might salvage another disappointing season.

Once again the First Division programme was a catalogue of inconsistency and the FA Cup didn't offer much consolation, although I was delighted to score a hat-trick against Hereford. Having knocked out the ambitious Southern League club, the famous third-round conquerors of Newcastle, we succumbed to Huddersfield and Frank Worthington in round five. It was the League Cup that produced our most impressive performances that season. I remember scoring two in two minutes late in a replay at Cardiff. That gave us a 2–1 win and a fourth-round tie against Don Revie's mighty Leeds United at Upton Park.

Although I hit the bar and Terry Cooper cleared two chances off the line, this match ended in a 0–0 draw. This was the great Leeds team of Giles, Bremner, Hunter, Lorimer and Clarke so we didn't think too much of our chances in the replay. As it turned out, we went to Elland Road and won 1–0 with a towering header from young Clyde Best after eight minutes of extra time.

The prize in the next round, believe it or not, was Bill Shankly's Liverpool who were at least as good as Leeds. I nearly missed this match with a troublesome hamstring injury. I didn't have many injuries and I hated missing games but I think I would probably have missed this one had the club's medical staff not persuaded me to have a cortisone injection into the back of the hamstring. There was little evidence at the time of cortisone's possible threat to long-term health so I agreed. It was the only time I had a cortisone injection and I'm not sure that I would agree to it now, but on that occasion it worked – up to a point.

More than 40,000 crammed into Upton Park and saw me score West Ham's equaliser after Bobby Graham had given Liverpool a 30th minute lead. But I was in pain and had to go off at half-time. Bryan 'Pop' Robson scored the decisive goal six minutes from time to give us a 2–1 win.

A fortnight later Pop hit a classic hat-trick against Sheffield United in the quarter-finals – one goal with his head, another with his right foot and a third with his left. He was one of West Ham's great marksmen, a penalty-box predator who scored 104 goals in two spells at the club. We beat United 5–0 that day, Best scoring the other two, and joined Chelsea, Spurs and Stoke in the last four of the competition.

We were drawn against Stoke with the first leg of the semi-final at the Victoria Ground early in December. Peter Dobing, a highly talented inside-forward who was then 33 but playing like a spring lamb, gave Stoke the lead after 14 minutes. I beat Gordon Banks from the penalty spot just before half-time and Clyde Best scored the winning goal with a spectacular volley that went in off the bar. It was a terrific match that contained a real footballing rarity – a Bobby Moore booking for a professional foul on Jimmy Greenhoff.

Having fought back from a goal down, we felt we had the momentum. This was reinforced by the following morning's newspapers that made much of the fact that only once before had a team that won the first leg of the semi-final failed to reach the final. A place at Wembley, it seemed, was within our grasp.

A week later we met again in another titanic clash at Upton Park. A defensive mix-up involving John McDowell and Tommy Taylor allowed John Ritchie to score in the 73rd minute. Locked at 2–2 on aggregate, we would still have won had it not been for the enduring excellence of my World Cup team-mate Banks.

Three minutes from the end of extra time he was penalised for bringing down Harry Redknapp. 'Penalty,' said the referee, Keith Walker. 'My job,' I thought. I put the ball on the spot and looked at Gordon who was smiling at me. In those situations, under lights at Upton Park, you could always sense the crowd willing you to score. 'Stick this away,' I thought, 'and we're back at Wembley.'

I struck the ball well and drove it, so I believed, beyond Gordon's reach. The shot was a replica of my penalty kick that had beaten him at Stoke a week earlier. This time, though, he anticipated the direction of the shot and saved it spectacularly. After the match he told me that he'd remembered my approach and run up to the ball when I'd scored from the penalty spot the week before. He guessed that I would hit it in exactly the same place and he was right.

I was so disappointed that I couldn't sleep that night but, where Gordon was concerned, there were occasions when you just had to hold up your hands and accept that you had been outwitted by the best in the business. He was still a wonderful goalkeeper and I wasn't surprised when the football writers voted him Footballer of the Year later that season.

So, a third game was necessary. Had it not been for Gordon's save we'd have been at Wembley. Losing 1–0 that night was a huge disappointment for me in a season of huge disappointments. Even today, people still remind me of that missed penalty.

We had to wait until 5 January for the third game, in front of 46,196, at Hillsborough. Compared with the first two meetings this was a game of little incident. Gordon twice saved brilliantly from Clyde Best and the Stoke fans jeered Mooro mercilessly following another undignified challenge on Greenhoff, who was a clever, elusive opponent. It ended 0–0.

Nothing that happened in the game matched the memorable coach journey to Hillsborough. The team had stayed overnight at Buxton, Derbyshire, and by the time we reached the outskirts of Sheffield the roads were choked with traffic. It was obvious we were going to be late for the kick-off. Ron Greenwood was desperate, but one of the lads shouted at the driver, 'Go up the other side of the road.' He thought for a couple of minutes, summoned up all his courage, and then did just that, driving through the traffic on the wrong side of the road. We arrived at Hillsborough just in time and discovered that the Stoke City team bus had been delayed too. 'Traffic,' we were told.

There was a postscript. After the match, our coach driver stuck his head sheepishly into the dressing-room and informed Ron that during the game someone had removed his petrol cap and filled the tank with sand. We had to wait for another coach to take us home and, just to make matters worse, when Ron tossed the coin for choice of venue for the second replay, he lost.

So on 26 January, nearly two months after the first match, we met again at Old Trafford, a venue that clearly favoured Stoke's travelling fans. The attendance figure for this game was just short of 50,000 and none of those who journeyed north from London or Stoke could have complained about the entertainment value that night.

It was a match packed with incident and controversy from the moment, early in the game, when Stoke's Terry Conroy collided with Bobby Ferguson, the West Ham goalkeeper. Conroy pleaded his innocence but it looked like a foul to me and Bobby, badly shaken, had to leave the field to receive treatment for a head wound. These were the days before five substitutes were allowed, so Bobby Moore volunteered to go in goal, largely because no one else wanted the gloves. He was still adjusting to his new role when the referee, Pat Partridge, awarded Stoke a penalty in the 33rd minute. We were delighted and somewhat surprised when Mooro saved Mike Bernard's initial shot but, sadly, he couldn't hold the ball and Bernard followed up to score the opening goal.

With Bobby Ferguson receiving treatment we were down to ten men but still managed to equalise through Billy Bonds just before the interval. Almost as soon as the second half kicked off, with a bandaged Ferguson back in goal, Trevor Brooking scored to put West Ham ahead. Could we hang on? No we couldn't! Stoke took every opportunity to exploit Ferguson's uncertain vision and scored twice, through Dobing and Conroy, to win a tumultuous match 3–2.

I remember Ron Greenwood complaining afterwards about Stoke's attitude to Bobby Ferguson in the second half. 'It wasn't what I would call good sportsmanship,' he said.

Tony Waddington, the Stoke City manager, described the match as 'out of this world'. He thought a Wembley final against Chelsea would be an anti-climax for his players after their classic, marathon series against West Ham.

Tony was a smashing guy, a manager of the old school, rather than one of the track-suited, academic types. He spent 17 years as manager of Stoke and was responsible for their first major success. After the semi-final against us, they beat Chelsea 2–1 at Wembley with the two old hands, George Eastham and Terry Conroy, scoring the goals. With that win Stoke City qualified for the UEFA Cup the following season. They were in Europe for the first time, a source of enormous excitement in a small town previously best known for its pottery and the novels of Arnold Bennett.

European football presented Stoke with a fresh challenge and Tony knew he would need to strengthen his squad. He particularly wanted an experienced striker to lead his attack. Perhaps he saw something in me during that series of matches against West Ham that convinced him that I was the striker he needed because one morning that summer Ron told me that Stoke had made a bid, matching West Ham's valuation. 'We don't want to lose you, but we won't stand in your way if you want to go,' he said. The message was clear enough to me. I packed my boots and, 16 years after first walking into Upton Park as a kid, took the family north to view the Potteries.

I would happily have given West Ham another couple of years

and Ron generously acknowledged the fact that my style of play had contributed significantly to the development of some younger team-mates. Years later in his book *Yours Sincerely* he wrote: 'He was always willing to help others. Clyde Best scored twenty goals in his first season basically because of the assistance he got from Hurst.'

But it was Tony Waddington who now wanted me to use my experience on Stoke's behalf. I remember driving north for pre-season training in the yellow Mercedes I'd bought when England played in West Berlin in May. I was very pleased with myself because I think I was among the first to realise how much cheaper it was to buy cars on the Continent. I'd paid £4,000 for the car in Germany, £1,000 less than the list price in England.

Initially, I stayed in the North Staffs Hotel, a large, imposing relic of Victorian England opposite the railway station in Stoke. This was not ideal, and for about two months George Eastham kindly allowed us to use his house on the outskirts of Stoke while he played in South Africa. Soon Judith found us a home – a detached bungalow with stables in five acres in the village of Madeley. She had moved up with our two daughters by the opening day of season 1972–73.

My Stoke City career started with a 2–0 win over Crystal Palace at the Victoria Ground. But we struggled in the early part of the season and it wasn't until Jimmy Greenhoff scored a hat-trick in a 5–1 win over Manchester City at the Victoria Ground that we began to find some consistent form. I'd scored a few goals but when Alf Ramsey named his first England squad that season my name was nowhere to be seen.

This confirmed what I suspected after the European Championship disappointment against the Germans. Alf was clearly looking at younger options. Malcolm Macdonald and Martin Chivers had already played for England, and Southampton's Mike Channon made his debut in the first game of that season, against Yugoslavia at Wembley. It was in the next match, against Wales in Cardiff, that Alf introduced Kevin Keegan.

But it clearly wasn't all going quite as Alf planned. This was the period building up to the fateful World Cup qualifying ties with Poland and at one point I believe he considered recalling me to the side. When he watched me play for Stoke against Arsenal my hopes were revived briefly, but there was no call-up. Many years later, when I was manager of Telford in the Southern League, Francis Lee gave me a lift home from a function in his chauffeur-driven limousine.

'You ruined it for Alf, you know,' he said. 'Once you'd gone, he couldn't replace you. He couldn't find anyone to do what you did in the England attack.'

It is a fact that in the 19 England matches between my farewell appearance against West Germany and Alf's sacking, he used Rodney Marsh, Martin Chivers, Malcolm Macdonald, Joe Royle, Mick Channon, Allan Clarke, Kevin Keegan, John Richards, Peter Osgood and Stan Bowles in a variety of striking partnerships.

I think Tony Waddington would have appreciated a Hurst recall to the England colours as much as Hurst himself. Gordon Banks apart, Stoke hadn't had too many England players wearing their red-and-white striped shirt. I think he felt that a recall would have been a public acknowledgement of his sound judgement in signing me at the age of 30!

But I didn't hear from Alf. I didn't let that spoil my enjoyment of that first season at Stoke. Rather like West Ham, they played good football. Tony's teams were always among the most attractive attacking sides and the fact that they were newly crowned League Cup winners gave them an extra swagger.

We finished 14th and should have done better. Our first-round exit in the UEFA Cup at the hands of West Germany's Kaiserslautern was a disappointment. We lost 5–3 on aggregate, but I was pleased to score in our 3–1 win in the home leg. Overall, my appetite for scoring goals showed no sign of diminishing. I was particularly delighted to score on my return to Upton Park just before Christmas. The crowd gave me a great reception but they weren't so happy when, after just nine minutes, I headed Stoke in front with my 11th goal of the season. It was a poignant day for me and I saw a lot of old friends, most of whom were delighted that I'd scored but finished on the losing side. West Ham won a terrific match 3–2.

A notable absentee from that match was Gordon Banks, who was recovering from a car accident in which he tragically lost the sight in one eye. He played just eight First Division games for Stoke that season – the last eight of his career in England. It was a terribly sad way to end a wonderful reign as the world's finest goalkeeper. By then he was 35, known throughout the world as 'Banks of England', and I think he would have played on and added to his 73 international caps. He came out of hospital full of good intentions and bristling with determination to play again and, in fact, did so – in America with Fort Lauderdale. With only one eye he was still good enough to be voted the country's best goalkeeper.

CHAPTER FOURTEEN

The prodigal son

WE HAD BEEN IN MADELEY FOR ABOUT 18 MONTHS WHEN, IN January 1974, Alan Hudson arrived on our doorstep, with all his baggage. Tony Waddington had paid a club record fee of £240,000 for him and asked Judith and me if we would help him settle in his new environment. What this meant was simply this – could he live with us for an indefinite period of time? Please!

It was a slightly unusual request but Judith said she didn't mind having a lodger in the house, so we agreed. What we originally thought might be weeks turned into months and, during that time, I think we helped provide Alan with the stable background that 'Waddo' thought he needed to be a success at Stoke. Alan had a rebellious streak. He wasn't a bad lad, but he was too easily led astray. My task, as a senior professional, was to keep him on the straight and narrow. There is no doubt in my mind that he was one of the outstanding players of the seventies and, had his attitude been right, I think we would remember him today as one of the greats of world football.

When he joined Stoke he was just 22 and had made a name for himself as the midfield creator in Dave Sexton's very exciting Chelsea side. As a kid 'Huddy' lived in a forties prefab, just a long goalkick from Stamford Bridge, and as a teenager in the sixties he had enjoyed all the social life that west London had to offer in those days.

He and his great pal and mentor Peter Osgood, who was four years older, supplied Chelsea with the attacking impetus that brought them the FA Cup (1970) and the European Cup-Winners' Cup (1971). They were, if you believed the stories of the time, the life and soul of the King's Road.

Alan, who missed the epic FA Cup final win over Leeds United because of injury, had all the midfield qualities that Waddo believed would make Stoke serious championship contenders. That was the theory anyway.

The previous season, my first at the Victoria Ground, I'd scored ten goals in 38 First Division appearances. It wasn't bad but I knew I could do better. After so long at West Ham, I knew it would take me time to settle into a new club and get on the same wavelength as team-mates unfamiliar with my playing style.

It was a strange environment at first, not just for me but for Judith, too. I had to get to know new playing colleagues and Judith, who liked to watch the games, had to get to know the wives. Just as there is a pecking order among players, so I guess there is a pecking order among wives. When you think about it, the arrival of the wife of a World Cup winner in a provincial club like Stoke was bound to start the tongues wagging.

One day Judith arrived for a game wearing the diamond cluster ring I'd had made for her. I believe she thought it a bit ostentatious but she wore it from time to time because it was a special gift from me. I know her mother thought it pretentious when she saw it for the first time and there were occasions when Judith would actually turn the diamond cluster into the palm of her hand in case people thought she was showing off. On this particular winter's day she was sitting in the directors' box at the Victoria Ground surrounded by the wives of other players.

'My hands are freezing,' she said.

'I'm not surprised,' said the wife of a team-mate. 'With a ring like that, pet, you won't be able to get gloves on.'

Actually, it didn't take long for us to be accepted as part of the family at Stoke. I already knew Gordon Banks and George Eastham, who had been with me in the England squads over the years. They were friends, which helped. There were other new arrivals at the club, too. Jimmy Robertson, the former Scotland, Arsenal and Spurs winger who signed from Ipswich, became a good friend along with Geoff Salmons, another talented winger who joined from Sheffield United, and later, of course, Huddy.

For all of us, Stoke City presented a new challenge. I remember thinking, after years in West Ham's claret and blue, just how strange I felt in a new strip. Somehow, the red-and-white stripes of the Stoke shirts just didn't quite feel right.

My first season wasn't helped by the fact that after playing against Arsenal with a heavy cold on a misty afternoon just after Christmas, I went down with pneumonia. I had a collapsed lung and after a fortnight in hospital, George Eastham suggested I go to play in the sunshine of South Africa for a few weeks to recuperate.

I spent nearly two months playing for Cape Town City, coached by Roy Bailey, who had been the goalkeeper in Alf Ramsey's Ipswich team that won the First Division title in 1962. Many years later his son, Gary, played for Manchester United and twice for England.

Judith followed me to South Africa with our two daughters. It was a wonderful experience for all of us. We lived in a comfortable hotel with Table Mountain visible in the distance. The weather was magnificent and we made the most of the deserted beaches. Cape Town remains one of my favourite cities. The only unpleasant memory is of the unease I felt at coming face to face with the realities of apartheid for the first time.

I was aware of what apartheid meant but like most young footballers of the time I had no experience of such a system of segregation. You can imagine the sense of shock therefore when, on arrival at the airport, the first thing we noticed were the signs outside the public toilets proclaiming 'Whites only'.

I'd grown up with black players at West Ham, including John and Clive Charles and Clyde Best, and they were treated like all the other players. In South Africa, though, I played in an all-white team in an all-white league. Thankfully, that sort of thing is no more than a memory to the people of South Africa.

When I returned, tanned and fully recovered, I found I had missed just four games, because of the severity of the winter weather. However, Stoke were locked in the relegation zone at the bottom of the table. My first game back was against West Ham at the end of February and we won 2–0, but we had a fight to avoid dropping into the Second Division.

It was clear to Tony Waddington, who had nursed hopes of challenging for the title, that he would have to strengthen the team just to avoid another relegation fight. He suspected the following season would be a dogfight in the lower half of the table because the Football League, for what they thought the best of reasons, was introducing a three-up three-down system of promotion and relegation.

This was designed to ensure that the competition at the top and bottom of the four divisions would remain exciting and relevant until the very last days of each season. With only two clubs going down each year it was felt that many matches lost their significance long before the season ended. Attendance figures were plummeting and this new system would give them a much-needed boost. However, it seems to me that the change to three up three down meant that from Christmas onwards at least half the clubs in the First Division were living with the threat of relegation. Safety and survival, inevitably, became the priorities.

The decline in attendances was, sadly, beyond dispute, but terrace violence was as much to blame as the football itself. The overall attendance figure for 1973–74, the first season of three up three down, showed a drop of five million fans on the 30 million who attended the same number of matches in 1967–68. Attendance figures for 1974–75 rose slightly, the crowds perhaps tempted by the importance of late-season matches, but were they entertained by the quality of the football they saw? On one Saturday in the last month of the season a quarter of the games ended as they had started – goalless.

I remember Tony Waddington telling me that the fear factor rose significantly among managers in 1973–74. First Division coaches who once used end-of-season matches to blood young players, dug in defensively to ensure they didn't lose. Not losing became more important than winning. That wasn't good for the game.

Tony Waddington was an adventurous spirit who, like Ron Greenwood, championed open, attacking football. There were, in fact, many similarities between Stoke and West Ham. They were solid clubs of sound ideals, both benefiting from principled leadership at boardroom level. Like Ron, Tony knew his position at the club was secure. He had been manager since 1960 and was responsible for bringing the legendary Stanley Matthews back to Stoke where he played until he was 50. Tony was on safe ground. He may have feared relegation but he clearly didn't fear it enough to allow the threat to compromise his beliefs.

So, when Alan Hudson, one of the great attacking midfield players of his generation became available, Tony was the first on the telephone to Stamford Bridge. Had he been a manager constantly worried by the threat of relegation, Huddy was probably the last player he would have wanted in his team.

Alan Hudson should have been the Franz Beckenbauer of English football. He had all the qualities of the great German captain but, unlike Franz, he didn't produce the goods on a consistent basis. Having said that, he was the best I played with apart from the World Cup-winning team.

There was a wayward side to his nature. He and Peter Osgood had fallen out with Dave Sexton, who felt that the attitude of both players was wrong. When Dave dropped them, both refused to train. This was a ridiculous swipe at authority and both players were immediately suspended and transfer-listed.

Tony made an enormous cash bid by Stoke's standards for Huddy, more than double the club record £100,000 they had paid Birmingham for Jimmy Greenhoff. Chelsea accepted, and on the morning Alan signed, Ossie made his last appearance at Stamford Bridge in a reserve match against Ipswich. Tony also made an attempt to sign Ossie – would that have affected my position at the club? – but two months later he joined Southampton for £275,000.

When Alan arrived at the Victoria Ground he was a stone overweight. He'd left his wife Maureen in London and it was obvious to Tony that he would need a 'minder' for his record signing. 'Will you keep an eye on him, Geoff?' he asked me. I think Tony saw me as a father figure. Judith and I were living in the country, outside Stoke, and he felt that the busy young London socialite would benefit from rural life. I wasn't so sure. Anyway, Judith said Yes and Alan moved in.

He was a bit cocky, basically a nice lad but vulnerable. There was a bit of the George Best about him. You couldn't meet a nicer guy than George but he has a little self-destruct button. There was nothing malicious about Alan but he invariably seemed to make the wrong decisions.

I think we helped him settle because he played some of the best football of his career at Stoke. Maureen came to stay occasionally and I remember her surprise when Judith explained that she had persuaded Alan to go shopping with her in the supermarket. Shopping was something Huddy didn't do in London, unless it was for the latest fashions.

Judith also introduced him to the kitchen and it was amusing to see the flamboyant young prince of the King's Road adapting to family life in Stoke-on-Trent. Eventually, he was making tea for us in the evenings. When we were watching TV at night I'd say, 'Who fancies a cuppa?' and Huddy would stroll out to the kitchen and return with a tray of tea and biscuits.

On the field, his impact was immediate. He played the last 18 games of 1973–74 and we lost only twice. We finished fifth in the First Division, a new experience for me. In all my years at West Ham we never finished above eighth. It meant a place in next season's UEFA Cup.

Alan was still a kid but he played brilliantly. In his second home game we beat his old club, Chelsea, 1–0 and in his third game at the Victoria Ground a crowd of 40,000 turned up to see Leeds United, who had led the table from the first day of the season. This was their 30th game and they hadn't lost any of them. My old mate Jack Charlton had gone by then but they still had Billy Bremner, Norman

Hunter, Peter Lorimer, Mick Jones and Allan Clarke. They remained an awesome team and you could sense the resignation among our supporters as they cruised into a two-goal lead through Bremner and Clarke. But Hudson started pulling the strings in midfield. Mike Pejic scored and then Huddy equalised. Denis Smith headed the winner for Stoke in the 70th minute.

It was a remarkable revival and proved to be the defining moment of the season for us. When Huddy signed we were in the lower half of the table, but with him prompting from midfield we climbed steadily upwards. We beat Leicester, Tottenham, Chelsea – Alan scoring the only goal at Stamford Bridge – and finally Manchester United in the last game of the season.

Sometime during that summer break, when Alan and I were both in London, he invited me out for lunch. We met around one o'clock in the afternoon in west London, had some lunch and then moved on to one of his favourite watering holes for drinks. Then we went to another of his favourite watering holes, then another and another and so on until, at about midnight, I forced myself into a cab leaving him in a bar. The next time I spoke to him I asked whether he often spent entire days drinking. 'No more than once a week,' he replied. That certainly wasn't the case when he was living with me, but it gave me some indication of the lifestyle he had at Chelsea.

I kept an eye on him during the time he lived with us but, as I said, he had a self-destruct button that, like George Best, he often pushed without warning. His first road accident, for instance, was something of a surprise because he was driving Judith's car. We had given him permission to borrow it, expecting to get it back in one piece. He wrote it off in a country lane.

The second crash came a couple of days before one of the biggest matches in Stoke's history – a UEFA Cup tie against Ajax in September 1974. Alan and I had a night out with Waddo at the manager's local pub in Crewe. Do players socialise with their manager in this way today?

By this time Alan was living in Barlaston. That night he was driving. We left the pub at closing time and he drove me home. Then he set off to his own house. I thought no more about it until the early hours of the morning when Maureen, who was still living in London, called to say he had been in a road accident. She explained where he was and I dressed quickly, climbed into my car and set off to find him.

He'd driven the car across a T-junction and buried it in a thicket. When I found him he was shaken and bleeding, but not bad enough to warrant a hospital visit. I took him home where we cleaned him up, bandaged his wounds and put him to bed. It was nearly 4 a.m. before Judith and I finally went to bed and as I dozed off I remember thinking to myself, 'I should have telephoned the police station.' When I got up in the morning, it was the first thing I did. By then, they knew Alan had been in an accident because someone had found the car. They'd had several police dogs out in the early hours of the morning looking for him, but they were very understanding.

Four days later Alan played in the Stoke side that met Ajax in the first-round first leg of the UEFA Cup. Still a bit shaken from his accident, he was largely ineffective when we really needed an influential performance from him. The Dutch club, the masters of total football, were widely regarded as the best club side in the world.

We drew 1–1 – Rudi Krol hitting a tremendous shot past John Farmer from 25 yards for the Ajax goal – and clearly faced a struggle in Amsterdam a fortnight later. By the time of the second leg, Huddy had recovered from the worst of his injuries but, as far as I was concerned, the opportunity was lost. We should have done the job properly at Stoke. Ajax held us to a goalless draw and were eventually knocked out of the UEFA Cup by Juventus. My own European club career ended that night in Amsterdam.

Alan rarely learned from his mistakes. He left bits of damaged cars all around the Stoke area. They built a roundabout just outside the city centre and forgot to tell him. One night he hit the roundabout at speed and left the car slewed across the middle. To this day it's known locally as the Hudson roundabout!

How sad it was, years later, to read that he had been seriously injured by a car while crossing a road in east London. I'm happy to say that he made a heroic recovery. I see him from time to time and still get enormous pleasure from his company.

He left Stoke in December 1976 and joined Arsenal for £200,000. He was reluctant to leave and Tony Waddington was reluctant to lose him. Alan had a few financial problems at the time and asked the club if they could help him with an extended contract. It was out of the question. A gale had carried away the roof of the Butler Street Stand and Stoke needed every penny they could get to repair the damage. An FA Cup third-round replay against Tottenham that season had to be staged at Port Vale because of the damage.

The game was changing and financial considerations were beginning to weigh heavily on managers and coaches. Tony Waddington was one of the first to recognise this. I remember him telling me, 'If we're not careful the game will soon be run by accountants.' What foresight! During my time there, Stoke City was a well-run club but the Victoria Ground was in constant need of refurbishment – not surprising, I suppose, when you consider that Stoke had been in continuous occupation of their ground for longer than any other club in British football. They had the same address from 1878 to 1997 when they moved into the shiny, new Britannia Stadium.

All this, combined with the growing bills in the Hudson household, spelled the end of his days at Stoke. Waddo was in tears as the prodigal son returned to the bright lights of London. I think he viewed Huddy as the key element in his long-term plan to challenge the First Division's big hitters – Liverpool, Leeds and Derby County. Tony had a deserved reputation for building attractive, attacking teams and that period with Hudson was probably as close as he got to creating a truly outstanding Stoke team capable of sustaining a challenge for the First Division title.

Huddy replaced Alan Ball in Arsenal's midfield and Terry Neill played him in the 1978 FA Cup final team beaten by Ipswich. But I never felt he was as happy at Highbury as he had been at Stoke. Whenever I've spoken to him about it he's always warmly recalled his years at Stoke. I think he had a particularly good relationship with Tony Waddington, who clearly idolised the Hudson style of play. Later, after a spell with Seattle Sounders in the United States, Alan returned to the Victoria Ground for his final three seasons. His career never quite lived up to its early promise.

It was at Stoke that he won his two England caps against West Germany and Cyprus in the spring of 1975. Alf Ramsey had called him into his provisional squad for defence of the World Cup in 1970 – he was just 19 – but never picked him to play, then or at any stage in the future. Alf liked his players to conform and Alan was a non-conformist. But Alf's successor Don Revie gave him a chance after Waddo had told the newspapers, 'Alan Hudson will get picked for a World XI before he gets picked for his country.' Alan played brilliantly in England's 2–0 win over the Germans at Wembley and was just as effective when Malcolm Macdonald scored all five in the 5–0 win over Cyprus. In that game, Alan was being marked by a waiter from Fulham and during an injury stoppage the waiter told him, 'I'm your biggest fan!'

Revie never picked him again. Alan believes it was because he had refused to attend the pre-match lunch with his England team-mates while on Under-23 duty as an over-age player in Hungary. Rather like Alf, Revie preferred players who observed his rules.

The moral of the Alan Hudson story is simple. Talent in itself is not enough. It has to be properly applied. There is more to being a great professional footballer than just skill with a ball.

Alan had far more ability than most of the other players during my time in the game. His passing, short and long, was sublime. Although predominantly right-footed, his vision, awareness and speed of thought allowed him to wriggle out of the tightest situations and set up attacking moves with the minimum of fuss. He also delivered the ball from corners and set pieces with unerring accuracy.

The history of the game is littered with similar examples of great players who failed to capitalise fully on their talent. The seventies provided us with Rodney Marsh, Frank Worthington, Stan Bowles, Tony Currie and Charlie George – all wonderful entertainers who never quite fulfilled their potential in my opinion.

Some might argue that George Best squandered a unique talent. But I would say that for five or six years he exploited his talent to the full, a fact widely acknowledged when he was voted European Footballer of the Year in 1968. You don't achieve that distinction alongside Matthews, Di Stefano, Law, Eusebio and Charlton if you are betraying your talent. His failure was an inability to sustain his position at the very pinnacle of the game, but at least he got there.

In skill terms, I was just a workhorse alongside some of them, but at least I was still working. Physically, it was becoming harder for me and I wish I had played alongside a couple of youngsters who could have done some of the running for me. Perhaps I could have stayed another couple of years at West Ham had another striker provided the young legs for me in the way that I had, initially, for Johnny Byrne. I could have given West Ham the same quality service that I gave Stoke.

I sometimes wonder what we might have achieved in 1972–73 had I stayed. West Ham finished sixth that season with Pop Robson scoring a very impressive total of 28 goals.

At Stoke, playing alongside John Ritchie or Jimmy Greenhoff, I was still expected to make the decoy runs out to the flanks, dragging defenders with me. Off the ball running was a big part of my game and I was still doing it at the age of 33. I needed a strike partner to take that burden from my shoulders. When no one came along to share the responsibility I knew my time was nearly up.

In my last season at Stoke, 1974–75, we again finished fifth, just four points behind the champions, Derby County, and two behind the runners-up Liverpool. During the autumn period I remember scoring the only goal in a 1–0 win over Queens Park Rangers that lifted Stoke to the top of the table. Another first for me!

The quality of Stoke's football at this time was outstanding but my enjoyment of it was shattered by terrible news from home. My younger brother Robert, just 28, had committed suicide, throwing himself under a train at Chelmsford railway station.

He was a big, good-looking boy. We'd been as close as any brothers during our early childhood but when I left home to join West Ham and live in digs, he was barely 11. From that moment football occupied my life, especially at weekends, and I saw less and less of him but my parents had made me aware over the years that he was becoming a bit of a problem. He did silly, juvenile things and they believed that his state of mind was seriously affected when his long-time girlfriend committed suicide.

He was closer to our sister Diane, who was two years older than him and two younger than I am. She saw far more of him in his teenage years and tried to teach him to play the piano. I often wondered whether he felt that he was in the shadow of a famous older brother, but Diane has told me that this wasn't the case. He wasn't the envious type.

He was a good all-round sportsman, had a trial with Crystal Palace and played cricket for Chelmsford. Diane says that the difference between the two of us was one of attitude. I was single-minded. He was easily distracted.

School was an ordeal for him. Sometimes he'd refuse to go. On these occasions he used to lock himself in the toilet. Even when he was apprenticed to a local butcher, my mother would find him sitting on a park bench when he was supposed to be at work.

Diane remembers him as a loving, affectionate boy with a stutter that he eventually overcame. Sadly, he fell in with the wrong crowd when he left school. He watched the World Cup final in 1966 on the communal TV at a home for young offenders. Apparently the other boys knew he was my brother and that gave him a special status among the inmates.

But his behaviour became increasingly eccentric. Occasionally he'd sleep in the garden or leave the house with his dinner plate, telling my mum and dad, 'I know someone who needs this more than me.'

My parents often took Robert and Diane to watch me play at West Ham but even these Saturday afternoons out had a dark side for Robert. 'Whenever I watch Geoff play, West Ham lose,' he used to say. 'I just bring bad luck.'

I think the loss of his girlfriend plus my mother's decision to leave home – my parents eventually divorced in April 1975 – had an effect that few realised at the time. He had just come out of a psychiatric hospital when he died. They believe he chose the day – Friday the thirteenth. As he set out for Chelmsford railway station he said that he was going to London for a job interview. The verdict at the inquest was misadventure.

His sudden death had a profound effect on me at the time. The club was sympathetic and supportive. I didn't play for about a month but otherwise was involved in every match that season. I scored a total of 11 goals, three in the League Cup, a competition that had been particularly kind to me over the years.

I scored my last goals in the League Cup in a game that had special significance for Huddy. We met Chelsea in the third round, six days after they had parted company with their manager Dave Sexton. As we travelled down to London Alan relayed all the gossip to the Stoke lads. Chelsea were clearly in a state of disarray and he was particularly keen to show the Stamford Bridge faithful what they had been missing since he moved north. We drew 2–2 and when Chelsea came back, still managerless, to Stoke a week later we drew 1–1.

The Stoke chairman Albert Henshall won the toss of a coin for choice of venue for the replay and when Chelsea returned to the Victoria Ground six days later, Ron Suart, their chief scout and a former Blackpool manager, had taken charge of the team on a caretaker basis.

It made little difference. We beat them 6–2. Huddy scored and was jubilant afterwards. I scored twice, giving me a career total of 49 goals in the competition, a record equalled 23 years later by Ian Rush of Chester, Liverpool, Leeds and Newcastle. Rush was the great goalscorer of his day. A lean, wiry Welshman of prodigious pace, he spent a season learning the basics of the trade at Chester before Liverpool paired him with the fabulous Kenny Dalglish. What an awesome partnership they formed in the eighties!

I like to think that Ian was a bit like me in that he could be relied upon to work for the benefit of the team. The game is full of predatory marksmen who loiter around the penalty area but the world's truly outstanding strikers are those who happily combine a goalscoring instinct with an appetite for hard work. Ian Rush was one, and I have to admit that he was a bit quicker than I was.

He benefited from the fact that he played in one of the greatest club sides of all time. At their peak Liverpool were far more dominant in European football than the modern Manchester United. Rush played alongside Dalglish in two of Liverpool's five European Cup finals. He also won the First Division championship five times and the FA Cup three times. People forget just how good Liverpool were. Over a four-year period in the early eighties they were unbeaten in 25 rounds of the League Cup. In total, Ian appeared in *six* League Cup finals, in the competition's various guises over the years – Milk Cup, Littlewoods Cup, Coca-Cola Cup. In my day, before the game sold its heritage to the sponsors, it was simply called the League Cup and I was proud, long after retirement, to know that my record of 49 goals remained intact. Then along came 'Rushie'!

In October 1995, a few months after playing in his sixth final, Ian scored his 48th League Cup goal in a 4–0 win over Manchester City at Anfield. Liverpool were beaten 1–0 by Newcastle in the next round and, with Ian then 34, I thought I would remain unchallenged as the competition's record-breaking goalscorer.

At the end of that season Ian moved to Leeds and although he played in two League Cup games for them he didn't score. Surely my record was untouchable. I remember making the Coca-Cola Cup draw live on television and being asked about it.

'He's just one goal away from equalling your record,' said the programme's host. 'What's your advice to him?'

'Retire!' I replied.

He obviously wasn't listening. His old pal Dalglish, by this time the manager of Newcastle, lured him to St James' Park for a final season. In October 1997, five days before his 36th birthday and two years after his 48th League Cup goal, the inevitable happened. Playing in the black-and-white stripes of Newcastle, he scored in a 2–0 win over Hull City. I was delighted for him! Truly I was! All I will say is that, according to the statisticians, he scored his 49 goals in 81 League Cup ties. I scored my 49 in 60.

You have to remember, too, that the pitches were much heavier in my day! And the balls! Seriously, though, the heavy pitches never troubled me. I remember feeling strong and on top of my game on the night we powered Chelsea off a muddy pitch at Stoke. Sadly for them, Chelsea never recovered from that thrashing. By the time they visited the Victoria Ground for a First Division match in early April, they were in serious trouble. A Hudson-inspired 3–0 win lifted Stoke to third in the table. At the end of the season Chelsea were relegated and Tony Waddington called me into his office and said that, although I had a year left on my contract, he wouldn't stand in my way if I wanted to move. 'West Brom think you could do a job for them,' he said with a smile.

It was no great emotional upheaval. I said goodbye to Huddy and Waddo and my boot boy, Garth Crooks, who was to have a great playing career of his own, and set off for Birmingham. We were reluctant to move house again because we'd bought the tenancy of a pub, The Sheet Anchor, in the village of Baldwin's Gate and I'd grown to enjoy pottering about behind the bar in the evenings. In those days a lot of players went into the pub business as their careers came to a close. Pubs and insurance were the two lifelines most of us clung to before Sky TV and the Bosman ruling ensured that most big-name players retired as millionaires.

Barry Adams, a friend and neighbour, and I had popped into The Sheet Anchor occasionally and it was invariably empty. We decided we'd like to refurbish it and the day the bank agreed to give me a small loan was my first step into the world of business and finance.

My presence behind the bar helped attract the locals and I did all the things landlords are supposed to do, including making sandwiches for the dominoes and darts teams. The darts lads were surprised one night when I accepted their challenge. 'Nearest the bull wins,' they said. I'd never played but we each put £1 in a pot for the prize money. I made one stipulation. Each player had to stand with his back to the board, bend forward and throw the dart between his legs. I won, but looking back, it's not a pastime I'd recommend.

Johnny Giles, the new player-manager of West Bromwich Albion, was quite happy for me to commute from Stoke. He paid £20,000 for me and thought my experience would help his young side win promotion from the Second Division. With hindsight it was a mistake to move to the Hawthorns. Playing in the First Division suited my game better. I was nearly 34 and my running power was beginning to fade. The physical demands of the Second Division meant that you couldn't get by on skill alone.

I scored against York and Charlton Athletic and played my last Football League game against Plymouth Argyle on 18 October 1975, nearly 16 years after my league debut for West Ham. Albion won 1–0. Johnny Giles dropped me from the side and didn't pick me again. You can't criticise his decision – six months later, he led Albion into the First Division. He had been a key figure in the Leeds success story and he was still an influential figure in midfield. Many felt he would eventually go back to Elland Road as manager, but he never did.

I have two abiding memories of my three months in the West Brom team. The first came in the second round of the League Cup. We were beaten 1–0 in a replay by Fulham but I had the chance to line up against two of my old England pals – Bobby Moore and Alan Mullery. As you might expect, nostalgia ruled in the bar after both games.

The second memory involved an England captain of the future. Bryan Robson was a lightweight, curly haired 18-year-old with a handful of games under his belt when he and I played together in the Albion team that year. He was a quiet boy in the dressing-room but he was keen and fearless and, as I recall from our training sessions, blessed with a biting tackle. It gave me a lot of pleasure watching his career develop over the years.

Albion released me from my contract in March 1976 and I decided at that point that my career in the Football League was over. I could have drifted down the divisions with a number of interested clubs but it wasn't for me. Although I had no chronic injuries I'd taken a physical battering and my back pain in later years was evidence of that. These days front strikers are much better protected by referees but throughout my career I had to endure heavyweight defenders thumping into me from behind. I wasn't quite in a wheelchair but I knew that wherever I went they would expect me to set an example and I felt I could no longer do myself justice. So, I let it be known that I wanted to stay in the game as a coach or manager. Sadly, this prospect didn't excite the game as much as I thought it would.

I received two offers. One was from Harry Gregg, the former Manchester United goalkeeper who was manager of Crewe at the time. He wanted me at Gresty Road as his player-coach. The other was from Telford United, an ambitious little club in the Premier Division of the Southern League. I met Telford's financial director, David Kirkland, in the pub I'd just bought in Eccleshall. Telford sounded like a progressive club, closely linked to the local community in Shropshire.

In those days Telford was a rapidly growing new town. The agreement with the club included coaching work for Telford Corporation in local schools for two afternoons a week. I thought about their offer for a week and then agreed to join them from the start of the following season.

By this time I'd agreed to spend the summer playing for Seattle Sounders in the burgeoning North American Soccer League. The Americans were trying to recruit the cream of the past generation of international players. Pele had joined New York Cosmos, Bobby Moore was going to play for San Antonio Thunder, George Best agreed to go to Los Angeles Aztecs.

Before flying out to Seattle I had a one-month commitment in Ireland with Cork Celtic. They asked me to play for them in the spring of 1976 by which time I was regularly watching Telford in preparation for the following season. The Telford vice chairman Gerald Smith used to drive me to Swansea on Saturday evenings after their game. I would take the overnight ferry to Cork, play on the Sunday afternoon and fly back to Manchester on Monday morning.

I enjoyed it, but a month was enough. Eventually we flew to Seattle where I spent five months playing in the Kingdome, an indoor stadium that housed around 60,000. We used to get about 25,000 watching our games. There were a few familiar faces there – Jimmy Gabriel, Mike England and my former West Ham teammate Harry Redknapp.

We travelled all over the States that summer, revisiting many of the venues that West Ham had played when Ron Greenwood was pioneering the old west with his young team in the sixties. Harry

Redknapp and I particularly remembered the Houston Astrodome, the vast and magnificent indoor arena where West Ham had played Real Madrid. When the referee tossed the coin before the kick-off that day Bobby Moore was given choice of ends. 'We'll kick with the air conditioning,' he said with a dry smile.

Inevitably, Judith and I spent a lot of time with Harry, his wife Sandra and their two sons Mark and Jamie, who of course followed in his father's footsteps. I'm sure Harry won't mind me saying that Jamie became a better footballer than his dad although he doesn't have his dad's pace.

I sometimes wonder whether there's much pressure on the sons of famous footballers. Do they feel that they have to emulate their fathers on the football field? When we first married I wanted a son. Now I have three lovely daughters – the youngest Charlotte was conceived on that trip to the States – and they have been the joy of my life.

We have many happy memories of Seattle. It's a beautiful city and we enjoyed our stay. I could have played for longer in the United States but, at that stage of my career, I didn't think it was the right move for me. My future at that time was back in England. The Sounders reached the play-offs, but I was keen to get back. We decided to return home on the *QE2*. The voyage took a couple of days longer than usual because of engine trouble – there is nowhere better to be delayed than in the sun lounge on the *QE2*.

I'm pleased now that I didn't start my managerial career at a bigger club than Telford because I may not have survived. There's a lot to be said for serving a managerial apprenticeship at the lower levels of the game. That is, after all, exactly what Sir Alex Ferguson did before establishing himself at Old Trafford.

The people at Telford were very supportive, particularly Frank Nagington, a lovely, old-style football club chairman who travelled to all the away games and had his own seat at the front of the team bus. It was part-time football and I think I made the mistake of accepting part-time attitudes. The players worked during the day so I accepted that sometimes they arrived 15 minutes late for training. This attitude doesn't work at any football club, whatever the level.

I learned my lessons very quickly. I realised that the attitude of the staff and players had to be 100 per cent professional if we were to succeed. I remember telling the players towards the end of my first season that attitudes would have to change.

'From now on,' I said, 'there will be more nos than yeses.'

I had been too soft. You could be honest and fair but you still had to make tough decisions. I had to sack people. Compromise was rarely the answer. It was difficult to be the man in charge of the unit having previously been just one eleventh of the unit.

I had inherited too many old professionals who were on the way down. I changed that and started introducing youngsters on the way up. I found the Telford board very patient and helpful throughout this period. I could sit down and talk over problems with them. I learned a lot at that little club and it stood me in good stead throughout my time at Chelsea and, years later, in my business career.

A lot of players in their mid thirties are desperate to stay in the game in some capacity because they can't face going out into the real world. The transition can be difficult. I was positive about my future but recognised that, in the first instance, coaching simply compensated for not playing. I was still pulling on a tracksuit and kicking the ball about in training as I had done for years. It was my life and I enjoyed it. I understand the anxiety some players have when they reach 35. They have been cosseted for two decades and suddenly they have to think for themselves. This is a frightening prospect for some.

Gradually I came to grips with the new demands of a job that, at Telford's level of the game, embraced so much more than simply coaching and selecting the team. I was, for instance, painting Telford's main stand in the late summer of 1977 when my country called upon me once again.

'Mr Hurst,' a voice shouted from the club office. 'There's a phone call for you. It's a Mr Greenwood.'

CHAPTER FIFTEEN

'Your country needs you! Again!'

RON GREENWOOD TOOK ME COMPLETELY BY SURPRISE ON THAT glorious summer's day in 1977. 'Your country needs you,' he said.

'Again?' I asked.

'Yes,' he said. 'Well, to be honest, I need you.'

When Don Revie dramatically walked out of the job as England team manager in July that year, my old West Ham boss was the man the Football Association turned to for salvation. Ron was 55 at the time but, in my opinion, the perfect man for the job. He had handed the responsibility for first-team matters at West Ham to John Lyall and I suspect that, having divorced himself from the players and training ground, he felt bored and disillusioned. Revie's decision to abandon England midway through his contract and secretly negotiate another job with the United Arab Emirates finally opened the door to international football for Ron Greenwood. It was about time.

Ron was a student of Pele's beautiful game, an innovative, thoughtful and scholarly coach respected throughout the football world. The FA gave him the task of restoring England's credibility on the world stage and I was flattered that he wanted me with him.

'You'll be aware by now that I've been offered the job,' he said. 'But I feel there's a big age gap between me and the players. I want you to help me communicate with them.'

It was five years since we'd worked together at West Ham, but I knew precisely what he wanted me to do. He needed a model, a demonstrator, someone to go on the training pitch and show the England players what he wanted from them. I was very familiar with his language, his coaching practices and I was still fit enough at least to go through the motions on the pitch with the players.

It was, of course, an unexpected bonus for someone on the first rung of the managerial ladder to be asked to help coach the England team. When Ron called his first squad together for training, I appreciated the response from the players. If I hit a good shot in training you'd hear them all cry, 'You never lose it, Hurstie!'

Obviously I did a lot of work with the front players, especially Kevin Keegan. Ron wanted me to demonstrate the near-post running tactics he'd pioneered at West Ham. I also devoted a lot of time to the goalkeepers, particularly Peter Shilton and Joe Corrigan. They always wanted extra work at the end of training and I was happy to do the shooting and crossing.

I was enjoying the job at Telford and they were honoured and delighted to learn that their manager had been offered a part-time role in Ron Greenwood's new England set-up. They had no objection and I think they enjoyed a little reflected glory when I drove south to join Ron and his players at the West Lodge Park hotel in north London to prepare for his first game against Switzerland at Wembley.

Initially, he was given the job on a caretaker basis for three games. But it quickly became apparent to the FA, and the players, that Ron Greenwood was not just an outstanding coach but a man of principle and vision whose legacy would include some far-reaching ideas about the development of the game.

He suggested to the FA's International Committee, for instance, that they appoint a team of coaches for England's international sides at all levels, with a system of promotion designed to ensure continuity. This, Ron claimed, would encourage the coaches at the

Top: Simply the best.

Above: Still together after all these years. The first reunion of the new millennium and I'm happy to say that the team spirit of 1966 remains as strong as ever.

That goal! Did it cross the line? Judge for yourself. As I struck the ball I fell and probably had the worst view in the stadium of the most controversial goal in World Cup history.

Right: I've spent the last forty years explaining to TV crews around the world what I thought happened. These cameramen were actually from Germany.

Pre-season 1966–67. Bobby, Martin and I enjoy our new status at West Ham's training ground at Chadwell Heath.

Right: My final days at Stoke but the photo suggests that at last I'm striking the ball correctly.

Familiar territory. Extra time again against West Germany, in the heat of Leon in 1970. But this time there was a different outcome, though I still don't know how we lost that game.

COLORSPORT

Yes, I know, it's an Arsenal shirt. My grandson Jack loves the Gunners and was mascot when they played West Ham in a Worthington Cup tie.

On holiday in Portugal with my grandchildren Amy, 13, and Jack, 11. If we look a bit red-faced, it's because we've been lying in the sun.

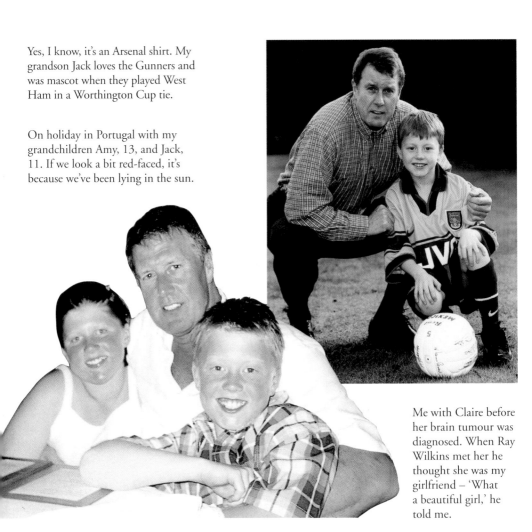

Me with Claire before her brain tumour was diagnosed. When Ray Wilkins met her he thought she was my girlfriend – 'What a beautiful girl,' he told me.

A fanfare of trumpets greeted the arrival of Hugh Grant when he joined Judith and me at Hampton Court Palace for the banquet to welcome Fifa's World Cup inspection team.

My introduction to the real world – my first day at the office in April 1984.

What would they cost today? Gary Lineker, Sir Stanley Matthews, Geoff Hurst, Sir Bobby Charlton, Sir Tom Finney and Nat Lofthouse – the newly installed England team for the World Cup bid line up outside Number 10 with Prime Minister John Major.

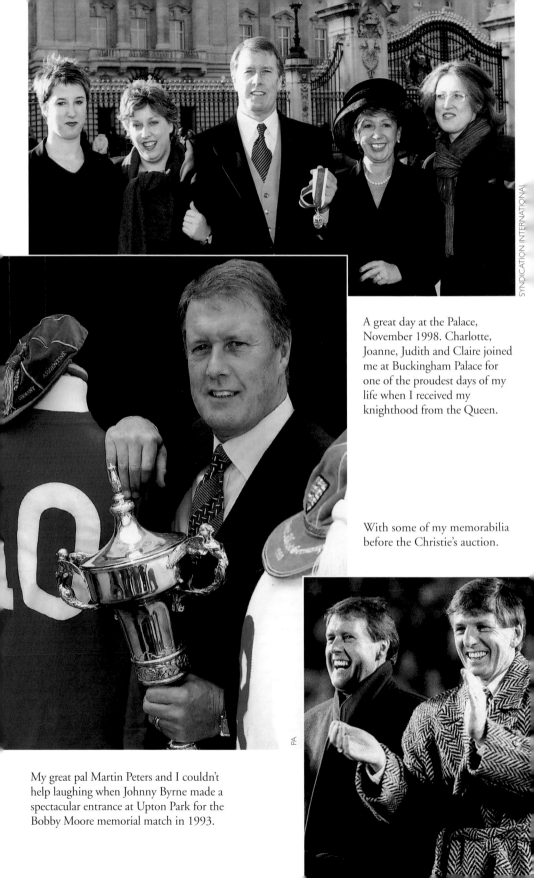

A great day at the Palace, November 1998. Charlotte, Joanne, Judith and Claire joined me at Buckingham Palace for one of the proudest days of my life when I received my knighthood from the Queen.

With some of my memorabilia before the Christie's auction.

My great pal Martin Peters and I couldn't help laughing when Johnny Byrne made a spectacular entrance at Upton Park for the Bobby Moore memorial match in 1993.

bottom of the ladder to work towards the top of the ladder while giving the FA the time to assess the qualities of each man.

He believed this would ensure continuity of tactics and personnel with coaches moving up the ladder from the youth levels as those above them retired. It was a system that had worked successfully in Germany and would mean that the FA no longer had to cast around the club game, as they do today, in search of a successor when the national team manager is sacked or resigns.

The FA, clearly impressed by the long-term value of Ron's proposal, immediately agreed to the plan. Ron didn't waste time. He knew the type of men he wanted around him. He chose Billy Taylor, the Scottish coach from Fulham, and myself to work with him at senior level. He gave Bobby Robson and Don Howe the England B team and Dave Sexton, Terry Venables and Howard Wilkinson the Under-21 side. Perhaps his most controversial decision was to appoint Brian Clough and Peter Taylor to run the youth side.

At the time Cloughie was the people's choice as England manager. If he was disappointed to be overlooked he disguised it well. I remember him telling Ron, via the newspapers, 'I'll crawl all the way to Lancaster Gate just to be involved.'

Ron valued the opinions of his team of coaches and I remember him asking us at one meeting early on to write down the England side each of us would select. We all selected different teams but Cloughie refused to write his down. He was a high-profile, unpredictable character and I always suspected that his involvement with the England youth team would be strictly short term. Sure enough, he eventually told Ron that Nottingham Forest's commitments meant he couldn't continue his part-time job with the FA.

Ron immediately gave the job full time to John Cartwright, a brilliant coach of young footballers. John had been an England youth international and a promising inside-forward at West Ham. When he failed to make the grade, he turned to coaching. Years later, when I went to work in Kuwait, I took him with me as my assistant.

The value of Ron's attempt to get the coaching infrastructure right was apparent when he finally retired in 1982. Bobby Robson, who had been the B team coach while manager of Ipswich, simply moved up a rung, taking Don Howe with him. It was precisely the seamless, effortless changeover that Ron envisaged. At that point the FA abandoned the venture, turning instead to Graham Taylor as Bobby's successor.

I feel it's significant that, since then, two more of Ron's original coaching team have had responsibility for the senior side – Terry Venables and Howard Wilkinson. Had the FA remained faithful to Ron's long-term plan there should have been no need to appoint England's first foreign coach when Kevin Keegan left.

It's also worth noting that, under former chief executive Adam Crozier, the FA advocated a ground-breaking innovation – a team of coaches from which each future senior national manager was selected. Sounds familiar, doesn't it?

When he announced his first squad of players for the Swiss match, Ron made an immediate impression, calling up seven of the Liverpool team that had beaten Borussia Moenchengladbach in the European Cup final in Rome four months earlier. This made good sense. England hadn't won for five games and the undignified departure of Revie left a sour taste that was to rumble on in the courts as the former Leeds manager fought successfully to lift the FA's ten-year ban on him. England needed a quick fix to steady the boat and restore some credibility and confidence. At the time, Liverpool were the standard bearers of the English game and Ron's first team included all the big names from Anfield – Ray Clemence, Phil Neal, Emlyn Hughes, Ray Kennedy, Ian Callaghan and Terry McDermott, who made his debut in that game against the Swiss.

Ian Callaghan was the only real surprise. I knew him well from England's World Cup squad of 1966. At 35 he was only a year younger than me, but he hadn't played for England for 11 years. His last cap had been alongside Jimmy Greaves, Roger Hunt and Bobby Charlton in the team that beat France 2–0 at Wembley in 1966.

Ron felt that if he was placing his faith in Liverpool he had to go all the way. Callaghan had been an influential figure in their success. So, too, had Kevin Keegan, but he had moved from Anfield to

Hamburg for £500,000 just after their European Cup success in Rome's Olympic Stadium.

Ron wanted a proven method of play in his first team so he picked Kevin, the former Liverpool hero, to lead the attack with Mick Channon and Trevor Francis. It looked very exciting on paper but the end result was a dull, goalless draw.

From Ron's point of view it was a worthwhile exercise. He got to know the players and, just as important, they got to know him. Soon after his appointment, I remember Ray Clemence calling me at home to ask about the new boss. The view of the Liverpool players and, I guess, a lot of other people in the game was that Ron Greenwood was a studious, schoolteacher type who used the blackboard to explain his ideas. This was wrong. When he pulled on a tracksuit and went out on the pitch, you saw him in the environment that best suited him. Bright, stimulating, full of ideas and opinions, he devised some of the most challenging training sessions that any England player had experienced. Football, he argued, was a practical subject. The only prop required was a ball!

Within a couple of days, Ron had established his credentials with the players. They clearly enjoyed working with him and he was lucky because they were a receptive bunch. Even the Liverpool players, who had achieved so much, were eager to learn from him. I was particularly impressed with them and it helped me understand why they had been so successful. I already knew Ian Callaghan, Ray Clemence and Emlyn Hughes from my own playing days with the England squad, but what I now noticed when they were together was just how down to earth they were. There were no stars and none of the huge egos that some carry around today. I remember having a drink with them after the Swiss game and thinking that, basically, they were no different in their attitude and behaviour from my lads at Telford.

I remember Emlyn Hughes, who had played under Alf, saying that Ron had brought back the family atmosphere to the squad. This was a good sign. Revie's attempts to foster the 'Leeds spirit' within the England camp and his love of in-depth dossiers on the opposition had fuelled an almost paranoid fear of the enemy. Life under Ron was more relaxed.

Ron had inherited a difficult World Cup salvage operation from Revie. A 2–0 defeat by Italy in Rome in November 1976 meant that England were on the back foot in the bid to qualify for the finals in Argentina in 1978. If England could beat Italy in the return match at Wembley, Luxembourg would be the key to qualification. Whoever scored most goals against them would probably get through to the finals.

Luxembourg provided the opposition in Ron's second game. We travelled to the Grand Duchy knowing we needed to score a lot of goals. Ron decided to play without a right-back. He fielded a back three – Trevor Cherry, Dave Watson and Emlyn – a strategy looked upon today as a relatively modern innovation.

We won 2–0, which was a poor result against a team of part-timers. Worse still, the hooligan behaviour of the mindless morons who attached themselves to the England team embarrassed us all. A couple of days later, the Luxembourg Football Association said that, in future, they would forfeit games against England rather than risk another visit by our fans.

A month later England faced Italy at Wembley. Both teams had eight points but Italy had a game in hand – Luxembourg in their final match. Ron gambled on fresh talent – two new wingers, Steve Coppell and Peter Barnes, and a new striker, Bob Latchford.

Kevin Keegan played alongside Latchford in what was one of the most vibrant, powerful and imaginative attacking England line-ups of my time as player, coach and spectator. Kevin and Trevor Brooking scored the goals in a 2–0 win and suddenly England were at the top of the group.

A month later Italy beat Luxembourg 3–0 and claimed the single qualifying place on goal difference. But the FA, clearly impressed by Ron's three games in charge, confirmed that the job was his on a permanent basis.

Throughout this period, I was managing Telford and as much as I enjoyed working with my part-timers there was something especially satisfying in watching players such as Keegan, Brooking, Wilkins and Coppell on the training pitch.

Ron was a big admirer of Steve Coppell, then a young winger with Manchester United. Busy and elusive, you couldn't fail to be impressed by his prodigious energy level. He played wide, but worked inside, did a good job defensively and crossed the ball with pace and accuracy. I would describe him as one of the first of what today we call wing-backs. I'd also have no hesitation in putting him ahead of David Beckham, one of his Old Trafford successors. Beckham crosses the ball superbly but overall, as a wide midfield player on the right, Steve Coppell gets my vote.

Ron, too, loved working with the players again. I think he had missed that involvement. It was the fresh challenge he needed and a fitting reward for a man who had devoted his life to the game.

In my opinion, he should have been given the job when the FA sacked Sir Alf Ramsey. I know he didn't have the club success that Don Revie achieved, but he was a student of the world game. He was ideally suited to international football.

Managing the national team is different from the job at club level. You don't have the access to players that club managers enjoy on a daily basis. The national coach usually has to wait at least a month for his next match before he can rectify problems. He rarely has his best team together for any substantial period of time. He's plagued by injury problems and is, to some degree, dependent on the goodwill and whims of club managers.

The England team manager should be a significant figure within society. He's a bit like the Prime Minister. He has to feel comfortable in the job and know that at least some of the people are behind him some of the time. That is important in retaining the respect of the players and people within the game.

He also needs to have the strength of character to shoulder the weight of responsibility that goes with the job. Defeat at club level is a matter of local disappointment. But when England lose, it's a national disaster. I've never quite understood why this should be the case. The England team last won a trophy in 1966 so just why expectation levels are so high in the modern game is a mystery. I think the media have to take some blame for fuelling this unrealistic sense of optimism and I think those who play for England would benefit if the expectation levels were more sensible.

All England coaches have to learn the importance of keeping their feet on the ground, and to be a bit shrewder tactically than the club coach. The international coach must improvise and bring together unfamiliar players within a team framework.

Ron could do all these things. In fact, I thought he filled the criteria perfectly. He certainly worked with the players far more than Alf did during my time in the squad. Alf wasn't a coach in the way that Ron was. He stood on the sidelines assessing the form of players. He was meticulous about defensive organisation and in nominating who took free kicks and throw-ins and who stood where at dead-ball situations. He could coach, of course, but it wasn't his forte. Some would say that he didn't have to do much coaching. He was certainly fortunate to be in charge of England at a time when he had an abundance of high-quality players from whom to select his teams.

Ron, on the other hand, was a creator, a teacher, and an innovator. He devised strategies and then went out on the pitch with the players to see whether his plans would work. When he pulled on a tracksuit he blossomed as a personality. Football was his whole world and at 55 he had the maturity to do the job in a relaxed, stimulating way that appealed to young players.

He restored the faith of the players and public at a time when the game's popularity was at a low point. Ultimately, he would have liked a major trophy as evidence of his contribution but those eluded him. He did, though, reach the finals of both the European Championship and the World Cup.

England qualified for the finals of the 1980 European Championship in some style. Seven wins and a draw from the eight games made us 'logical favourites' according to the amiable manager of Italy, Enzo Bearzot. Ron knew Enzo well enough to realise that, by declaring England favourites, he was hoping to lift some of the pressure from his own team. The Italians were the host nation and expectations were high.

As it turned out, neither team won it. Ron was optimistic, I know, and he believed his confidence was well placed after a 2–0 win over Spain in Barcelona during the build-up period. This was among the best performances of Ron's time as coach. Trevor Francis and Tony Woodcock scored the goals but, just before the championship, Francis was injured. Not only did he miss the tournament but also Nottingham Forest's European Cup final win over Keegan's Hamburg in Madrid.

At this time, the English game had a clutch of international-class strikers and although none scored quite as regularly as Keegan, they at least gave Ron options. Apart from Woodcock, Francis and Keegan, he had Latchford, Kevin Reeves, Paul Mariner, Trevor Whymark, Alan Sunderland, Peter Withe, Garry Birtles and David Johnson available. Two goals by the Liverpool striker Johnson against Argentina, who fielded 'new wonderkid' Diego Maradona, gave England a hugely encouraging 3–1 win over the world champions at Wembley.

The newspapers were beginning to bang the patriotic drum as they do on these occasions. Could England win the European title? They were all saying yes in big headlines until a month before the kick-off when we travelled to Wrexham for the annual Home International Championship clash with Wales.

The Welsh were determined to impress their new manager, Mike England. We were beaten 4–1, our first defeat on Welsh soil for 25 years. Puzzled and disappointed, Ron made nine changes to the team for the match against Northern Ireland at Wembley three days later. It had little effect. We drew 1–1, but required an own goal from Blackburn's Noel Brotherston to save our embarrassment.

The newspapers weren't quite so bullish now. At times like this it's important that the coach remains upbeat. Ron did, and ensured that the rest of his staff kept the mood in the dressing-room light and optimistic.

A 2–0 win over Scotland at Hampden Park – how I enjoyed waving to the crowd that day! – restored a bit of confidence and when the squad gathered again to prepare for the European finals there was a genuine feeling among the players that they could win the title in Italy.

We were based in a large, old hotel in Hertfordshire and Ron allowed the players far more freedom than they get today. Occasionally it was abused and someone was late returning after a night out but, by and large, the players behaved well. He even allowed some of the horse-racing enthusiasts – Emlyn Hughes, Mick Mills and Phil Thompson – to hire a helicopter to transport them to the Derby.

Just before we flew to Italy we were invited to a cocktail party at 10 Downing Street. Mrs Thatcher moved easily among the players and had obviously done her homework. When we posed for pictures one of the photographers handed her a football.

'They'll get you to head that if you're not careful,' Ron said to her.

'I thought that was Mr Brooking's speciality,' she replied. It was far from his speciality, of course, but she knew that he'd just won the FA Cup for West Ham against Arsenal with a rare header.

A couple of days later we flew to Italy. Ron and the FA's travel department had scouted the area thoroughly and found a small private hotel in the hills south of Turin. The nearest town was Asti, one of the most important centres of the Italian wine industry and particularly well known for the sparkling Asti Spumante. The training ground was next door to the hotel. The food and facilities were excellent. That just left us the football to get right – but that was the hard bit!

Eight nations were competing in two groups of four. The other three in our group were Belgium, Italy and Spain. Ron impressed on the players the importance of starting well against Belgium. What we could not legislate for was the atmosphere in which the match would be played. We had a huge army of supporters in the old Stadio Communale and they were deliriously happy when Ray Wilkins gave England an early lead with a remarkable goal. The Belgians were using the offside trap as a calculated strategy and it was causing us problems until Ray chipped the ball over their defence, ran through the wall of advancing players, gathered the ball again and lobbed it over the goalkeeper Jean-Marie Pfaff.

It was a wonderful example of a clever player using his skill and intelligence to outwit the opposition single-handed. But within a couple of minutes Jan Ceulemans equalised and that, for some reason, signalled the worst reaction from the England fans. A small group of supporters started fighting behind the England goal and, as the violence took hold, the police began to fire tear gas into the crowd.

The clouds of yellow smoke began to billow down the terraces and I could see Ray Clemence rubbing his eyes in our goal. Ron immediately appealed to the UEFA officials and the match was stopped. Other players were clearly affected by the smoke.

Once the police had control of the terraces, the referee started the match again. The stoppage was for about five minutes but the game never recaptured the intensity of the early stages. It ended 1–1 and was followed by the usual hooligan debate.

Ron was clearly distressed by the trouble on the terraces. All of us were. We were embarrassed and ashamed to be English. It's hard to explain how you feel. It's very difficult for players representing their country to perform to their full potential in such circumstances. From England's viewpoint, the incidents that day set the tone for the rest of the tournament.

It was an ominous sign of the way things were going throughout Europe at that time. English football supporters had an appalling reputation, dating back to the sixties, and little of any significance had been done to address the problem. The same old excuses were trotted out after each incident. It was a problem way beyond the control of the football authorities but it wasn't until a series of terrible disasters in the eighties that the government did something about it. The clubs and the game's authorities were obliged to implement the recommendations in the Taylor Report. Thankfully, the hooligan problem is no longer as bad but, as we saw during the 1998 World Cup in France and Euro 2000 in Belgium and Holland, there is no room for complacency.

The one consolation for us, back in our headquarters in Asti, was that the other match in our group, between Spain and Italy, had ended in a goalless draw. That meant the group was still wide open.

But, as Ron pointed out to the players, we had to beat Italy in our second match in Turin to have any realistic hope of reaching the final. A crowd of 60,000 squeezed into the Stadio Communale and there were nearly as many policemen.

As a spectacle, the game was only slightly better than the match with Belgium. Ray Kennedy hit a post, but Kevin Keegan, playing alongside the debutant Garry Birtles, was practically marked out of the game by the formidable Marco Tardelli.

We sat on the bench telling ourselves that this was a match that would be decided by a single goal. It was, and Tardelli, deserting Keegan for once, was the man who scored it. That defeat ended our hopes of winning the championship. In our last match we beat Spain 2–1 in the searing heat of Naples and although it was an irrelevance, the football we played was our best of the tournament.

The quality of the football throughout the fortnight was, at best, functional. Ron found the lack of originality depressing. The most accomplished and adventurous team, West Germany, deservedly won, beating Belgium 2–1 in the final in Rome.

But if the European Championship was a disappointment, the following season was a disaster for England. Our chances of reaching the World Cup finals for the first time since 1970 looked pretty good when we were drawn against Hungary, Romania, Switzerland and Norway. FIFA had extended the final tournament to 24 nations and this meant that two from each European group would qualify for Spain in 1982.

We couldn't fail, or could we? By this time we had some truly outstanding young players emerging at international level – Terry Butcher, Kenny Sansom, Glenn Hoddle and the lad I played with briefly at West Bromwich Albion, Bryan Robson. They brought youthful enthusiasm to a squad that contained other players of enormous experience. Among these you would include the two goalkeepers, Peter Shilton and Ray Clemence, Phil Neal, Mick Mills, Kevin Keegan and my old West Ham team-mate Trevor Brooking.

With this blend of youth and experience, Ron began the qualifying campaign in handsome style, beating Norway 4–0 at Wembley. Within six months the newspapers and the TV pundits were calling for his head.

The criticism that followed a 2–1 defeat against Romania in

Bucharest was only partly eased by an unconvincing 2–1 win over Switzerland at Wembley. Then it all began to go seriously wrong for Ron. In the space of eight weeks, as he prepared for vital World Cup qualifying ties in Switzerland and Hungary, England played five matches at Wembley, failed to win any of them and scored just one goal. This was a sequence of home results unprecedented in the history of the English game. We lost to Brazil, Scotland and Spain and drew 0–0 with Wales and Romania. The baying for Ron's head reached a crescendo when England crashed 2–1 to Switzerland in Basle, the scene of further ugly hooligan behaviour.

I knew Ron well enough to realise that he wouldn't cling on to the job if he felt it was time for a fresh face to take the helm. He would do the honourable thing and resign long before anyone thought of sacking him. What I didn't know at the time was that within a few minutes of the Swiss defeat Ron had made up his mind to retire. He kept his decision to himself because a few days later we were due to play Hungary in Budapest and he wanted one more game in charge. Apart from wanting the chance to rectify the defeat in Basle, Ron particularly wanted to pit his wits against the Hungarians who had been so influential in forming his own footballing philosophies back in the fifties.

We stayed in Regensdorf, just outside Zurich, to prepare for the Hungary game because the facilities were so good. Unbeknown to us on the staff, Ron told Dick Wragg, the chairman of the FA International Committee, that he was going to announce his retirement on his return to London. When we finally arrived at our vast hotel beside the Danube in Budapest, no one within the squad realised what had happened. There was, though, an intensity among the players in training. They knew that they would have to win if England were going to qualify for the finals.

And win they did. As if stung by the mounting criticism, England produced one of their best performances to beat Hungary 3–1 on a sultry night in the Nep Stadium with two superb goals from Brooking and a Keegan penalty.

The following morning, as England's charter plane climbed into the sky above Hungary, Ron and I sat together at the back of the section reserved for the players and staff. The media party, as was always the case, was confined to the rear seats where they drank, played cards, smoked cigarettes and argued among themselves.

Ron said, 'I've got something to tell you. I'm retiring. I've had enough. There will be a press conference at the airport but I think the players should be told first. I want you to tell them for me.'

I told him that I really didn't feel comfortable doing that, but he was insistent. It was clearly a difficult moment for him. So I stood in the aisle and told the players that Ron had decided it was time to go. They were clearly shocked. They started talking in little groups. Then the senior players conferred and Keegan and Brooking were given the task of talking the boss out of his decision. They sat down with him and before the plane touched down in London they were smiling. Somehow they'd talked him into changing his mind.

The FA's Dick Wragg, with his familiar pipe, was waiting for Ron in the baggage area when we arrived. He was clearly agitated. Ron quickly walked up to him and told him that he'd changed his mind. All the players were watching and waiting for a reaction. The smile on Dick's face told its own story.

But the drama was not yet over. The next qualifying tie was against Norway in Oslo where the unthinkable happened. England lost 2–1, the emerging midfield-powerhouse Robson scoring our goal. The delight of the Norwegians was perhaps best captured by their commentator Borge Lillelien. He it was who screamed into his microphone, 'We are the best in the world. We have beaten England. Lord Nelson . . . Lord Beaverbrook . . . Sir Winston Churchill . . . Sir Anthony Eden . . . Clement Attlee . . . Henry Cooper . . . Lady Diana . . . we have beaten them all. Maggie Thatcher, can you hear me? Your boys took a hell of a beating.'

You couldn't argue with that. Our World Cup fate was now in the hands of others. Romania and Hungary were clear favourites to go through, but Switzerland proved to be England's unlikely rescuers. They beat Romania in Bucharest, lost in Hungary to spoil their own chances and then drew at home in their return game with Romania. England's better goal difference meant that a draw in the final match, against Hungary at Wembley, would be enough.

The Football League cancelled the First Division programme on the Saturday before the match and this meant Ron could pick from an injury-free squad. It rained on the night of the game but it didn't worry me as I sat on the substitutes' bench with water running down my back. England won 1–0 with a goal from Paul Mariner, finished runners-up to Hungary and so secured a place in the finals in Spain.

Sadly, Steve Coppell was badly injured by a Hungarian called Jozsef Toth that night. It was a knee injury that would eventually end his career. Even sadder, my coaching colleague Bill Taylor was taken ill during the build-up to the Hungary match. He watched the game on TV but died a fortnight later at the age of 42. He had been a very popular figure with Ron and the players. His place on the coaching staff was taken by Don Howe, who was Terry Neill's assistant at Arsenal at the time.

The World Cup itself was the highlight of Ron's career, and after the problems experienced getting there, it provided a worthwhile and satisfying way to end his management reign. England were unbeaten in Spain. We defeated France, Czechoslovakia and Kuwait in the first round and drew with West Germany and Spain in the second round. All we lacked was the flash of quality and inspiration to take us to the semi-finals. We lacked the killer touch of a Paolo Rossi, who scored for Italy when it mattered most – three against Brazil, two against Poland in the semi-finals and one against the Germans in the final.

Ron prepared thoroughly for the finals and spent a lot of time travelling around Spain with the England team doctor, Vernon Edwards of Watford, and the FA administrative officer, Alan Odell, assessing hotels and training facilities. We even played a testimonial match against Athletic Bilbao in the stadium that would stage our first three games, San Mames. It was a public relations triumph.

But there was a serious downside. Two of our most senior players, Brooking and Keegan, were making painfully slow progress in recovering from injuries. I used to run every day with Kevin, who was desperate to play. He and Trevor shared a room. When Ron secretly flew in the West Ham doctor Brian Roper to give Trevor an injection in his troublesome groin, Kevin decided that he needed to do something equally dramatic. He persuaded Ron to allow him to fly back to Hamburg to see a specialist who was used to treating his back.

Kevin drove himself through the night to Madrid where he caught a flight to Germany. Three days later he was back at our hotel in Bilbao. 'I feel a lot better, boss,' he reported.

In the end, Keegan and Brooking played for just 27 minutes of that World Cup in 1982. I suspect we may have progressed further had both been fit.

Otherwise, we had a sound squad of players. Ray Wilkins, Graham Rix and Bryan Robson excelled in midfield. We also had two of the world's greatest goalkeepers in Peter Shilton and Ray Clemence.

There was so little to choose between them that Ron played them in alternate matches for much of his time as manager. This was not, in my opinion, a satisfactory compromise because neither of them were happy with the situation. Had I been manager, I would have picked one as my first choice and stuck with him. Perhaps Ron was too nice a guy. He knew that by picking one he would upset the other. He genuinely felt they were equal but in the end, just before the 1982 World Cup, he decided he had to make a choice. He chose Shilton as his number one. I think it was the right decision. Clemence was upset and sat on the bench throughout the tournament but statistics suggest that Ron made the right selection. Shilton conceded one goal in five games.

The real problem for England was an inability to score in the games against the Germans, who were the European champions at the time, and the host nation Spain. The German game was a dull stalemate, greeted by whistles and jeering from the 75,000 spectators in the Bernabeu Stadium. It meant that everything now depended on the final two matches of the round – Spain's games against West Germany and England.

I went with Ron and Don Howe to watch Spain play the Germans while our players watched the match in the hotel. Spain looked no more than a moderate side as the Germans beat them 2–1. We had to beat Spain by two goals to reach the semi-finals.

Ron put Brooking and Keegan on the substitutes' bench and with the game deadlocked at 0–0 sent on his two trump cards with 27 minutes remaining. Both could have scored. Kevin had the best chance, but his header from Bryan Robson's cross flew wide.

I sat there thinking to myself that a fully fit Keegan, at the peak of his game, would have buried such an opportunity. It is difficult, though, for a substitute to come off the bench and adjust quickly to the tempo of the game, fit or otherwise. In the dressing-room afterwards I remember Kevin slumped with his head in his hands. 'How did I miss that?' he kept saying.

He didn't know it then but that was his last game for England. The man Ron had groomed as his successor, Bobby Robson, was already planning for the future and it didn't include Kevin. Ron was settling into retirement when Bobby named his first squad in the autumn of 1982. There was no place for Keegan. 'I didn't even get a letter of explanation,' Kevin complained at the time. Well, Kevin, none of us did – not me, not Bobby Charlton, not Bobby Moore. We all used to receive letters from the FA telling us that we had been called up but no one received a letter thanking us for our services.

Of course, the FA may argue that because one coach discards a player, it doesn't mean the player's international career is over. A successor may recall the same player at some stage in the future. Even so, I think that when a player acknowledges that his England career is finished, his service to his country should be recognised by a letter of thanks. It may be something for the FA to think about.

CHAPTER SIXTEEN

The Blues

IN THE SUPERSTAR STAKES KEVIN KEEGAN TOWERED ABOVE ALL rivals. Twice European Footballer of the Year, his importance to Ron Greenwood's England was roughly the same as petrol to a motor car.

In action, nobody took their eyes off him, such was the sense of anticipation when he received the ball. Away from the field of play, his fame and charismatic personality attracted throngs of admirers and more than once I saw him stop traffic in cities throughout Europe. He was the player every manager in the world wanted in his team. I was no exception. When I was manager of Chelsea, I wanted him at Stamford Bridge – and I nearly got him.

It was through working with Kevin and players of his class in the England squad that my own stature as a coach developed. One day, in the summer of 1979, when I was again working on a range of improvements to the Telford stand, I had a telephone call from Danny Blanchflower, who was the Chelsea manager. I was still happily committed to Telford and had just turned down an offer to take over at Peterborough. When Danny called he asked if I would consider going to Chelsea as his first-team coach.

Chelsea, of course, presented a slightly different proposition. They were then, as they are today, a club of great reputation and awesome potential. Did I want to be part of that? Did I want to test my own coaching ability at club level in the highly competitive field of First Division football?

Well, Second Division, actually. Chelsea had just been relegated after one of the worst seasons in their long and distinguished history. The club was already in serious decline when Danny succeeded Ken Shellito as manager in December 1978. They had tried to tempt the famous Yugoslav coach Miljan Miljanic to Stamford Bridge but after ten days studying the problems at Chelsea he declined their offer to become 'technical director'.

They were bottom of the table when Danny took over, initially on a monthly contract. Within hours of his arrival he saw the full enormity of the task ahead in a 7–2 defeat at Middlesbrough, a match that marked the return of Peter Osgood after five years away with Southampton and Philadelphia Fury.

Inevitably, Chelsea finished bottom of the table, having won just five of their 42 games in the First Division. Danny was confident he could steer them out of the Second Division but, rather like Ron Greenwood, he felt he needed a younger coach to help him get his message across to the players.

The prospect appealed to me but I asked for time to think about it. I knew Danny, but not well. Our playing careers had just overlapped. He retired in 1963 having played outstandingly for Glentoran, Barnsley, Aston Villa, Tottenham and Northern Ireland, whom he led to the quarter-finals of the World Cup in 1958. Just as I found my feet in the game, he reached the pinnacle of his playing career as captain of the wonderful Tottenham team that won the league and FA Cup double in 1961, the first club to achieve such a feat in the twentieth century. He followed that by winning the FA Cup again (1962) and the European Cup-Winners' Cup (1963). We forget these days, but Bill Nicholson's Tottenham were the first British side to win a major European competition.

Since then Danny had played a lot of golf, managed Northern Ireland and written a provocative and widely read column in the *Sunday Express*. A charming Irishman, he was a bit of a romantic and in his newspaper column had once described Chelsea as a 'social club'. I was to discover just how correct he was in that assessment.

I later learned, too, that Danny had initially turned down the offer from the club chairman Brian Mears to take over as manager, but after further thought he changed his mind. I suspect he realised that after such a long time out of the game he would find it difficult to adjust to the demands of modern management. I think his suspicion was right.

Football had changed enormously in the time that Danny had been away. He retained his idealistic view of the game and couldn't understand those who didn't feel the same way. Financial restrictions were still in place because of the club's debts and this meant he had little money to spend in the transfer market. In a sense, he had one hand tied behind his back from the moment he took over.

I knew all these things when I agreed to join him. It was simply too big a challenge for me to ignore. Dave Sexton, the manager who led the club to the FA Cup (1970) and European Cup-Winners' Cup (1971) before Mears sacked him, had advised me to take the job. Like me, Dave had been involved in Ron Greenwood's England set-up.

'Chelsea? Take it!' he told me. 'There's no limit to what they could achieve in the right hands. If you're successful, they'll turn up in their thousands.'

I left Telford with some sadness. Chelsea represented a significant step up from the Southern League but I left behind a well-run club and some wonderful people who had helped me cut my teeth in football management. Gerald Smith, who was by this time chairman of Telford, came to visit me at Stamford Bridge soon after I moved down. As I showed him round the ground I remember telling him how much I'd valued the support of the Telford board. 'It would be nice,' I told him, 'to have such familiar and supportive people with me now at Chelsea.'

I'd learned how important it was to have people around you with whom you could talk on a regular basis and on whom you could rely for support and advice. I have no doubt that my time at Chelsea would have been more successful had I had the kind of boardroom support I enjoyed at Telford.

I'd also learned at Telford the value of good man-management techniques. It was my first taste of telling people what to do and I quickly realised that some had to be told in a different way from others. Some players responded best to a consoling arm around the shoulders and a pat on the back. With others, you had to shout and thump the table to get any reaction at all.

Of course, I'd watched experienced coaches in the past dealing with players of different temperaments. I'd learned that it was important to pick out the troublemakers early and get them out of the dressing-room. There are disruptive influences in all dressing-rooms and the players themselves obviously know the identities of the troublesome ones in their ranks. You win the respect of the majority by dealing with the dressing-room anarchists decisively.

Working with Danny was a stimulating experience but I quickly realised that there was no quick-fix solution to Chelsea's decline. Their problems were deeply entrenched and could be traced back to the club's ambitious redevelopment plans that had been announced seven years earlier. The idea had been to create a 60,000-seat luxury stadium at a cost of £5.5 million. Although the project was dramatically modified in the following years, the building of the magnificent new East Stand had produced debts of around £3.4 million. Worse still, during the two years it took to complete the work, the club's fortunes on the field plummeted. They were relegated from the First Division in 1975 and although they went back up in 1977, the stand became a symbol of the club's decline.

Inevitably, the debt hindered the progress of essential team rebuilding. But the 1979 Second Division season started encouragingly enough with a draw at home to Sunderland followed by wins against West Ham at Upton Park and Wrexham at Stamford Bridge.

Then disaster struck. Having drawn 2–2 at Plymouth in the League Cup, the Third Division club beat us 2–1 in the replay at Stamford Bridge. In those days, the League Cup, like the FA Cup, was viewed as a valuable source of extra revenue. This, for a club in

Chelsea's position, was important. Defeat in the League Cup at the first hurdle was a serious business.

The setback against Plymouth was quickly followed by Birmingham City's 2–1 win at Stamford Bridge. Suddenly Chelsea were in the bottom half of the table and sliding. Sat in the dug-out, Danny and I could sense the gloom of the fans. I don't think I was alone in sensing Danny's imminent resignation.

He said nothing to me but that September, just nine months after taking over, he announced that he was returning to the safer pastures of journalism. He explained to the media that he felt the club should appoint a younger man 'more in touch with the values of the modern game'.

I think Danny found that the social life in west London was simply too tempting for the young players at Chelsea. He wanted them on the training pitch but once the morning session was over, they wanted to be out and about in the West End. It had been the same when Peter Osgood and Alan Hudson were younger. I wonder whether Chelsea's position in the heart of a great capital city, bursting with temptations and pitfalls for young players, explains why one of the richest clubs in the Premiership never quite fulfilled their potential until recently.

So, suddenly Chelsea were in the middle of another crisis, looking for their fifth manager since sacking Dave Sexton four years earlier. As first-team coach I was placed in caretaker control and, with a team selected by Danny, went to Shrewsbury for my first game in charge. We lost 3–0 and slid to 18th in the table, the lowest position in the club's history. Asked for my assessment of the situation by the media, I remember saying in bullish fashion, 'I think we can improve with the existing players.'

While Brian Mears and the Chelsea board drew up a shortlist of candidates to succeed Danny, I dedicated myself to the task of reviving a team that had lost its way. I made a couple of changes to the team that had lost at Shrewsbury for our next game at home to Watford. A crowd of more than 21,000 saw us win 2–0. We won the next four games and climbed to fourth in the table. Suddenly, we were promotion hopefuls!

In the newspapers I read the usual speculative pieces about possible new Chelsea managers. These included Terry Venables, then with Crystal Palace, John Bond, then with Norwich, and Fulham's Bobby Campbell. When asked my opinion, I told the newspapers that my message to the club was simple – 'If you don't make up your mind soon, I'll quit.'

Eventually Mears invited me to an interview in a Chinese restaurant in Richmond. He was accompanied by one other club director, Sir Richard Attenborough, CBE. They asked all the usual questions and were quite clearly impressed by the fact that under me the team had won five consecutive matches. Finally, as we picked at the carcass of a crispy aromatic duck, they offered me a three-year contract which, in principle, I was happy to accept.

The salary was to be decided a few days later at a meeting with Martin Spencer, who was Chelsea's chief executive. When we met, Martin suggested I write on a piece of paper the salary that I'd consider acceptable. He said he would also write down the salary that he was prepared to pay. We each turned over the pieces of paper to reveal the sum. Remarkably, it was the same figure – £28,000 a year. The deal was done. I was the manager of Chelsea FC.

Sir Richard was clearly a committed Chelsea fan although I saw little of him in the months that followed because he was abroad most of the time filming *Gandhi*. Mears was more than simply committed. For him, the club was almost a family heirloom. His grandfather, J.T. Mears, and great uncle Gus founded the club in 1905 and his father Joe was in charge from 1940–66. Brian himself sat on the board from 1958–81 and was chairman from 1969.

He was a lovely, courteous man but lacked the qualities necessary to run a club of Chelsea's size successfully. I have to admit that he seemed to take his responsibilities seriously. He was in his office at Stamford Bridge every day – one of the first chairmen to work at his club on a regular basis – but it was, as Danny said, more like a social club at times.

They'd lost their training ground at Mitcham as part of the financial cutbacks. When I arrived, Chelsea's players trained at the Metropolitan Police Sports Ground at Imber Court in Surrey.

Nothing wrong with that, except that we were not allowed to use the football pitches. We could train only on the grass areas between the pitches. One of my first tasks therefore, was to find a proper training headquarters and I was instrumental in hiring the university sports ground the club used in Sipson Lane near Heathrow airport until 2005.

The club, in my opinion, was in disarray. I was very serious about the job. I wanted to be successful. If the club could not afford to buy players, we had to produce our own. When I was a youngster at West Ham, Chelsea had a wonderful reputation for producing outstanding kids including Jimmy Greaves, Terry Venables and Bobby Tambling. What had happened? Where were the good youngsters now? One of the first things I did when given the job was to release the youth development officer and advertise in the national newspapers for coaches. I didn't want to hand jobs to my friends in the game. I wanted to see what sort of response I'd get from the adverts.

One of the first replies came from Gwyn Williams, a school-teacher in Ealing, west London. He was a sports coach, disillusioned with teaching. We met and talked and I gave him the job of running the youth development at the club. He's still there today, the only survivor from my time at Stamford Bridge.

I also interviewed my old West Ham team-mate Jack Burkett for the job, but I felt that Gwyn was better qualified for the role of youth development officer. We needed to revive the youth policy and I felt he could do it. The kids at the club when I arrived were of indifferent quality and few made the top level apart from Colin Pates, who wasn't a bad player.

Getting money from the club for staff and improvements was a constant battle. Gwyn needed a car to do his job properly and I told him the club would supply one. Once a week he would come to see me. 'Any sign of my car?' he used to ask. After several months I took him to a car showroom myself. 'Give this man a car,' I said to the manager. 'I'll take the responsibility for it.' I was to discover that one of the most important figures at Stamford Bridge at this time was Martin Spencer. Like any good accountant who specialised in advising companies in serious financial trouble, his favourite word was 'No!'

I'd inherited Danny Blanchflower's team but knew I had to replace a few of the older players. I sold Eamonn Bannon, David Stride and Trevor Aylott for a total of about £250,000 and asked Brian Mears if I could have some money to buy players. I had my eye on an England Under-21 striker called Andy Ritchie, who was at Manchester United but couldn't get into the first team.

'Of course, we've got money to buy players,' he said. 'I think we've got about £500,000 in the transfer fund. Just check with Martin.'

Encouraged by this news, I left Brian and walked a matter of 20 yards to the office of the club's chief executive.

'The chairman's just told me we've got about £500,000 to spend on players. I just want to check that it's OK to spend it,' I said to Martin.

'No, it isn't OK,' he said. 'We have no money to spend on players.' This situation was as confusing to me as it was to Brian Mears.

There was little sign of the situation improving significantly. You didn't need to be a financial wizard to realise that, with the current debts, borrowing more was an invitation to disaster. What little money we had available went on smaller items such as kit for the youth team. Gwyn complained that the youth team had to use the hand-me-downs from the senior teams. By the time this kit had worked its way through the system there were usually two or three shirts missing.

Salaries, too, had to be tailored to meet the financial restrictions placed on the club. I was lucky when Micky Leach, who was to die so young and tragically in 1992 after a long fight against cancer, agreed to join the coaching staff. Mick was a very good midfield player with Queens Park Rangers, Cambridge and Detroit Express and did a great job for me as youth team coach.

I was fortunate to inherit Brian Eastick, a talented and diligent reserve team coach, but I needed someone to work with me at first-team level. I gave this some thought when the adverts didn't produce the kind of people I was seeking. I decided to try to tempt Bobby

Gould to London. Although he'd been at West Ham, I didn't know him from his playing days. I'd met him and been impressed by his enthusiasm at a management course we'd both attended three years earlier at Bisham Abbey in Buckinghamshire.

At the time, he was still scoring goals for Hereford in the final days of a remarkable career that had taken him around the country from Coventry, Arsenal, Wolves and WBA to Bristol City, West Ham, Bristol Rovers and Hereford. He was living in Bristol and asked for time to think about it because Hereford wanted him to become their player-coach. Eventually, he came back and said yes to a three-year contract.

I was delighted. He turned out to be a very supportive number two, very good for boosting morale among the players. In the end, he had a far more successful managerial career than I did. He took Wimbledon to the FA Cup final in 1988 and managed Coventry, Bristol Rovers and Wales. We worked well together. His input in the dressing-room and on the training pitch was significant. Between us we established a good rapport with the players.

We were fortunate in that one of the all-time Chelsea greats, Ronnie Harris, remained an influential figure in the dressing-room. A formidable defender, who had often given me a hard time in my playing days, he was 35 and coming towards the end of his career. Nonetheless, he did a fantastic job for me that season.

I played him in the centre of midfield, organising, delegating and encouraging the young kids in the team. They responded positively to his leadership. He was still as tough as old boots and watching him in action, I was reminded more than once of the Harris tackles that used to thunder into me from behind. As much as I hated playing against him, I fully appreciated his qualities when I had him playing for me. As a pro, he was a great example to the youngsters. He was never late for training. He did the job, soaked his sore feet in hot water to relieve the aches, and then went home.

At the end of that season he wanted to go to Brentford as player-coach and after a record 795 first-team appearances in 19 seasons for Chelsea, I didn't think it would be fair to stop him. We were not the same team without him.

Having been confirmed as manager on a permanent basis, my first games were a local derby with Fulham that we lost 2–0, and a visit to Sunderland that we lost 2–1. The next game was a ten-goal thriller against Leyton Orient at Brisbane Road. We won that 7–3 with Lee Frost, a young winger from the Elephant and Castle, scoring a hat-trick. Because of a bout of injury problems late in the week, we had no central strikers available for the Orient game. I remember devoting that week's final training session to coaching young Lee to play up the middle alongside another young winger, Clive Walker.

It was one of those occasions when a coach has to improvise and make the best of what he has available. We devised a simple tactic. I wanted no balls played to the feet of either Frost or Walker. I told the pair of them to drop short, spin away from their markers and use their pace to chase the balls we planned to hit over the Orient defence. On the day it worked a treat.

When West Ham visited us four days later, a crowd of 30,859 squeezed into Stamford Bridge and Lee scored again in a 2–1 win. It was the last of the five goals he scored in his 12 games for Chelsea. He was a promising youngster but, in Chelsea's situation at the time, I had to sift out those who were merely promising and rely on those whom I knew could do the job. The following season Lee moved to Brentford.

The one player I knew I could rely on, if I could lure him to Stamford Bridge, was Kevin Keegan, the England captain who was playing for Hamburg in Germany. He wanted to return home. We'd spoken in Belfast during England's 5–1 win over Northern Ireland and the prospect of playing for Chelsea seemed to appeal to him.

Financially, of course, I knew it would be a daunting challenge for Chelsea. I kept all this to myself but, soon after the club offered me the job on a permanent basis, Kevin came to London with his agent Harry Swales. We met discreetly at Stamford Bridge one Sunday morning.

I telephoned the chairman, who was ill in bed at home. 'You'd better get down here,' I told him. Within an hour, Brian was in my office. In principle, a deal was considered a realistic possibility by all the involved parties, with the exception of Mr Spencer, of course.

We had to convince the man who held the purse strings that Chelsea could afford such an ambitious project.

Brian sold the idea to Martin Spencer and they decided to seek a sponsor for the deal. Martin realised that Kevin would almost pay for himself in extra revenue.

The Ford Motor Company became involved and although I was never aware of all the details, I understood that the club had financial backing for a £2 million package that included a £400,000 transfer fee, a £1 million payment to Kevin plus a salary of £25,000 a year. Although £400,000 was nowhere near the transfer record at the time – Steve Daley and Andy Gray had both moved clubs that autumn for £1.5 million – the overall package represented a vast investment by Chelsea.

For a time it looked a real possibility. I was excited but worried in case our interest leaked out. If that happened, many other clubs would suddenly become involved. Sure enough, one day the *Evening Standard* billboard in London screamed at me: 'Amazing! Chelsea move for Keegan.'

The game was up. Arsenal quickly muscled in, followed by Barcelona, Real Madrid and Juventus. Lawrie McMenemy, the manager of Southampton, began craftily wooing Kevin. Lawrie seemed to build his teams around experienced international players. On his staff at the time he had Charlie George, Dave Watson, Chris Nicholl, Alan Ball and Mick Channon.

A few weeks later, just after Kevin had been voted European Footballer of the Year, I saw him with the England squad preparing for a European Championship qualifying tie against the Republic of Ireland at Wembley. He told me the news I didn't want to hear and then went out and scored twice in a 2–0 win that was perhaps most notable for the debut of Bryan Robson. A couple of days later, Southampton officially announced that Kevin would be joining them at the end of the season. Kevin said that one of the reasons he chose Southampton was that, 'I'll be playing in the same team as Mick Channon, my best friend in football.'

That was little consolation to me. Kevin did a great job for Lawrie at Southampton and, I think, would have done the same for me at

Chelsea. He was one of those top-of-the-range footballers who, a bit like myself I suppose, had worked hard to maximise his potential. You couldn't go wrong with Kevin Keegan. With his enthusiasm, his discipline and his appetite for hard work, he would have lifted us at a critical time in the season. No one could fault the commitment of some of my young players but we were short of quality.

By December, with Clive Walker and Mike Fillery scoring the goals, we were at the top of the table, but I was bitterly disappointed when Wigan, from the Fourth Division, beat us 1–0 in the third round of the FA Cup on a cold January night.

I knew that we weren't a good team. I'd made an impact on arrival, as a lot of new managers do, and that momentum carried us through the season. Pates apart, I didn't think the young players we had were likely to achieve much in the game and most of the older players in the squad had achieved all that they were going to achieve. Peter Osgood was back, but he wasn't right for the club at this time. A cult figure from his first ten years at the club, he'd been re-signed by Ken Shellito, the manager before Danny, but hadn't contributed much. I fined him for reporting late for training.

Peter didn't like it. I think he felt he deserved better treatment from an old England team-mate. He had no greater admirer than me. At his peak he was a superb player. He was in the 1970 World Cup squad and we had roomed together on England trips. But in the end I let him go. It was difficult, but something I couldn't back away from. It was obvious that his best days were behind him. He'd been a great player for the club; there was no doubt about that. His reputation and his rapport with the fans made the situation all the more difficult for me. It's never easy removing an idol from a club, particularly for a new manager.

I'd always admired the way Liverpool had been able to ease out their ageing stars, right back to Ian Callaghan, Ian St John and Emlyn Hughes, without provoking a backlash. I handled Ossie's departure as delicately as I could and I thought it significant that he didn't play for anyone else after leaving Stamford Bridge for a second time.

The limitations of the team were apparent when we lost 5–1 at

Birmingham in March. We were still top of the table, but cracks were beginning to appear.

I squeezed about £300,000 out of Spencer and with that was able to buy Colin Lee from Tottenham, Dennis Rofe from Leicester City, and Colin Viljoen from Manchester City. Rofe made an immediate impact at left-back, but Lee, the goalscorer I needed, was bedevilled by injuries, and Viljoen was a misjudgement on my part.

Viljoen and Lee were both absent when we entertained our west London neighbours QPR on 2 April. They beat us 2–0 but we retained the leadership of the Second Division. Even so, I wasn't in the best of moods that day.

The night before the match, as had been the case for some months, Judith and I had stayed in the small, comfortable hotel in South Kensington owned by Ray Wilkins' in-laws, Gladys and Colin Bygraves. Occasionally, on a Sunday, we'd go out for lunch with Ray and his wife Jackie.

I'd been staying in the hotel since taking the Chelsea job while Judith looked for a house. She'd finally found the house she wanted in Cobham, Surrey, and we'd moved in the day before the match against QPR. Just before the kick-off that afternoon, the police asked to see me. Apparently, the previous night burglars had broken into our new home, picked up several unpacked tea chests, loaded them into a van and driven away. Our house in Stoke had been robbed in the past but it was a bit much being burgled before we'd even unpacked. The police were sympathetic, of course, but we never saw the stolen items again.

In fact, about a month later, when we had just completed decorating the house in Cobham, Judith said, 'Let's finish the dining room.' It wasn't until then that we realised they'd stolen our dining chairs!

The theft of personal mementoes was probably the thing that hurt most and was the main reason why, years later, I decided to auction many of my trophies and medals. I remember losing several little treasures during a burglary while Judith and I were in Seattle in 1976. As we walked down the gangway of the *QE2* at Southampton, a friend was waiting for us.

'You've been robbed again,' he shouted. 'The police reckon it's the same bloke. This time he's taken thirty pairs of Judith's knickers!'

That 2–0 defeat to Rangers was probably the turning point of the season. Although still top, Leicester City were gnawing away at our lead. We lost 1–0 at Filbert Street and drew with Luton and Preston. When we beat Notts County 1–0 with a goal from Gary Chivers, we were still second.

In those days, three clubs were automatically promoted. So promotion was still a very real prospect when we travelled to Swansea for the penultimate game of the season. A Tommy Langley goal gave us a 1–1 draw but, just as relevant, was the chance Mike Fillery missed. A cross from the right gave him a scoring opportunity that he should have buried. Had he scored that day, we would have been promoted.

Looking back, that miss was probably one of the key moments in my life. I didn't realise it then, but it was the first stage of a process that would show me an alternative life outside football.

Of course, at the time we didn't know how critical that miss would prove to be to Chelsea. We had dropped a valuable point and slipped to fourth in the table. Nonetheless, Bobby and I convinced the players that we could still clinch promotion in our final game.

More than 28,000 crammed into Stamford Bridge for the last match against Oldham. At the end, after Walker (two) and Fillery had given us a 3–0 victory, hundreds of singing fans thronged the pitch assuming that promotion had been secured. Wrong! Sunderland, still to play their final game, were one point below us. We waited nine days for West Ham, fresh from their FA Cup victory over Arsenal, to visit Roker Park. I wasn't surprised when Sunderland won 2–0. They climbed above us to finish second. We were joint third with Birmingham on 53 points, but had an inferior goal difference. Had Fillery scored that day in Swansea we would have had a point more than Birmingham and goal difference would have been irrelevant. Had Fillery scored, promotion would have established my management credentials in my first season in the job.

I was bitterly disappointed and questioned the wisdom of the Football League in allowing Sunderland to play West Ham just two days after my old club had scored a famous Wembley victory over Arsenal. They had been celebrating for 48 hours. Were they really bothered about winning an end-of-season match that was of academic interest to them? I thought the circumstances of that day were unfair to Chelsea.

With hindsight, missing out on promotion was not a bad thing from a personal point of view. There was still no money to spend on players and I soon realised that promotion would have brought even more problems. We would have struggled in the First Division and, in the end, I suspect the club would have sacked me.

Ultimately they sacked me anyway and that gave me the opportunity, for the first time in my life, to assess a future outside the confines of professional football. But, for the moment at least, Bobby Gould and I were the recipients of loads of sympathy from within the game. Nothing could disguise the fact that we'd had a magnificent season, despite all the problems at the club.

Once it was all over Bobby and I sifted through the debris of the season, examining where we might have gone wrong. We were both learning and shared a fierce determination to get it right the following season.

As soon as I returned from England duty at the European Championship in Italy, I began planning for my first full season in charge at Stamford Bridge. We still had no money to buy players but, after the previous season's narrow failure, I was optimistic that we could sustain another promotion challenge.

We started badly, failing to win any of our opening five fixtures. It became apparent to me that, with Ronnie Harris gone, Viljoen wasn't going to play much part in our promotion drive. I had big hopes for him but in all he played just 22 first-team games in two years at Chelsea.

Our first win of 1980–81 came with Colin Lee's first goal of the season – 1–0 away to Cambridge United. Suddenly it all began to fall into place and by early December, after just one defeat in 16 games, we were second in the table, a single point behind the leaders, West Ham.

Then, inexplicably, it started to go wrong. We lost 2–0 at Grimsby on 13 December and won only three of the remaining 20 Second Division games. They were the only three games, in fact, in which we managed to score. The other 17 games didn't produce a single Chelsea goal. The goals just dried up. Colin Lee finished the season as top marksman in the Second Division with 15 goals, but only one of them was scored after December.

The crowd became restless, then the crowd in the boardroom became restless. I remember David Mears, Brian's brother, screaming at me from the front row of the directors' box because I'd substituted Peter Rhoades-Brown. Spencer and I fell out in a big way when I learned that he was trying to sign players behind my back. He made an optimistic attempt to bring Johan Cruyff to Stamford Bridge, perhaps to do what we'd hoped Kevin Keegan would do. When asked, I truthfully told the media that the deal was nothing to do with me.

When reporters asked for my comments after a 1–0 defeat by Cardiff in April, watched by just 11,569 at Stamford Bridge, I told them that I felt the board should give me their full backing. This was a bit naïve of me because the story appeared in the newspapers as a 'back me or sack me' ultimatum. That was all the invitation they needed. At midday on 23 April, after a 2–0 home defeat by Luton, I was summoned to the chairman's office. A friend of mine on one of the newspapers had warned me what to expect. How he knew I can't imagine. 'Wear a tin hat,' he said.

Brian Mears and I sat across the table from each other. We had a strange conversation. He waffled around the subject for some minutes. When he finished speaking it wasn't clear what he was trying to say.

'Are you sacking me?' I asked.

'Yes,' he said.

Until that morning, I hadn't been expecting the sack. We'd missed promotion again, I knew, but we were 12th in the table. There was no fear of relegation. Bobby Gould took charge for the remaining two matches and shortly after the last game, a 3–0 defeat against Oldham, Mears announced that he was standing down as chairman.

The sack upset and angered me. I telephoned home and Claire answered. I waffled to her, just as Mears had to me.

'Dad, have you been sacked?' she asked.

I'd been in football for 25 years and it was the first time someone had told me that I wasn't good enough. It was hard to take. It was the low point of my career. It couldn't get any worse – or could it?

In the aftermath of the sacking, Mears made several accusations. In one he claimed that I'd ordered the Chelsea head groundsman to cut the lawn in our garden at Cobham. My view was somewhat different. The groundsman and Judith's father, Jack, were pals. Jack enjoyed looking after our garden and, after his death, Judith used to talk to the groundsman at Stamford Bridge. One day she said, 'If my dad could see the mess Geoff's made with that Flymo he'd turn in his grave.' As a result of that conversation with Judith, the grounds-man offered to cut our lawn.

Mears also claimed that I once refused to attend an urgent meeting at Stamford Bridge because I was babysitting. I have no recollection of this. He must have known how dedicated I was to the job and I can only imagine that he was confusing me with someone else.

Some weeks after my sudden departure I received a letter from the club. I'd had 15 months to run on my contract and my view about that was quite simple. Providing they paid up the 15 months' salary I was owed, that was the end of the matter. I'd put it down to experience. When I read the letter, I was really quite surprised at the contents. Basically, they were refusing to pay up the 15 months' money that was owed to me. This, they claimed, was because of my negligence. According to Chelsea, I had been negligent in my role as club manager.

I read the letter to Judith. I don't think I've ever seen her so angry. Chelsea's claim was absurd. I hadn't been the most successful manager in the club's history but to accuse me of negligence was offensive and demeaning.

I went to see my lawyers and they explained the options. One of these, the most straightforward, was to take my case to an industrial tribunal. This is what I chose to do. As part of my preparations for the case I requested Chelsea's board-meeting minutes during my time as manager at the club. I wanted to see how many times, if any, they had recorded the fact that I had been negligent. There was nothing in the minutes to suggest that I had been negligent at any stage during my 19 months at Stamford Bridge.

What intrigued my lawyers was an item minuted some time after I had been sacked. Inadvertently, the club had sent me minutes not only for the period I'd requested but for some weeks afterwards. This was a serious oversight on Chelsea's part and, for me, underlined the administrative chaos at the club at that time.

These minutes recorded an extraordinary conversation between members of the Chelsea board. During the course of this conversation, it was clear that they were trying to establish their reasons for sacking me. It was also clear that this was the first occasion on which the board members had discussed it.

It was explained to me by my legal advisers that this record of the Chelsea board meeting meant that, having sacked me, they now had to find a reason for doing so. They didn't have a reason before the event. Now they were looking for one.

Armed with this information, my lawyers told me that Chelsea did not have a hope of winning the case. We turned up at court on a Monday morning. By lunchtime it was all settled – out of court. Chelsea agreed to pay me the 15 months' money they owed. I didn't gloat. I was satisfied with the outcome but would have preferred to keep my job as Chelsea manager. Despite the problems, I enjoyed my time at Stamford Bridge and years later saw what a man with vision, energy and a sense of purpose could achieve.

Viscount Chelsea briefly succeeded Mears as chairman before selling out to Ken Bates in 1982. Love him or hate him, you have to acknowledge that Bates fulfilled much of the club's potential. He turned Chelsea into a huge success story. Unlike Mears, he was never afraid to make difficult decisions; nor was he afraid to upset people.

Could I have worked for him? I would have enjoyed finding out. It's too late now, of course, but there's no doubt that as a chairman, Ken Bates was a hard act to follow even when his successor, Roman Abramovich, had one of the world's biggest fortunes.

I didn't realise it at the time, but my brief stay at Chelsea was my final tilt at management in English football. People sometimes ask me why it was that so few of the World Cup-winning team enjoyed any sustained success in football management. I think it was a matter of circumstance rather than anything to do with the calibre of the individuals involved. Of the 11, only George Cohen, Ray Wilson and Roger Hunt chose not to have a stab at management at some serious level. The other eight had mixed success but only Jack Charlton would claim to have enjoyed a long and productive managerial career. He coached Middlesbrough, Sheffield Wednesday and Newcastle before hauling the Republic of Ireland from the backwaters of international football to compete with the world's best.

I think one successful coach from any team of 11 players isn't a bad ratio. How many of Chelsea's league championship-winning team of 1955 went on to become successful managers? Only one – Ron Greenwood.

CHAPTER SEVENTEEN

The real world

SISTER MARY AGNES SMILED KINDLY AS I EXPLAINED MY SITUATION in her oak-panelled private study at The Notre Dame School for Girls in Cobham.

I was approaching 40 and out of work for the first time in my life. It was a new, uncomfortable experience. I'd applied for about 15 jobs following my sacking at Chelsea but didn't get a single interview. It was important to be seen to be applying for work while awaiting my wrongful dismissal case. I'd made the whole business with Chelsea public and that may have been the wrong thing to do. It's possible that other club chairmen viewed me as a potential troublemaker. I signed on the dole.

Sister Mary listened patiently. I needed to work, I told her. I wanted a job. I had a wife, three daughters and a big mortgage. The three girls loved The Notre Dame School but the fees, for a man out of work, were crippling.

'I wonder whether you could bear with me for a while until I get myself sorted out financially,' I asked her. Thankfully, she was very understanding.

It was a difficult time for me. I didn't want to be seen hanging around dressing-rooms and training grounds hoping someone would take pity on me. The more I thought about it, the more I realised that I didn't really want to become part of the managerial merry-go-round. I wanted a job that was reasonably secure. In football, you can be talented, industrious and dedicated and lose your job because the ball hits the wrong side of a post and bounces out. You can show exactly the same qualities in business but survive the occasional mishap and keep your job for years. I spent the last 20 years of my working life in the same business. How many football managers these days keep the same job for 20 years?

Early in the summer of 1981, I felt a sense of purpose once more when I joined Ron Greenwood and the England squad for two European Championship qualifying ties in Switzerland and Hungary. Ron and the lads were sympathetic and supportive. 'Don't worry, Hurstie, you'll soon get another job,' seemed to be the general feeling.

When I returned from my coaching duties with England, a friend who was a travel agent offered Judith and me a few days in a lovely hotel in Marbella. While sitting by the pool one morning, I met a chap who spoke enthusiastically about the life insurance business. He worked for Hambro Life and told me what a wonderful job it was, providing big annual commissions for successful salesmen. That'll do for me, I thought.

Along with the pub business, selling life insurance was the favourite refuge of retired footballers who didn't remain in the game in some capacity. A lot of players, professional footballers since leaving school, were not willing to risk venturing into the real world.

Jimmy Greaves worked for Abbey Life and as soon as I returned home I called him. He arranged for me to have an interview with Paul Riviere, the manager of Abbey Life in Southwark. Paul was enormously helpful and we became good friends. He recruited me for Abbey Life, paid me a small retainer and gave me a blue Ford Cortina. Delighted with myself, I immediately wrote out a cheque for Sister Mary Agnes.

The first thing I had to do in my new role was attend a two-week induction programme in Southwark. They taught me the basics of selling, the structure of selling and the product knowledge that is essential if you want to be a successful salesman. There were about ten other potential salesman on the course with me and I was met with the usual raised eyebrows and dropped jaws when I reported on my first day. We all got along well, though. They were a good bunch of lads; all ages and from all walks of life. Suddenly, I was no longer a well-known footballer and World Cup hero. I was another man-in-the-street struggling to pay the mortgage. In the space of a fortnight, my life turned around completely.

The induction course taught me how to approach people. Until this time, everyone had approached me – for autographs, for charity events, for photographs, for interviews, for TV appearances, for supermarket openings. Now I had to learn how to approach strangers. It taught me something about humility – not a bad lesson for some of the egotistical young players in the modern game.

I spent hours practising. I used to rehearse the routine at home in Cobham, using Judith as the client. Even for rehearsals I made sure I looked my best – suit, tie, crisp white shirt, highly polished shoes. Carrying my briefcase, I'd walk up my own garden path to my own front door. When I knocked, she answered and I began my patter – serious, but bright and cheerful too. The first time I did this it all went smoothly. After about a dozen attempts I was quite confident. Judith played her role patiently but it was clear she was getting a bit tired of it.

A couple of days later, I thought I'd test the routine without warning her. Booted and suited, I strode boldly up to my front door. Bang! Bang! Bang! 'Good morning, Madam,' I said. 'My name is Geoff...'

Before I got any further she said, 'Not you again! Get lost!' and slammed the door in my face!

There were no short cuts in selling. You had to be patient, polite and persistent. Initially, you had to learn your script parrot fashion but, as confidence grew, your delivery became more natural. Cold calling is important in the early days for any salesman, but as you progress you attract more and more business through references, recommendations and renewals.

Paul Riviere, my new boss, was a Chelsea fan. I was enormously encouraged when he told me that I approached my new life with the same dedication and energy I'd devoted to my job at Stamford Bridge. He introduced me to cold calling, a thankless task but essential if you want to be a successful salesman.

On my first day, I went through the Yellow Pages and started making telephone calls randomly. The first half a dozen calls produced nothing. Then, on my next call, a woman answered.

'Good morning, Madam. May I introduce myself? My name's Geoff Hurst and I represent Abbey Life.'

Before I could go further she said, 'I think you'd better talk to my husband.'

A couple of seconds later the husband came to the phone. 'Hello,' he said. 'My wife tells me you're Geoff Hurst. If you're —ing Geoff Hurst, my wife's —ing Marilyn Monroe!'

There were setbacks and moments of disappointment, but I persevered, gradually found my feet and began to enjoy the little triumphs that came along from time to time. Inevitably, I contacted friends in football and people I knew, if only by reputation. The more people I saw, the more comfortable and confident I became.

I remember my delight when Brian Clough, the manager of Nottingham Forest, agreed to see me before a game. I drove to Nottingham with Paul Riviere and Brian gave us 30 minutes to explain what we had to offer. We sold him nothing, but the mere fact that he'd shown an interest gave me a sense of satisfaction.

Paul and I meandered back that night and it was past 4 a.m. when I finally got home. Judith was not pleased with me. In fact, she was so displeased that she threw my briefcase at me. It burst open and the papers and brochures spilled on to the carpet. She stormed off back to bed. I left the papers on the floor because Judith can't abide mess and untidiness. I knew that, first thing in the morning, she'd get out of bed and pick them up. I was right.

'The house looks lovely this morning, my angel,' I said, but she still wasn't happy with me.

Judith has been a pillar of support throughout my life and her encouragement and advice were critical during this uncertain period of transition. I valued her opinions and her judgement and in moments of doubt we found support in each other.

As a professional footballer, my life had been mapped out by my club, or by the fixture lists or England's international commitments. But now there were different avenues to explore and Judith and I discussed all the options. We decided that I should continue to coach the England squad while Ron was the manager because I could fit this in with my work for Abbey Life.

When Anglia TV asked me to do some work for them, we closely examined what they proposed and realised that I could also squeeze this into the weekly schedule. Football punditry was still in its infancy but they wanted me to join their commentary team of Gerry Harrison and Steve Ryder, a youngster then who was to become the top BBC sports presenter. I regularly watched matches in the Anglia region and worked in the studios in Norwich on a Sunday morning, preparing the programme. I enjoyed the work and it kept me involved in the game at club level.

It was hard sometimes, commuting to East Anglia at the weekends and selling insurance during the week, but it made me realise that, if I wanted, I could make a life for myself outside football. In that year, I earned £23,000. In my last year at Chelsea I'd earned £28,000. The fact that I'd done so well in my first year with no experience of business encouraged me to believe that I could have a successful career outside football. It was another step in the sequence of events directing me away from football.

Nothing had diminished my determination to succeed or my appetite for hard work but I realised that I'd have to slow down, otherwise something disastrous would happen. It nearly did one night, late in 1981, when I was driving home from Norwich in thick snow knowing that I had to be up early for a sales conference the following morning.

While overtaking another car somewhere near Newmarket I lost control of my blue company Cortina, rolled down a bank and finished upright, still strapped in my seat, in the middle of a field. I was conscious but frightened to move anything. It was dark but I could feel the warm sticky blood on the back of one hand.

Gradually I realised that I wasn't seriously hurt and within a minute or two the couple from the car I'd tried to overtake found me in the middle of the field. The man peered at me in the gloom and said, 'My God! It's Geoff Hurst. Look! Look! It's Geoff Hurst.'

We were all in a state of shock but once they'd helped me out of the wreck of my car and we'd established that I could walk, I was OK. They suggested they give me a lift. It seemed the best option. They were on their way to a dinner party. They said they would happily drive me to the house where I could use the telephone.

We arrived at the house in a state of some excitement. They knocked and once inside pushed their way down the hallway crying, 'You'll never guess who we've got with us. Go on, have a guess. You'll never guess.' They left me standing on the doorstep, muddy and freezing with a blood-stained handkerchief wrapped round one hand. 'For God's sake, *guess!*' I was muttering to myself.

Finally I was ushered into the warmth of the house. They were really nice people. I was washed, fed and bandaged. I called Judith and told her the car had broken down. They gave me a lift to the railway station and I caught a train to Liverpool Street. The next day the police told me that the car was a write-off. 'You were lucky to survive,' they said.

In the spring of 1982, a chance meeting with a man in a village pub in Essex opened the door to a new life that would eventually mean severing my last connections with football. Ron Pleydell was the chairman of Motor-plan, a company that administered used-car warranties, underwritten at Lloyds, in the motor trade. It was a thriving, bullish company in London and the south east but they wanted to develop their potential nationally. When I walked into the pub, Ron Pleydell, like the entrepreneur that he was, saw a business opportunity. He asked if I would undertake some public relations work for him. I was very interested in what he proposed and initially agreed to promote their company. Within a few weeks, I'd signed a one-year contract with the company.

I realise now that I was reaping the benefits of the good image I'd enjoyed throughout my playing career. It wasn't a manufactured image. It was natural, the result of a good upbringing, disciplined schooling and the values that West Ham taught all young players.

At the time I felt that if I was going to put my name to a product, or a company for that matter, I should find out as much about it as possible. So I decided to join the company's 40 self-employed reps on the road and see how it all worked. I began to learn about the business and, armed with my new knowledge from Abbey Life, quickly fell into selling mode.

Within six weeks, Motor-plan offered me a full-time job on their sales force. This, I thought, was the secure job with long-term prospects that I needed. I thanked Abbey Life and Paul Riviere for all they had done for me, and established myself in the Motor-plan offices at Chadwell Heath, ironically no more than a mile from the West Ham training ground.

I was beginning to come to terms with the fact that professional football was no longer a significant part of my life. It had been, but now I was seeking new challenges. I recall saying to Judith one evening that I'd made a decision not to return to football. She was very surprised but I felt I could make a successful life outside the game.

My image was good and I was beginning to realise how important that was. Almost everything that came my way after leaving football could be traced back to a good reputation and public image.

I missed some elements of the game more than others but I'd just about consigned my football career to history when, out of the blue, all my plans were thrown into turmoil. Albert Wade, a West Ham fan who worked in investments in Kuwait, called one day with a proposition.

'D'you fancy working in Kuwait for a couple of years?' he asked. 'Kuwait Sporting Club want you to be their coach.'

Judith and I talked it over and said no. Albert was persistent.

'Why not go and have a look,' he said. 'Take Judith. First class, good hotel. Just a few days.'

I was in a dilemma. I'd made my decision. I was going to finish with football after fulfilling my coaching obligations to Ron Greenwood and the England squad at the World Cup in Spain that summer. I wanted to try something new with my life.

Judith and I flew to Kuwait City where we were met at the airport and escorted to our hotel. In the car we had to suppress our laughter as we read the English-language *Kuwait Times*. A front-page story, headlined 'Man arrested for raping camel', told how vets had examined the camel and found it to be in a pretty poor condition following the ordeal. During the course of our visit Mohammed Al Sagar, the vice chairman of Kuwait Sporting Club, interviewed me. I asked about the fate of the camel and Mohammed seemed to find the story as amusing as Judith and I had done.

The Kuwait Sporting Club offered me £50,000 for the first year, £55,000 for the second, a free luxury apartment for the family, a Chevrolet saloon, free health treatment, school fees paid for three daughters and almost four months holiday a year. We flew back to London, still unsure. We could talk about nothing else.

I'd made up my mind to turn it down and was actually writing the letter declining the offer when Judith said, 'We'd be mad to turn it down. The money's too good to refuse.'

She was right. I threw the half-written letter away and started another one. This one said that I'd be delighted to accept the kind offer. I took the job for the money. It delayed my transfer from the football world to the business world by two years.

In early May 1982, just a month before I flew to Bilbao with the England squad for the 1982 World Cup, I told Motor-plan that I'd had an offer that was too good to turn down. Then I told Kuwait Sporting Club that I would be joining them after the World Cup.

Kuwait, strangely, were one of England's three first-round opponents in Spain. As unranked amateurs they had started the tournament impressively, drawing 1–1 with Czechoslovakia. Then, in the stifling city of Valladolid in the centre of Spain, they met the highly fancied French team of Platini, Tigana and Giresse. It was in this match that I had my first taste of the complexities of the Arab personality.

Towards the end of a game that Kuwait were losing, little Giresse chased a ball from Platini through a motionless defence and scored. The Kuwaitis had stopped playing because they'd heard a whistle. The fact that the whistle had been blown by a fan on the terrace behind their goal was an irrelevance. When the referee awarded the French a goal there was mayhem on the pitch.

Kuwaiti dignitaries in the stand appeared to be beckoning the players to leave the field. As the players began to walk off, the referee changed his mind and disallowed the goal. Carlos Alberto Parreira, Kuwait's Brazilian coach, appealed to his players to stay on the pitch. They agreed reluctantly and eventually lost the game 4–1.

I watched that match with Ron Greenwood because England met Kuwait next. They had some clever players and claimed proudly that the modern game in Kuwait was based upon principles championed by Brazil. They had entrusted their development to the Brazilians since Mario Zagalo, one-time World Cup team-mate of Pele, went there to work in the seventies.

England beat them 1–0 in Bilbao, a Trevor Francis goal the highlight of a disappointing game, and progressed to the second round with a 100 per cent record. Kuwait failed to win a match and finished bottom of the qualifying group.

It was unfortunate for them that the World Cup finals coincided with Ramadan. Some of the more religiously observant of the Kuwait players took to the field on empty stomachs, having refused food between sunrise and sunset. Some even refused to drink water during the interval. The England physiotherapist Fred Street, a very popular figure with the players and staff during my five years with Ron Greenwood, believed that such abstinence could be harmful, especially when temperatures were nudging 100°F in Spain.

I was to come across this strict fasting and the five daily ritual sequences of prayer increasingly in the months ahead. It took me some time to adapt to life in this small Arab sheikhdom that was among the world's leading oil producers.

First, though, I needed to see my new players in pre-season training. As financial support was no problem, I booked the entire squad into Eltham College in south London for a month's pre-season training. I had a few small problems with senior players who had brought their wives along and it occurred to me that, as they were amateurs, I had to devise ways of disciplining them. You fine professional players who step out of line, but you can't withhold the wages of amateurs, can you?

I discussed this at some length with the coach I'd appointed as my assistant. John Cartwright, who was in the process of establishing a reputation as one of the finest coaches of youngsters in the game, had played with me at West Ham when we were boys. I wanted someone to look after the Under-21 players at Kuwait Sporting Club and he was the man I chose for the job.

I was a year younger than John so he was already on the groundstaff when I arrived at Upton Park. A clever, talented inside-forward, his first-team opportunities were limited by the emergence of Ronnie Boyce and the signing of Phil Woosnam. He played just a handful of first-team games although I remember playing alongside him in a 1–1 draw against Newcastle at Upton Park in April 1961.

Dealing with Arab footballers was a new and, at times, complex experience for both of us. Once in Kuwait, we established a set of rules and explained them to the players. Most of them understood English and those who didn't listened to the translation by the club's English-speaking trainer, Nasser Kabbaz. He was to become an important figure in interpreting the finer points of our rules and regulations. He was a typical trainer, the kind you find at football clubs around the world. He loved the game, loved the players and would do anything for the benefit of the club.

As I had discovered at Telford, it was essential to approach the challenge in a professional manner even if the players themselves were not professional. So we decided, for instance, that those reporting late for training would not play for whatever number of matches we felt appropriate.

A clear, warm desert morning greeted the first training session of the Hurst–Cartwright regime. All the players arrived at the scheduled time except for one – Saed Al Houti. Club captain, midfield general, captain of Kuwait, World Cup hero in Spain a few weeks earlier, Saed enjoyed superstar status.

John and I were warming up the rest of the squad when the superstar ambled on to the pitch. I saw his team-mates looking at me over their shoulders to see how I dealt with this breach of club discipline. I knew it was important to get it right because it would set the tone for my relationship with the rest of them. As Saed approached the group I put my arm up, like a policeman stopping the traffic, and beckoned him to leave. I wanted the other players to see that my arm was raised because they wouldn't be able to hear what I was saying to Saed.

I said to Nasser, 'I want him to go home. He's suspended for reporting late for training. Make sure he understands.'

The other players were clearly shocked by the severity of my reaction, but not as shocked as the 20 members of the committee responsible for all aspects of the club's welfare. The morning training session had only just finished when I received a call from Mr Al Sagar.

'What's happened to Saed?' he asked desperately. 'We must talk about this.'

'OK,' I said. 'I'll see you in the morning.'

'No! No!' he said. 'We must talk now.'

Within 30 minutes John and I were in my air-conditioned Chevrolet, driving through the heat of the mid-afternoon to the offices of Kuwait Sporting Club. John, I remember, was particularly chirpy.

'You've done it this time, Hurstie, haven't you?' he grinned. 'Have you got the passports ready for a quick getaway?'

I recalled the advice I had been given from Albert Wade, the go-between in the process that brought me to Kuwait. He had worked closely with the Arabs for a long time. He told me never to back down. In Kuwaiti culture, if you backed down you lost face. They interpreted this as a significant character weakness.

To this point I'd found my new employers polite, understanding and hospitable. In fact, the only slight concern I had in any of my dealings with the club's senior figures came on the day the finance director showed me round the ground, insisting that we walk hand in hand! This unexpected familiarity provoked just a tremor of unease at the time! But this was the custom. When you go abroad to work, you have to accept you are living in a different culture.

When John and I arrived at the club's offices, all the committee members were seated around a vast boardroom table. We were greeted formally and asked to explain the decision to send Al Houti home from the training ground. I told them what had happened.

Had we warned the players of the consequences if they broke the new rules?

'Yes,' I replied. 'All the players were aware of all of the rules.'

They told me that what I had done in dropping the national team captain was, politically, very difficult for the club. I told them that if they wanted a politician to run their football team, I was not the man for the job.

'We have Mrs Thatcher in England,' I said. 'She may be available.'

'Might you reconsider your decision?' I was asked.

'Not a chance,' I said. 'In fact, not only is he dropped because he's broken a rule but I feel that he's not good enough to be in the team anyway.'

Gasps of horror came from around the table. There was much scratching of beards and heads. John and I were asked to wait in another room. Two hours later Mohammed Al Sagar emerged.

'Thank you very much,' he said. 'We're happy with your explanation. You have our full support.'

It was an important victory for me. Saed Al Houti wasn't happy, though. He played no more than a handful of games for the club during my time there.

We enjoyed our two years in the desert. From the football point of view, I was proud to lead the club to the national Cup final, but we never seriously threatened Arabi, the dominant team in the 13-club league in Kuwait. Although Brazilian coaches were increasingly popular, Arabi had thrived under the guidance of a former opponent of mine – Dave Mackay. He was a legend at Tottenham when I played against him in the mid sixties and later, as Derby County manager, he won the First Division title in 1975.

A sociable, boisterous Scotsman, he had been the life and soul of Bill Nicholson's fabulous double-winning side and was just as popular among the Brits in Kuwait. Although not as strict as some other Arab countries, Kuwait was nonetheless dry. It was illegal to bring alcohol into the country, but that didn't stop people trying.

Because of my tax situation, I spent the time between seasons in the United States. During one trip home, Judith, travelling alone, brought with her several litres of bourbon, vodka and gin. As the airline wouldn't allow her to take the bag holding the drink into the cabin, she reluctantly agreed to allow the bag to go in the hold.

Mistake! Waiting to collect her luggage from the carousel at Kuwait airport, she could smell her bag before she actually saw it. All the bottles had broken and when she picked up the bag and joined the queue for customs and immigration she smelled like a walking brewery.

'Anything to declare, Madam?' smiled the customs officer.

'Not any longer!' she said.

During the course of 1983, Ron Pleydell, the chairman of Motor-plan, visited me in Kuwait to stress that his company still wanted me to work for them when my contract finished. They were actually chasing me now so, in a sense, I was in a stronger position than before. I agreed to join them when my contract finished and negotiated a position as sales director and shareholder. I purchased 19 per cent of the company, which was £38,000 worth of shares, with the money I'd earned in Kuwait.

In January 1984, three months before my contract was due to expire, Motor-plan asked me to attend a meeting in London. The other directors wanted to ascertain the strength of my commitment to the company. They were worried that I might use them simply as a stepping-stone while I waited for another job in football. I'd already told them, very clearly, that Motor-plan was my first option. My second option would have been to stay in Kuwait with a return to football in England a very poor third option.

We met at the chairman's house in Doddinghurst, a village in Essex. Tony Bilton and Peter Head, the company's two other directors, attended. It was a strange meeting. In front of the chairman, in his house, the two other directors insisted on talking to me alone. Ron left the room while they interrogated me. I explained to them that I had decided that football was no longer an option. Had I wanted to continue in football, I would probably have stayed in Kuwait. They had offered to extend my contract with a significant salary increase. I had declined the offer.

After about two hours of talks, Tony Bilton stood up and said that he had to leave because he had a social engagement that evening. I'd flown all the way from Kuwait for this meeting and, as you can imagine, I wasn't impressed. Nonetheless, having satisfied them that my intentions were honourable, it was agreed that I would start work in May.

We packed up in Kuwait and I handed over to John Cartwright, who did a great job as my successor before returning to the UK where he became assistant manager of Arsenal and coached the England youth team.

My tax adviser suggested I return home no earlier than 6 April, so on that very day in 1984 we turned up with all our baggage on our doorstep in Cobham. As much as I'd enjoyed the desert, it was good to be back in England in the spring. I planned to have four weeks' rest before starting work again.

The following day Ron Pleydell called me to say that one director was ill, and another on holiday. Could I go into the office in Chadwell Heath the following day? I thought at the time that perhaps they were testing my commitment to my new job.

I agreed to start work immediately so on 8 April 1984, just 48 hours after returning from Kuwait, a new life began with no football involvement. For the first time, I was not pulling on a tracksuit as either a player or a coach. I'd made a conscious decision to put football on the back burner and I intended to stick with it. I wasn't sure whether I would enjoy the nine-to-five routine that forms the framework of the week for most working people, but I was determined to have a real crack at it.

This was the real world. I was awake at 6 a.m. every day. I devoted Monday and Friday to office work, but Tuesday to Thursday was spent travelling all over the country selling the company. I quickly realised that past glories counted for very little in the business world. I remember waiting to talk to a big Ford dealer in Essex. I gave my business card to his secretary and sat patiently in the showroom. He eventually came into the showroom and flicked the card at his secretary. The card slid off her desk and as I bent down to pick it up he announced in a pompous voice, 'I don't deal with ex-footballers.'

Experiences like that were disappointing, especially as I had promised myself never to trade on my name and reputation as a footballer. I always introduced myself as 'Geoff Hurst, the sales director of Motor-plan.' I never mentioned football unless someone mentioned it first. I remember one senior director at another Ford dealership studying my business card. It said 'Geoff Hurst, MBE'.

'Hurst?' he said. 'Yes, I know a Hurst at Fords.'

'No relation,' I said.

'Uhm,' he said. 'What does the MBE stand for?'

'Oh dear!' I thought. I said, 'It stands for . . . er . . . mechanical breakdown expert.'

'Oh! Really?' he said.

Two weeks later I met the same man. I wasn't looking forward to it, but as soon as he saw me he said, 'Good morning. My staff told me who you were as soon as you left. You must think I'm some kind of idiot.'

Others, of course, went out of their way to please and impress when they knew we'd be meeting. I appreciated all the efforts they made but, to be honest, would have preferred the same treatment as everyone else.

I remember arriving at Newcastle-upon-Tyne railway station early one morning where I was met by Geoff Holiday, a great guy who was the Motor-plan rep in the area at the time. I was due to be there for a few days so I had my overnight bag and suit carrier with me. He had a small estate-type van so we put the luggage in the back and I climbed into the passenger seat.

As we drove through the early morning traffic in Newcastle, I could feel the seat of my trousers becoming damp and cold. I ignored it at first but soon I could feel the dampness in my back too. I was going to be in and out of the car all day. Apart from feeling wet and cold, the suit would be stained.

I said to Geoff, 'I'm feeling a bit damp. I think you must have left the windows open in the rain.'

He was clearly embarrassed. 'Look, I'm sorry,' he said. 'We've got a pet dog. It sits on the seat sometimes. When I knew you were coming up here I tidied the car and noticed dog's hairs on the seat. So I shampooed it.'

'How thoughtful,' I said. At the next stop I took my clothes out of the suit carrier and sat on that for the rest of the day.

Geoff Holiday was typical of most of the people I met and worked with. They were helpful, friendly and considerate. But when you're out there selling, more people say no than yes. It was difficult to accept at first but I wouldn't let anything put me off.

Having been feted for most of my adult life, rejection was a new experience. I gritted my teeth and got on with it. The induction course at Abbey Life had taught me how to handle rejection. It occurred to me that, as with most things in my life, I wasn't very good when I started. That includes playing football and selling insurance. I learned both the hard way – but I learned.

I didn't miss the world of professional football. There was no element of the game that I felt I needed to make my life complete. I was able to detach myself from it completely. Occasionally I went to watch a match, but it was occasionally. I gave no interviews, refused requests to appear on TV and invitations to celebrity dinners. I turned down anything to do with football. It wasn't a matter of being disillusioned or bitter. I just didn't want to do anything that conflicted with my business life.

The only real difference this absence of football made was a physical one. As any professional will tell you, when you're fit you glow with health and vitality. For the first time I wasn't playing or training, but I was still in reasonable condition and had no weight problem.

When Motor-plan decided to sponsor Dennis Waterman's Showbiz Football team, I played a few times. Actor Warren Clarke was in the team, and Martin Peters, who worked with me at Motor-plan. We used to travel up and down the country for charity matches and after one game on a hot summer's day, I said to Martin, 'That's it. I've had enough.' Martin tried to talk me out of it but I simply didn't want to play any more. I still received lots of requests from people to appear in charity matches but I declined them all.

'I've hung up my boots,' I told them all. 'I've retired.' And I had.

CHAPTER EIGHTEEN

Tears

LIKE ANY OTHER COUPLE, JUDITH AND I HAD OUR UPS AND DOWNS, our moments of triumph and disappointment, but nothing in life prepared us for the news that our daughter Claire had a brain tumour.

She was 22 and about to present us with our first grandchild. One day she telephoned Judith from her office. Midway through the conversation she began talking strangely. 'Gobbledegook,' was how Judith described it later. A colleague took the telephone from Claire and explained to Judith that she wasn't feeling well. That evening Claire came to see us. She was explaining what had happened earlier in the day when she suddenly began talking strangely again.

We thought she was demonstrating what had happened at the office. She wasn't. She was having another fit. We called the doctor immediately but it was another three years before Claire's problem was correctly diagnosed.

Those three years were nightmarish for all of us, but particularly for Claire. Apart from the varied medications she had to take, she had EEGs on her brain, she was told her problem was hormonal, she was told she was having a nervous breakdown and she was told the problem was stress-related. One doctor even asked if she was a member of a religious cult.

Throughout 1988, the year Amy was born, Claire had numerous tests and visited several doctors and specialists. Some we had faith in, some we didn't. One consultation with a lady neurologist was an appalling experience. We travelled a long way to see her and I have this vision even now of her peering suspiciously at us from behind a door. She had the touch and charisma of a rogue elephant. She told Claire that she should have a biopsy, contrary to all the other advice she'd received. She then told her, without a hint of sensitivity, 'You could die from this you know.' As we walked back to the car with Claire, Judith looked as if she had aged 20 years.

In a sense, it didn't help that the number and regularity of her attacks began to diminish. Perhaps, whatever the problem, it was healing naturally. That wasn't the case. Her attacks returned with the birth of Jack in 1990, and they got worse.

This was the low point of my life. Not much has reduced me to tears but this did. I remember sitting on the kitchen floor with Judith and our two younger daughters, Joanne and Charlotte, and we were all crying. Every parent will understand. This was my little girl. What was going to happen to her? We had shared so much. This was the little girl I took to Romford in her pram and inadvertently left in a shop when I met Jimmy Greaves. This was the little girl I gave away on her wedding day.

At that moment I would have sacrificed all the Cups, medals, fame and glory for a guarantee that my daughter would be cured of whatever it was that was causing her such distress. Nothing puts the trivia of life into sharper perspective than serious family illness.

Judith and I sought comfort and strength in each other. As parents, when you go through something like this, it's essential that you support each other. Some days you feel strong and she feels weak, on other days you're weak and she's strong.

This was a sad time. Bobby Moore, a good friend to both of us, was declining before our eyes. Judith and Tina were still very close and kept in touch. Judith knew he was dying but she didn't tell me.

Not long before he died, in February 1993, he called me at home.

By this time we were back in Chigwell, Essex, where Bobby's children and my children had played together years before. Claire was born the same year as their eldest child, Roberta, and their second, Dean, was born a year before Jo.

It was a strange phone call from Bobby. Judith recognised the significance of it immediately. I didn't realise it at the time but it was his way of saying goodbye.

A few days later, driving in the north of England, I heard the news flash on the radio. I knew he was seriously ill but it was still a brutal shock to be told by a voice on the radio that Bobby Moore had died. He was part of my life and only eight months older than I was.

Judith and I drove down to West Ham to pay our last respects. The gates at Upton Park were covered in flowers, scarves and messages from fans. They'd built a shrine to Bobby. It was a moving, tearful occasion for both of us. Claire, Jo and Charlotte were upset too. They knew how close we had been to Bobby and Tina.

As a family, we were in need of a ray of sunshine. It came, at last, when through Paul Riviere I met Dr Adrian Whiteson of the British Boxing Board of Control. He was familiar with brain-related problems and introduced us to the man who convinced us that Claire's illness could be diagnosed correctly – Peter Harvey, a neurologist in Harley Street. Claire went to see him and he immediately recommended a scan. The scan revealed a brain tumour. It had taken three years to get this far.

Quite naturally, we wanted the best treatment for her. Peter Harvey recommended Professor Lindsey Symon, CBE, a Scottish surgeon who had been a captain in the Royal Medical Corps. A keen golfer and member of the Royal and Ancient, he proudly told me that he'd played a few rounds with George Graham.

It was such a relief to find someone in whom we had total confidence. Claire felt very comfortable with him. The only problem was that he was planning to retire, but he agreed to monitor the tumour for three years before deciding whether to operate. Claire wanted him to perform the operation, which he did in January 1995 at the National Hospital for Nervous Diseases in London. The treatment she received couldn't have been bettered. Seven years after she first thought something was wrong, she finally came home, pale and with her head still shaved, but she was smiling again. We all were.

Claire's illness dominated family life and had been emotionally draining for all of us. There were other worries, but these were merely financial. Business matters came a poor second to the long-term welfare of the family.

In 1989 a company called Diamond Group Holdings had acquired Motor-plan and, shortly afterwards, collapsed with debts. Due to an oversight during the course of their acquisition, Ron Pleydell, Tony Bilton and I were still guarantors for the Motor-plan building in Chadwell Heath. The building was valued at £400,000 and we had a mortgage of £200,000. As the three principals, we held a joint and several guarantee, which meant that any of the three of us could be held liable for the total debt.

This worrying state of affairs wasn't picked up until 1993 when the building, now leaking and derelict, was sold for £75,000. The mortgage hadn't been paid for years and the total debt had mounted to something like £600,000, owed to the First National Finance Company.

Pleydell, the Motor-plan chairman, had left the company and had been declared bankrupt so he was clearly in no position to pay. That left Bilton and me and as far as the First National Finance Company was concerned, I was the more attractive target. Perhaps believing that the potential publicity would embarrass me, the bank started to lean on me for the money. An offer was made but initially turned down. Repaying a sum like £600,000 would mean selling the house and would have ruined me financially. I was prepared to accept a share of the responsibility but repaying the total was out of the question as far as I was concerned.

Eventually, I was put in touch with lawyer David Tiplady of D.J. Freeman, a company experienced in this kind of problem. They decided to get the PR guru Max Clifford involved. I met Max, we agreed on a strategy and with his help the matter was resolved in 1998 when I paid a settlement figure of £150,000.

By this time London General Holdings, a subsidiary of AON, owned the Motor-plan business. I now worked for them, and have done so on a consultancy basis since retiring from my full-time role in 1998.

In March 1993 I was thrilled, and slightly surprised, when the American managing director of London General Holdings, David Cole, made me managing director of the domestic appliance division, based in Kingston, Surrey. It was a big opportunity for me and for five years I put into practice all that I had learned in management with Telford, Chelsea, Kuwait and Motor-plan. I appointed two key people, Ian Kenny and Taj Mian, and from 1993–98 turnover rose from £15 million to £85 million.

Although Claire's illness dominated my thoughts, that period of my business life gave me as much satisfaction as anything I had achieved in football. I had learned the business the hard way and my perseverance had paid dividends.

My philosophy in business was quite simple. I treated people properly, I liked to set a good example, I applied common sense and discipline and I worked hard. They were many of the qualities I had learned as a kid at West Ham. They apply in the modern world just as much as they applied then.

I'd devoted almost 15 years to establishing myself in the business world and I think my diligence and determination were well rewarded. For almost ten years of that time, I'd had practically no significant contact with professional football, but as I edged into my fifties, the game started to beckon again.

In 1986 Judith and I had decided, almost on a whim, to re-visit Mexico, a country we had enjoyed enormously during the 1970 World Cup. When Colombia withdrew as the 1986 hosts, Mexico filled the breach. When a travel agent asked if I would like to go for a few weeks, escorting a bunch of supporters, I said, 'OK, providing Judith comes too.'

If you can handle the dust, heat, noise and chaos, Mexico has a special appeal. A sense of humour helps, especially when you climb into one of the hundreds of beaten up taxicabs that cruise the city streets. In one such old banger, Judith, two Manchester City fans and I were ferried to England's game against Morocco in hot, humid Monterrey.

As we bumped along the city streets in the glare of the midday sun, the driver suddenly exclaimed, 'Caramba!' In his hand was the gear stick that had come away from its housing in the steering-wheel column. To return it to its proper place in the steering column he had to remove the dashboard.

Thankfully, we arrived safely and witnessed a very disappointing goalless draw in which Bryan Robson was injured and Ray Wilkins sent off for throwing the ball at the referee in frustration. This was completely out of character for Ray but, nevertheless, a player of his experience should have known better.

Strangely, with Wilkins and Robson missing from the next game, Bobby Robson's team seemed to have a better balance. This time Peter Reid and Trevor Steven joined Glenn Hoddle and Steve Hodge in midfield. England beat Poland 3–0, their first victory in the World Cup, with Gary Lineker scoring all three goals.

Lineker, of course, ended the tournament as the World Cup's top marksman with six goals and, soon afterwards, secured a lucrative transfer to Barcelona. It was bitterly hard on him and his teammates to be edged out in the quarter-finals by Argentina and Diego Maradona's handball goal.

The BBC persuaded me to go to their studios in Mexico City on the morning of the Argentina game. They wanted me to appear in their build-up programme. They agreed to pick Judith and me up from our hotel, drive us to the studio, then to the Azteca Stadium for the game and pick us up afterwards for the return to the hotel.

The first couple of stages went smoothly. I did the programme and the taxi drove Judith and me through the dense Mexico City traffic to the stadium. The driver dropped us just outside the stadium, next to a vast inflated packet of Camel cigarettes. 'Señor, I pick you up here,' he said, gesturing to the floating cigarette advert.

As luck would have it, we watched the match from seats that probably gave the very best view of Maradona's controversial goal. He'd had very little influence on the match in the first half but five minutes after the interval he rose with England goalkeeper Peter Shilton and quite clearly punched the ball into the net. I saw it. Everyone around me saw it. We were sitting in a multinational section and they all leapt up and shouted, 'Handball'. The Tunisian referee didn't see it, nor did his linesman. Astonishing!

We were sitting about 30 yards from the edge of the pitch, directly opposite the linesman who gave the goal. It was a remarkable incident, the single most graphic example of cheating I saw in my career.

I once put the ball in the net with my hand, but at least I owned up to it. Maradona was quite shameless about it. 'The hand of God' is how he described it. Four minutes later he showed just what he could do legitimately when he scored a stunning individual goal to secure Argentina's place in the semi-finals.

I was angry and frustrated as I left the stadium with Judith. We hurried out of the ground. Where was our landmark, the giant packet of Camel cigarettes? Unbelievably, during the course of the match, they'd deflated it and taken it away. I had no way of knowing where the taxi might be. We spent hours with 100,000 others trying to find our way back into the city.

I enjoyed Mexico and the 1986 World Cup. Bobby Moore was there and the visit revived memories of 16 years earlier for both of us. For me it was a welcome break from the demands of business. I was soon back on the road and it would be another six years before I dipped my toes into the football world again in any significant way.

In 1992, 20 years after I left West Ham, they invited me back to act as a host in one of their hospitality suites, which was supremely ironic considering there was an occasion when I was refused entry to the ground. That incident underlines the careless manner in which some clubs continue to treat their former players.

It happened on a matchday and I'd been asked to give a TV interview inside the ground. I had valid tickets for the sponsor's lounge but one of the club doormen refused me entry because I didn't have match tickets. What most annoyed me was that Brian Blower, the club's commercial manager at the time, was standing ten yards away. He was fully aware of what was happening but refused to intervene.

There's huge scope for clubs to use their former players commercially. But some still cling to the old days, before the abolition of the maximum wage and the retain and transfer system, when professionals were viewed as club servants. Other clubs, though, are becoming increasingly aware of the benefits of involving their ex-players in the matchday hospitality packages.

I accepted West Ham's invitation and after Bobby Moore's death I became the host in the 1966 Lounge in the stand named in his honour. I was therefore able to watch all of West Ham's home matches each season. This gave me the opportunity to keep in touch with the teams and players in the Premiership. It meant that I could have a valid opinion about the modern game.

To be truthful, much of what came my way in the nineties would, I'm sure, have gone to Bobby Moore had he been alive. He would have been the automatic first choice and it's sad to think now that he didn't have the chance to capitalise on the growing popularity of football that followed the introduction of the Premiership.

This even revived my enthusiasm for the game although nothing – absolutely nothing – gave me more pleasure than watching Claire return to work in February 1996. She needed six weeks of radiotherapy after her operation and, even now, has to make annual visits to the Royal Marsden Hospital. She fought her illness with magnificent stoicism and her mother and sisters fought every inch of the way with her.

On the day before she left hospital her hair had not grown back, so Judith asked Jo and Charlotte to buy six hats each and bring them to the ward. Judith was sitting with Claire in the hospital waiting for the hats to arrive. They heard the sisters giggling before they saw them. From the depths of the ward Jo and Charlotte tottered into view, each with six hats balanced on their heads.

By the time she went back to work, as the secretary to the local vicar in Weybridge, Claire had regained her health and her hair. For me it was like scoring another hat-trick in the World Cup final.

CHAPTER NINETEEN

'You can kiss the World Cup goodbye!'

I FIRST SUSPECTED THAT ENGLAND'S BID TO STAGE THE 2006 World Cup faced insurmountable difficulties during a conversation with the Duke of York. 'What's all this about a gentleman's agreement with the Germans?' he asked during an informal chat with Tony Banks and myself. I was surprised, and impressed, to learn that the Duke's grasp of football politics stretched to Sir Bert Millichip's alleged 'gentleman's agreement' with the German Football Federation. That agreement hovered like an albatross over England's bid to host the 2006 finals. England's campaign had to overcome several major obstacles but, as Prince Andrew's question demonstrated, none gnawed away as consistently during the life of the four-year bidding process as the 'gentleman's agreement'.

The Duke and I met in Doha, the capital of Qatar, a small oil sheikhdom on a peninsula on the west coast of the Persian Gulf. A former British protectorate, the Qataris remain very pro-British.

Prince Andrew was there in the city's main shopping mall to open the British Council Football Nation Exhibition, a project born out of a recognition that sport is an undervalued asset in British diplomacy. I was there with Alec McGivan, England's campaign director, and Tony Banks, the then Minister for Sport, to seek support for England's World Cup bid. It was our fourth visit to Qatar and we'd flown there direct from Saudi Arabia where we'd met their Sports Minister, Prince Sultan.

It was November 1999 and I had been on the World Cup campaign trail for more than two years. It was an honour to be involved. When the Football Association asked me if I would like to be a Bid Ambassador, along with Sir Bobby Charlton and Gary Lineker, my response was immediate.

On the home front, worries about Claire were receding. She had made a magnificent recovery and was leading a full life again. On the business front, I had made a conscious decision to slow down. In fact, this opened new doors. It wasn't the idea at the time but Dave Davies, my agent in matters related to football, was finding me an increasing number of speaking engagements at football dinners.

Although I was still working from my office in Kingston, I had more time to spare and when the FA came to me with their proposal, I was happy to devote that time to England's World Cup cause. If successful, it meant that, 40 years on from 1966, England would host the World Cup in 2006, the year of my 65th birthday. In my neat, orderly fashion, I could think of no more appropriate way of stepping out of the limelight and embracing my retirement years.

For England to host the 2006 World Cup quickly became a private dream. It was obvious, too, that just as in 1966, home advantage would prove critical if England were to have any realistic hope of winning the title in the future.

The Football Association announced England's bid immediately after the successful Euro '96 tournament in England. The strength of the bid lay in the success of the domestic game, the modern stadia, many rebuilt since the Taylor Report, and the global popularity of the new Premiership.

McGivan, the man who approached me initially, had been part of the Euro '96 success story and gathered around him another energetic and committed team of campaigners. Although small in stature, he had a prodigious appetite for hard work. He was also a natural campaigner. He had a political background and was one of the first to join the Social Democratic Party when the famous Gang of Four left Labour's ranks in 1981. He may not have struck the man in the street as an inspirational leader, but I was impressed with his contribution. His attention to detail was legendary and, as the campaign unfolded, you could see his mark on everything we did.

I don't think the general public has very much idea of what's involved in an enterprise of this kind. I didn't have the faintest idea myself until I had a look at FIFA's list of minimum terms and conditions with which the host nation must comply. I didn't realise, for instance, that FIFA insist on guaranteed hotel accommodation. That's not just a few rooms here and there. They wanted 35,000 rooms with signed contracts guaranteeing the availability of this accommodation six years ahead of the potential tournament. Alec needed the intervention of the government to meet this particular challenge.

In all matters relating to government, Tony Banks of course was a valuable ally. Once a tub-thumping local London politician and pal of Ken Livingstone in the old GLC days, he was at the time of the bid the Labour MP for West Ham and, crucially, the Minister for Sport.

Although the Tory Prime Minister John Major had officially launched the World Cup campaign at Downing Street in February 1997, a general election the following May put the Labour Party in power. Support for England's bid had been a party manifesto commitment and the new Prime Minister, Tony Blair, quickly voiced his support.

Tony Banks, the new Minister for Sport, was a well-known Chelsea fan and, as I worked with him, I was able to judge his knowledge of the club. There was no doubt that he had a long-standing allegiance, although he swore that he'd never jeered or abused me, even in my darkest hours as manager at Stamford Bridge!

His support for the World Cup bid, and the involvement and enthusiasm of the Prime Minister, proved to be major assets throughout the campaign and made a deep impression on many of the FIFA dignitaries we entertained. At his own request, Tony was relieved of his wider duties as Minister for Sport to concentrate on the World Cup as the Prime Minister's special envoy for the bid. He was a major player in the final year of the campaign.

As I got to know him, I realised that much of what I'd heard about him was unjustified. I found him quite straightforward, if outspoken at times. He was never involved in political cover-ups, he explained, because he never told lies in the first place. 'I've never had anything to hide,' he said. I like people who are honest and say what they think.

He was very popular with the members of the bid team and most of the FIFA people we met and, fortunately, his candour backfired only occasionally. At lunch in the British Embassy in Paris in 1997, for instance, in front of three FIFA Executive members, he wondered aloud why Britain didn't have just one team in the World Cup because that would give us a much better chance of winning it. Similarly, I recall that as a member of the Labour opposition, he publicly supported the World Cup claims of South Africa against England, a statement that he simply had to learn to live with during the course of the bidding process.

With Tony and Alec and other campaign members, I probably flew more than 100,000 miles to 20 countries in Europe, North America, the Caribbean, the South Pacific and the Far East. In the last six months of the campaign it was almost a full-time job.

Some days I'd be asked at the drop of a hat to fly somewhere, attend a dinner or greet a foreign dignitary at some function or other. I remember one chilly morning in December 1998 receiving a call from the FA. I was sitting in my office in Kingston. The FA's chief executive, Graham Kelly, had just resigned and the executive committee had passed a unanimous vote of no confidence in the chairman Keith Wiseman. He clung to power for another three weeks before quitting. It quickly became clear within Lancaster Gate's corridors of power that Kelly's resignation would be interpreted by mischievous sections of the media as a big blow to the World Cup bid. The FA wanted me to face the press on the steps of Lancaster Gate on behalf of the bidding team.

'Will you come and do a turn?' asked Steve Double, one of the FA press officers at the time. 'Everyone else in the campaign team is abroad.'

'When do you want me?' I asked.

'Now!' he replied.

Within about an hour I was at Lancaster Gate. David Davies, head of public affairs, briefed me. Then I went outside to answer the questions from reporters gathered on the steps of Lancaster Gate. They wanted to know whether Kelly's resignation would damage England's World Cup bid. I was able to assure them that it wouldn't. Privately, I felt that his resignation, and the later departure of Wiseman, might be no bad thing for the bid, although I didn't say so at the time.

I'd attended plenty of functions with Keith Wiseman and Graham Kelly, two rather grave, dour figures. I thought neither was very comfortable with the kind of socialising necessary to win friends and influence people. At one high-powered lunch in London with FIFA representatives I noticed Graham Kelly sat, shoulders hunched, with his briefcase on his lap.

Both men were sincere and devoted to the well-being of English football. Kelly, of course, was perhaps the finest administrator in football, having learned the basics of the business under the legendary Alan Hardaker in the old Football League days at Lytham St Annes.

But I felt that neither was good at what the Americans call 'schmoozing' or 'pressing the flesh'. This is the art of working a room full of people, shaking hands, slapping backs and making small talk. I learned the value of this during my own business life and, in World Cup terms, it was an important part of the vote-winning process.

With his wife Ann, Geoff Thompson, the FA vice chairman who succeeded Wiseman, was far more comfortable in the social arena. In the turmoil that followed the resignations, Thompson served as acting chairman until his election as chairman six months later.

With hindsight, I don't think the Kelly–Wiseman crisis was particularly damaging to the World Cup bid but it did reveal a serious, on-going problem for English football. When England won the World Cup in 1966, the president of FIFA was Sir Stanley Rous.

I remember him as a benevolent, white-haired old gentleman, but he was far more than that. A former sports master at Watford Grammar School, he refereed the 1934 FA Cup final. He was secretary of the Football Association for nearly 30 years and in that time he re-wrote the rules of the game and revolutionised the way referees handled matches. But it was his diplomacy and energy during 14 years as FIFA president that established England's place among the great powers of the modern game. England's influence began to wane as soon as the Brazilian Joao Havelange succeeded him as FIFA president in 1974.

It has continued to diminish. It was no secret in 1998 that the FA was increasingly dissatisfied with the fact that England was a member of neither the UEFA nor FIFA Executives, on which Scotland's David Will represented the four home unions of the UK. It was felt that it would be beneficial to be on the 'inside' and therefore able directly to promote the bid. England and Wales favoured Will's departure in the hope that this would help secure Keith Wiseman a place on the FIFA Executive. Then a payment of £400,000 to be made to the Welsh FA came to light. The FA council asked Wiseman and Kelly to account for this and they maintained that the proposed payment was a justifiable continuation of previous loans. However, their failure to go through the accepted channels of approval by the FA Executive left them open to some criticism and they felt compelled to resign.

It was a sad chapter. It appeared that the FA's proposed candidate for a place on the FIFA Executive had been discredited in people's eyes. I fully understood the desire to win a place on the FIFA Executive. Many, including some powerful FIFA voices, considered this to be crucial in helping England host the World Cup.

There were other more damaging obstacles to England's bid. Whatever the rights and wrongs of Sir Bert Millichip's alleged 'agreement' to support Germany's 2006 bid in return for their backing for England's Euro '96 bid, the fact was that UEFA, while not officially taking sides, did everything it could to ensure a German victory. Crucially, this issue appeared to deprive England of majority support within our own Confederation.

The election of the new FIFA president in the summer of 1998 provided me with a further intriguing insight into the complex world of football politics. The two contenders were the UEFA president Lennart Johansson and the FIFA general secretary Sepp Blatter.

On the one hand England, as a European nation, would be expected to support the UEFA candidate Johansson. Not to do so would further alienate those in Europe who had given their backing to Germany in the World Cup race. Blatter was on record as favouring an African candidate for 2006.

The main difficulty for the English bid was that Blatter's closest supporters were also those England needed to attract for the World Cup vote. The FA was urged to back Blatter if it wished to find favour with those outside Europe.

For the FA it was impossible to be enthusiastic about either candidate. Voting for Blatter guaranteed nothing but not voting for him would have alienated nearly all of England's potential support outside Europe. England's support for Blatter was not a debt repaid by the FIFA president.

The problems surrounding the redevelopment of Wembley also plagued us during the life of the bid. The rebuilding of the world's most famous stadium had been enshrined as one of the main reasons why England should host the tournament. But timetables were delayed and questions asked. The potential problem of the Wembley project was headline news in Japan's English-language newspapers during the 2002 World Cup draw in Tokyo.

Similarly, the issue of Manchester United taking part in the FIFA Club World Championship provided another dilemma for the campaign. As champions of Europe, Manchester United were expected to represent UEFA at the Club World Championship in Brazil in January 2000. FIFA made it quite clear that if they refused, our World Cup rivals Germany would be invited to send the Champions League runners-up Bayern Munich. This would have been a great public relations coup for the Germans.

I was at an elegant dinner in London with Alec McGivan and Chuck Blazer, the FIFA member for the USA, when Blazer made it quite clear that United's refusal to play in Brazil would seriously jeopardise our World Cup bid. 'You should do everything in your power to get United there,' he told Alec. 'Otherwise I think you can kiss the World Cup goodbye!' This was the fourth meeting I'd attended with FIFA executives to discuss the issue of United's participation in the Club World Championship. It was becoming a matter of increasing concern to us.

Ultimately, the FA decided that the least bad of several bad options was to grant Manchester United an exemption from the FA Cup. Blatter, while welcoming the decision, didn't seem to appreciate the dilemma FIFA had created or the sacrifice English football had made. From the bid's point of view, the gains were limited but it would have been catastrophic not to fulfil the commitment.

Considering all the problems, I believe that Alec McGivan and his campaign team, about 20 strong, negotiated the pitfalls magnificently. It was a privilege to work with them. I don't think I can recall working with a more committed or energetic team of people at any stage in my career. Such was the confidence they generated that at one point I believed that we had a real chance. However, I quickly learned that in football politics what is said is not always what is meant.

In March 1998 Havelange, then 81 years old, came to London for a meeting at Downing Street with the Prime Minister and senior FA officials. After the meeting, Havelange declared to waiting reporters, 'England is my personal choice for 2006.'

I remember thinking to myself, 'If that's not a two-goal lead in the first ten minutes I don't know what is!' My view changed when Havelange was alleged to have said the same thing to the South Africans.

Perhaps the most important event of the entire campaign was the 1999 FA Cup final. All 24 members of the FIFA Executive were invited to London for a long weekend. In the event, 16 attended.

Every detail had to be right from the moment of their arrival, often in the small hours of the morning, until their departure – red roses for buttonholes, special meals for vegetarians, prayer arrangements for Moslems. It was a brilliantly organised programme that included lunch at Highgrove with Prince Charles, dinner with the Prime Minister at 10 Downing Street, an FA reception and lunch at Wembley on Cup final day, a gala dinner at the Natural History Museum and lunch on the Thames. Much goodwill was generated although, according to Judith, most of the wives went home muttering about diets!

Six months after the FA Cup final, the FIFA inspection team arrived to look at the stadia where the proposed World Cup matches would be held. This, too, was a vitally important part of the bidding process and, once again, the organisation was outstanding. They spent four days examining the facilities at Anfield, Villa Park, Old Trafford and Sunderland and at the end Alan Rothenberg, the American chairman of the FIFA inspection committee, had nothing but praise for the arrangements and the stadia.

On the final day of their inspection tour the FA entertained them lavishly at a marvellous banquet at Hampton Court, the great palace built by Cardinal Wolsey on the Thames at Richmond. Among the guests that evening was the actor Hugh Grant, who is a Fulham supporter. Judith and I were asked to escort him to the top table on his arrival because he knew very few people at the dinner. Quite coincidentally, as the three of us entered the medieval splendour of the banqueting hall, we were greeted by a fanfare of trumpets.

'That must be for me!' smiled Hugh, tongue in cheek.

'Oh no!' said Judith. 'It's for me!'

At the end of dinner, Hugh addressed the assembled guests. He explained that he was a Chelsea fan in his youth.

'Their fans are not so cultured,' he said. 'If a girl walked round the pitch they used to shout at her, "Show us your tits, love!" '

Alec McGivan was next to speak.

'I don't quite know how to follow that,' he said.

During the course of the evening Rothenberg, a lawyer who had successfully led the American bid to host the 1994 World Cup, told Judith that he would ensure England were awarded the 2006 World Cup if she admitted that England's third goal in the 1966 final hadn't crossed the line. Judith asked whether he had put the same proposition to me.

'Yes I have,' replied Alan. 'Geoff said that, whatever the prize, he would have to say that the ball crossed the line. What are you going to say, Judith?'

She thought for a moment and then replied, 'I shall say that the ball didn't cross the line. But once you've given us the World Cup, if in fact you do, I shall change my mind again!'

'Typical woman,' I thought, but her attitude was probably right. Some months later I was staggered to learn that, after all the praise they'd lavished on our stadia, the FIFA inspection report placed the facilities in South Africa and Germany in the top category of 'very well qualified' with England in the lower category of 'well qualified'.

This was another nail in the coffin but events that occurred during the European Championship in Belgium and Holland in June 2000 finally put England's bid beyond salvation. The worst nightmare came true on the streets of Brussels and Charleroi when drunken English fans rioted. The TV pictures of the violence were relayed around the world.

The UEFA Executive issued a public warning that further hooliganism could lead to the exclusion of the England team from the remainder of the tournament. Several of our supporters within FIFA stated that it would now be difficult to vote for England as World Cup hosts.

The World Cup bid, representing years of hard work, was in tatters. Alec McGivan telephoned all the key members of the campaign team for their opinions. Should we withdraw our bid? I said no. Emotionally, we wanted to fight on but there was a sound view that a dignified withdrawal was preferable. The FA board eventually concluded that we should fight on, try to win as many votes as possible and put a brave face on defeat.

We'd always realised there was a risk of hooliganism at Euro 2000 but the fact that this took place just three weeks before the voting for the 2006 World Cup is what proved to be so damaging. Initially, the vote was due to take place in March 2000. It was FIFA's decision to delay until July. Whether the true reason, as stated by FIFA, was to allow the bidders to make further presentations or whether someone had calculated that postponement could boost South Africa's chances if there were trouble at Euro 2000 we may never know.

One of the most frustrating things for me, as a fan, has been the licence the authorities have allowed hooligans over the years. I remember yobs fighting on the terraces, outside grounds, on railway platforms and in city centres back in the sixties. These people, and we are now talking about generations of them, have been a disgrace to the country for decades. It wasn't until the terrible disasters of the mid-eighties that the government finally took control of the situation, and football, as a result of the Taylor Report, began a programme of stadia redevelopment that significantly restricted the potential for violence inside the grounds.

Although we've got to grips with the problem in football grounds in the UK, we still export the problem abroad; and whatever the authorities say, hooliganism is as rampant as ever in the streets of our cities on a Friday or Saturday night.

Had the necessary legislation been in place, the police could have prevented troublemakers travelling to Euro 2000. Does the will exist within society to solve this problem? If it does, there's very little evidence of it.

So, some weeks before the great and good of world football met at FIFA's Zurich headquarters for the vote, most of us accepted we had no chance of winning. There was a lot of last-minute lobbying and 48 hours before the vote *The Times* described the mood in the England camp as 'defiance tinged with outlandish optimism'.

The Dolder Grand Hotel and FIFA House buzzed with gossip and intrigue and news of deals, double deals and double crosses. We learned of inter-Confederation deals and tactical voting. South America, for instance, switched their second-preference support away from England to Africa. Accepting that Brazil couldn't win, they asked Africa to promise support for a bid in 2010 in exchange for giving the three South American votes to South Africa. My old rival Franz Beckenbauer was spearheading the German bid and, in the newspapers the following day, he described the private deal between South America and Africa as 'offensive'. The deal between Germany and Asia, revealed by the voting the following day, was apparently something different!

We felt we had the best bid and, on reflection, I still feel the same way. It was no consolation to learn, just 24 hours before the voting, that several influential FIFA members were scathing about the inspection report, recognising that England had suffered an injustice.

Just hours before the voting, Alec McGivan and Tony Banks were locked in conversations with Chuck Blazer (USA) and Jack Warner (Trinidad and Tobago), who were happy to honour their commitment by voting for England in the first round. But they would support England in the second round only if we were to win at least six votes in the first. Alec and Tony argued that five, not six votes in the first round, should be the conditions of CONCACAF's support in the second. But Chuck and Jack wouldn't budge.

The result of the voting was announced to the world by Sepp Blatter on 6 July. That morning, a final meeting of our campaign team was interrupted by a telephone call from David Will, the Scottish vice president of FIFA. He told us the outcome of the voting just as we were about to leave for the auditorium where Blatter would make the official announcement.

To everyone's amazement, Germany had won by 12 votes to South Africa's 11 with one abstention, New Zealand. In the first round of voting, Germany finished with ten votes, South Africa six, England five and Morocco three. At each stage the nation finishing last is eliminated. In the second round, Germany had 11 votes, South Africa 11 and England, with just two, were out. For the third and final round, Germany and UEFA had succeeded in doing a deal with Asia whose four votes, along with UEFA's eight, had given the Germans a winning total – not enough had South Africa secured New Zealand's vote and enjoyed the casting vote of Blatter.

By the time of the vote, New Zealand's FIFA member Charles Dempsey was in the air flying home via Singapore. He had voted, as instructed by the Oceania Confederation, for England. When England dropped out, he faced intolerable pressure from Germany, South Africa and Blatter, and decided to abstain.

Personally, I felt sorry for him. A sprightly 78-year-old with a

Scottish accent, Charlie and I met during my campaign visit to Oceania. I was worried that I'd call him Jack after the boxer and, on the flight out, I kept telling myself that I must address him correctly. Of course, as soon as we met I called him Jack. 'Everyone does it,' he laughed.

Charlie provided me with my only leisure time in more than three years of campaigning – a round of golf in Auckland. I went home via Tonga and Vanuatu, two tiny, beautiful islands in the South Pacific, both members of the Oceania Confederation. When I met the King of Tonga I was able to tell him, truthfully, that I could remember watching his mother in the Queen's Coronation parade in London in 1953. The trip home from Vanuatu to Surrey took 36 hours.

It was all part of the flag-waving campaign for our World Cup bid but that day in Zurich, I wondered how much of it had been worthwhile. We'd been outmanoeuvred by the Germans, who had the full support of UEFA.

We were prepared for our disappointment but the South Africans were devastated. They'd worked as hard as us and believed they had won. That evening our campaign team had a party, the centrepiece of which was the penalty shoot-out involving Bobby Charlton and myself in one of the hotel's function rooms.

With hindsight, I can see that, to be successful in the future, England need greater representation among the decision-makers of world football. England are unlikely to host the World Cup in the future if we continue to lack influence at the highest levels of the game.

With the system of rotating the host nation among the continents proposed by Blatter, England couldn't now expect to stage the World Cup until 2014 or, more likely, 2018. The Germans are hosts in 2006, South Africa in 2010 and the 2014 World Cup is likely to go to Asia or America. At least a system of rotation would end the voting fiasco.

I'd like to be involved again in some capacity because I believe it helps to have high-profile ex-international footballers on the team. Franz Beckenbauer has done a wonderful job for the image of

Germany over the last couple of decades and Bobby Charlton and I have tried to do something similar. Bobby is a huge 'name' around the world, at least as well known as Franz. But Franz is the vice president of the German Federation and for England to capitalise fully on Bobby's reputation, he should have some significant role within the Football Association.

Had Bobby Moore still been with us, I'm sure he, too, would have made an ideal World Cup ambassador for England. He had all the necessary qualities, just like Beckenbauer. When I heard that I'd been recommended for a knighthood, one of my first thoughts was that this was an honour that should have gone to Bobby. He should have been knighted for his services to football.

The first I knew of the recommendation was when a letter arrived from Downing Street. I came down to breakfast one morning in June 1998 and Judith handed it to me. She'd already read it. When I finished reading I looked up and she had tears in her eyes. Initially, I thought it might have been a joke but there was no way of knowing. You have to keep the news confidential. We weren't sure until a month later when the press began to call on the day before the official announcement. When the first call came, I ran up the stairs in my pyjamas shouting, 'It's true. It's true.'

The newspapers wanted me to go to Wembley to pose for the photographs that appeared in the following day's newspapers. I asked if they could send me a few copies of the pictures as keepsakes but none arrived. Weeks later, a man turned up on my doorstep with a sheaf of them. I told him that I'd been promised pictures similar to these by the cameramen who took them. 'Where did you get them from?' I asked him. He said he bought them in Petticoat Lane Market.

I was sent plenty of the photographs taken outside Buckingham Palace on the day of my investiture. I spotted a familiar face – Arthur Edwards, the *Sun*'s royal photographer – among the ranks of cameramen. A long-time West Ham fan, he made sure I received a few prints of one of the most memorable days of my life.

Judith's family came over from the United States and we all travelled into town for the investiture at the Palace. I was a little anxious, as you'd expect, but the Queen knows how to make you feel comfortable. She asked me if I was still involved in football. In the evening, we gave a dinner for 50 friends in a hotel in London.

If I'm honest with myself, I think my role in the World Cup bid was probably influential in the decision to offer me a knighthood. It must have helped, I suppose, when shaking hands and meeting people in foreign places if our high-profile bid was fronted by two Knights of the Realm – Sir Bobby and Sir Geoff.

It always puzzled me that Bobby Moore was the only player in 1966 honoured with the OBE. He was the captain, of course, but that victory had been a great team effort. My feeling at the time was that the entire team should have been honoured.

It wasn't until 2000 that the 'Forgotten Five' as the tabloids dubbed them, finally received the honours they deserved. Nobby Stiles, Alan Ball, Ray Wilson, Roger Hunt and George Cohen were the five members of the 1966 team who had not been honoured at some stage in their careers. I think even without the World Cup win of 1966 each made enough of a contribution to the sport to be worthy of recognition. Ian Wright didn't have to wait 34 years for his MBE and, great goalscorer that he was, he never got even close to a World Cup final.

A wrong was righted when the Queen handed the five of them their MBEs. It had always concerned me that recognising some and not others was, in a sense, projecting the idea that some had contributed more than others. That wasn't the case. Ours was a team victory, just as losing out to the Germans in the race to host the World Cup was a team defeat. The important thing in both circumstances is that you learn the lessons.

CHAPTER TWENTY

Can we have our ball back, Mr Haller?

SEVERAL LESSONS EMERGED IN THE AFTERMATH OF ENGLAND'S failure to secure the 2006 World Cup and one of these concerned the importance of media support during the campaign process.

The ingredients of a successful bid, whether it's for the World Cup, the Olympic Games or any other major sporting event, are broadly similar and all rely to a greater or lesser extent on positive, sympathetic and fair-minded media coverage.

I fully acknowledge the right of the media to comment and, if justified, criticise but I felt that much of the media coverage during the bidding process for 2006 was unhelpful. At no time did I ever feel that the media as a whole were pulling for England. There were one or two supportive elements but, in the main, the media coverage ranged from indifferent to hostile.

There was plenty of opportunity for controversy of course – the gentleman's agreement, hooliganism, Wembley, Manchester United in Brazil – and any domestic criticism was immediately relayed by the news agencies and Internet to every corner of the globe. Opinion in London often appeared as sensational fact in some other part of the world.

On various occasions I recall influential FIFA dignitaries, including Chuck Blazer (USA), Isaac Sasso Sasso (Costa Rica) and Mong-Joon Chung (Republic of Korea), asking me to explain why the domestic media were so against the bid. It was a difficult question to answer. I remember the enthusiasm with which the declaration that England would host the 1966 World Cup was greeted and, naïvely, I expected similar tub-thumping patriotism this time.

As a player and manager I'd few serious complaints about my media treatment and I'd been out of the public eye for a long time when I was suddenly introduced to the frenzy of modern journalism. Over a period of two days I watched with amusement as two of the nation's biggest selling tabloid newspapers battled over a World Cup story that was pure trivia compared to the significance of England's bid.

I had no idea of the drama that was about to unfold as, one spring afternoon in 1996, I drove towards Shrewsbury to fulfil a speaking engagement at a sporting dinner. I was in a good mood. Claire was happily recovered and back at work, Judith had kissed me goodbye that morning and, apart from West Ham's customary end-of-season collapse, life was good. During the course of the drive from London to Shrewsbury I received five or six calls in my car within the space of an hour. The first was from Dave Davies.

'The *Sun* has just been on,' he said. 'They want you to go to Germany and bring back the ball.'

'What ball?' I asked.

'The World Cup ball,' he replied. 'The one you scored the three goals with at Wembley in 1966. The orange one. You know, THE ball!'

'Are you serious?' I said.

'Yes,' he said. 'They're offering you four thousand pounds to go to Germany with a couple of their reporters.'

He explained that a magazine called *Total Football* had run a feature story headlined 'Hurst in ball snub shock' that had excited the interest of the national media in both Germany and England.

Mention of the ball brought memories flooding back. I never knew what had happened to it, although I knew that Helmut Haller was seen walking from the pitch with it. I wasn't too bothered about the ball at the time. Apart from the jubilation I felt, my main concern on returning to the dressing-room that afternoon was ascertaining whether or not I had in fact scored three goals.

Gottfried Dienst had blown the full-time whistle immediately after I struck the shot for England's fourth goal. Play never resumed. Was it all over before the shot hit the net? Everyone was congratulating me on my hat-trick, but I wasn't convinced. I left our dressing-room and went back on to the pitch. Sure enough, the big electronic scoreboard still carried the result: England 4 West Germany 2. In the aftermath of the final, I just assumed that I'd be given the ball at some stage as my reward for scoring three goals, but I never was.

Some years later, Helmut Haller and myself were invited to face the media at a Wembley press conference before an England–West Germany game. For some reason I was asked about the 1966 ball.

'I don't know what happened to it,' I said. 'As you know, it's the tradition in this country to give the ball to the scorer of a hat-trick, but the last time I saw it Helmut was walking off the pitch with it.'

Helmut was asked if he knew what happened to the ball. I think he was joking when he replied through an interpreter, 'In my country, if you score the first goal in the World Cup final, you keep the ball!' Everyone chuckled because, of course, Helmut scored the opening goal in the 1966 final.

I didn't see Helmut again until July 1985 when we played the Germans in a re-run of the 1966 World Cup final. It was a charity match, played at Leeds, for the families of the victims of the Bradford fire disaster. We won 6–4 and I scored another hat-trick but there was still no sign of the old orange ball.

But now, at last, I had a chance to retrieve it – and collect £4,000 from the *Sun* too.

'Say yes, I'll do it,' I told Dave Davies.

A few moments later Dave called me back.

'Apparently others are interested in the same project,' he told me with a note of gravity that only agents can muster. 'This has to be done quickly. We must go to Germany tomorrow.'

That presented problems, but I agreed.

About 20 minutes later the mobile rang again.

'Hold everything,' Dave shouted down the phone. 'The *Mirror* are making a better offer – six thousand. But the real bonus is this. They're bringing the ball to you. You don't have to go to Germany. Do I look after you or what?'

'Much better,' I said. 'Let's accept the *Mirror* offer.'

Could this be true? It seemed ridiculous that this relic from 1966 was about to become the star prize in the on-going circulation battle between the two heavyweight tabloids. Both papers, of course, have big football readerships and recapturing 'the ball' for the nation would be presented as a great patriotic triumph. Teams of reporters and photographers were sent to Germany to retrieve what *The Times* described in a leader column as a football icon of 'mystical significance'.

I later learned that academics at Leicester University had produced a thesis on the subject of the World Cup ball, explaining that nostalgia for England's only tournament victory reflected a desperate desire for sporting success, evidence that England remained a significant player on the world stage.

The race to retrieve the ball contained elements of high farce as reporters from London squabbled and fought in airports and restaurants, on autobahns and at M25 service stations. While all this was happening, high-level negotiations were taking place between editors, senior football figures and diplomatic staff from the German Embassy in London.

Meanwhile, I drove on towards Shrewsbury, blissfully unaware of all this but amused that the old leather ball was now considered such an epic symbol of English greatness. The mobile rang again. This time it was a photographer from the *Daily Mirror*, Kent Gavin, whom I'd known from my playing days.

'I'm your minder,' he said. 'I'll be doing the pictures. I'll talk to you again later.' Before I reached Shrewsbury, Kent called again. 'Don't go home tonight,' he said. 'We're having a bit of a punch-up with the *Sun* over this one. You mustn't go home. We've booked you into a hotel in Hertfordshire, the place where Gascoigne got married.

Don't tell anyone you're going there. I'll call you later.'

So that night, after my speaking engagement, I slipped quietly out of Shrewsbury and, with one eye on the rear-view mirror, drove to Hanbury Manor, a large, Jacobean-style hotel in 200 acres of Hertfordshire countryside. My room had been booked in the name of Albert Hall!

'It's Albert here,' I told Judith when I phoned her from the room.

'Albert? Albert who?' she demanded. 'I know it's you. What's going on?'

Early the following morning, Kent Gavin called. He was downstairs in the hotel lobby.

'Come down and have some breakfast,' he said. 'Then we're going to look round and find the right location for the pictures. They're bringing the ball to the hotel.'

Over the course of the next hour or so I learned from Kent what had happened to the ball in the years since 1966. As we suspected, Helmut had taken it home with him. The magazine *Total Football* had confronted him at his sports shop in Augsburg and asked him the whereabouts of the ball. He eventually conceded that he'd given the ball to his son Jurgen for his fifth birthday. He was now 35 and for many years the ball had remained untouched in Jurgen's cellar. When challenged, Jurgen is supposed to have said, 'Why should I return it? I'm very proud of the ball. It was a gift from my father.'

In the end the pressure from the media persuaded the Haller family to think again. The other consideration of course was this. The *Sun*, I was told, had offered £20,000 for the ball. A German TV station had offered £45,000 and the *Daily Mirror* had offered £80,000. At that moment the most expensive leather football in history was in a helicopter with Helmut Haller and his entourage. The *Mirror*, having agreed to pay £80,000, were looking for a sponsor to share the financial burden. I later learned that this was Richard Branson.

The idea was simple enough. Haller would land with the ball. We'd take the pictures, shake hands and he'd take off again. I'd then go with the ball to London and do more pictures with Richard Branson.

We were still looking at different locations around the hotel when Kent's mobile rang. After a few hurried words he said, 'Quick. We've got to go. They know we're here.'

Within five minutes we were both in a *Daily Mirror* car with chauffeur, heading for another hotel. By a strange coincidence, the *Mirror*'s fallback plan involved West Lodge Park Hotel, which was also in extensive grounds with a helicopter-landing pad. This hotel was at Cockfosters, close to the M25 motorway in north London. I hadn't been there since Ron Greenwood was the England manager. It used to be the base hotel for the England squad prior to matches at Wembley.

We arrived in the middle of a wedding reception and decided to stand in the car park to await the arrival of the helicopter. I remembered watching a helicopter land in the same spot in 1980 to ferry Emlyn Hughes, Phil Thompson, Terry McDermott and Mick Mills to the Derby during the preparations for the 1980 European Championship.

Throughout this time Kent was taking calls on his mobile phone. Our helicopter, it seemed, was in the vicinity, but it was being chased by the *Sun*'s helicopter. Finally, Kent was told, 'We'll be on the ground in three minutes.'

Sure enough, the *Mirror* helicopter swirled into view, landed in front of us and out jumped a smiling Helmut Haller with the football. We shook hands, mumbled a few pleasantries which neither of us understood and posed for the photographs. Was it the real ball? I think so. The leather was in reasonable condition, although the bladder had deflated. I noticed the faded signature of Pele; at some stage after the match he had autographed the ball.

Within minutes Helmut was strapped back in his seat. He was grinning from ear to ear as the helicopter lifted off the ground. Kent gave the rolls of film to a *Daily Mirror* despatch rider who was taking them straight to the offices in Docklands.

I now had to go with Kent to meet Richard Branson at Waterloo station in London. I was going to be photographed with Richard and the ball on one of the platforms, but it had to be done discreetly. We waited in the shadows of an archway at Waterloo. A figure drew up on a motorbike. He was wearing a helmet with a dark visor. It was Richard Branson. Kent took more photographs, Richard and I shook hands and I climbed back into the *Daily Mirror* car.

Some bright spark in the *Mirror* office had dreamed up yet another element to the story. They wanted me to go with Kent to a playing field and re-create the three goals! I tried hard not to laugh.

We drove out into Essex, to a remote playing field near Ongar. We had recreated the first goal, Kent snapping away furiously, and were about to start on the second when Kent's mobile rang.

'We've been spotted again,' he said. 'We've got to go.'

We climbed into the car and had started along a narrow lane when we noticed a car some distance behind us.

'No problem,' said Kent.

As we turned out of the narrow lane into a busier road, our driver signalled to the driver of a van parked about 50 yards away. As we pulled away, the second *Mirror* car drove across the exit to the lane, blocking the car that was following us. It was like a Hollywood movie.

'That's stuffed them,' grinned Kent.

We finally finished the photographs in another remote field and the *Mirror* appeared to be very happy with their investment. They still have the ball and Richard Branson uses it occasionally for promotional work. Helmut Haller returned to his sports shop and told whoever wanted to know that he gave the money to charity.

Had I been given the ball in the first place I don't know what I would have done with it. Probably it would have sat untouched in a dusty cupboard for decades, along with much of the other memorabilia. I've gathered plenty of souvenirs from my football career and all of them were to go to the children. This was something that Judith and I decided when they were toddlers. But how do you divide a World Cup winner's medal between three daughters? To be honest, apart from a handful of items that had some special appeal, none of the three girls was genuinely interested in the collection.

After a lot of family soul-searching, Claire, Joanne and Charlotte agreed with Judith and me that the best thing to do was auction the bulk of the memorabilia and invest the proceeds.

Another thing to bear in mind was the fact that we'd already lost a significant part of the collection in burglaries. In the last break-in, the robbers snapped a lot of trophies and statuettes from their plinths and left them strewn about the house. As a consequence of this, everything was locked away and no one ever saw any medals or trophies. We decided that it would be better to sell it all, donate some to the Bobby Moore Cancer Fund and the Brain Tumour Foundation and invest the rest for the girls.

So, a couple of years ago, Christie's auctioned the lot and raised about £250,000. I was particularly proud that the red shirt I wore in the final in 1966 attracted a world record £80,000.

It was a great pity that the FA Premier League Hall of Fame on London's South Bank didn't survive because I know many players who, like me, would appreciate a safe and permanent home for some of the personal memorabilia that would interest the public. The Hall of Fame was a super concept.

Peter Osgood asked me to become involved when a friend of his, Gary Trowsdale, tried to introduce the idea to London. I'm usually very cautious about committing myself to this sort of thing but I thought Gary had some terrific ideas. The problem was that not everyone else agreed. We struggled to raise the finance but nonetheless opened with great hope for the future in the County Hall building in June 1999.

Tony Banks took time off from England's World Cup campaign to perform the opening ceremony. He was pleased to do it but it did present him with something of a dilemma. As a London politician he used to work at County Hall in the days of the GLC. When the building was sold to Japanese owners he vowed that he would never again set foot in the place. As chairman of the Premier League Hall of Fame, I asked him to open the attraction officially and he agreed as long as he didn't have to enter the building. We compromised. We held the opening ceremony in the arched entranceway to the building. He fulfilled his commitment without breaking his pledge.

It was a privilege to meet some of the first 12 inductees to the Hall of Fame. All these players meet whatever criteria you choose – Alan Shearer, Dennis Bergkamp, Peter Schmeichel, Les Ferdinand,

Ian Wright, Gianfranco Zola, Tony Adams, Ruud Gullit, Ian Rush, Mark Hughes, Eric Cantona and David Seaman.

The fact that five of them are from abroad illustrates the way the modern game has gone in the last decade. Zola was an absolute delight to meet. I was there with him when they made the wax model that was to be used in the Hall of Legends.

Sadly, the project failed because of lack of investment. Other sports in other countries have similar exhibitions. It's a shame that the birthplace of the greatest game on earth has no Hall of Fame in which to honour and cherish the sport's legendary figures.

CHAPTER TWENTY-ONE

Forty years on

I'M NOT ONE OF LIFE'S GRUMPY OLD MEN BUT, EVEN SO, I'M irritated when people hover around in the street or in a restaurant trying to take photographs of me with my family or friends. It used to be an occasional annoyance but it has been turned into a regular intrusion by the advent of new technology. Many people can now take photographs with their mobile phones. When I'm spotted, especially when I'm sitting in a restaurant, the first photographer to stand up gives confidence to a second and a third and so on. Then they start calling their pals and more turn up. Thankfully, it doesn't happen too often – but it does happen.

I'm in my sixties now and not instantly recognisable like many of today's football stars. It makes me wonder what it must be like for people like David Beckham, Wayne Rooney or Rio Ferdinand. These are truly global celebrities. Apart from having to deal with the antics of professional photographers they, too, must sometimes resent the intrusion by members of the 'amateur paparazzi' armed with their phones. Many may simply be seeking a souvenir of a chance encounter with someone famous. But others see a photo of a footballer in a nightclub with a girl, for instance, as a money-making opportunity, such is the voracious appetite of some media outlets for tittle-tattle.

It is the way of the world now and it has taken professional footballers a long time to realise that they are considered by many to be public property. This is clearly not how it should be. They surely have the same right to privacy as anyone else. But, like everyone else, they also have a duty to behave appropriately, and some of them don't. Some of them behave appallingly when they are in public and this has, I fear, tarnished the image of the professional footballer.

It isn't always easy for young footballers, especially those with more money than sense. They are drawn into a world that some are simply not equipped to deal with. For this reason I believe that the professional game should do more to warn young players of the pitfalls they face and prepare them for life in the public eye. It wasn't really necessary when I was a young player because, with TV still in its infancy, the media interest wasn't as intense and it tended to be far more respectful. Similarly, the man in the street still observed the old-fashioned courtesies that players like Bobby Moore, Martin Peters and I grew up with.

Today's world is a harsher, more complex place. Stars like Wayne Rooney and Rio Ferdinand are simply products of a society that sometimes seems to take more pleasure in destroying reputations than creating them. I believe that a gullible young man like Rooney, an awesome talent fabulously rewarded, would benefit enormously from specialised advice about lifestyle and behaviour. I'm not talking about him in isolation but a lot of famous young players. They should be brought up to appreciate the value of a good image in professional sport.

A good image has financial benefits, I'm certain, but just as important is the message that polite, dignified, respectful behaviour sends to the youth of the nation. Footballers are idolised today and, as role models, they surely have a duty to uphold standards of behaviour considered acceptable by society. I think the football authorities, in conjunction with individual clubs, should consider a mentoring service that helps young players make the right choices when they're away from the protected environment they enjoy at their clubs.

The success I had when I finished playing football was due almost exclusively to the fact that I had looked after my image. Employment opportunities in promotions and marketing came along regularly because people felt that my association with a product would be beneficial. Even today my links with companies like McDonald's and the Royal Group can be traced back to the image I established during my playing days. Some might argue that today's salaries are such that professional footballers have no need to think about the long term. They make so much money that providing it's properly invested many will never need to work once they hang up their boots. This may be true but doesn't excuse unacceptable conduct or lessen the responsibility of the role model to behave in an appropriate fashion.

If I was a club manager today – remember I spent two years in charge at Chelsea – I would ensure that my players behaved on and off the field in a way that upheld the sporting traditions of the club and the professional game as a whole. If the young Wayne Rooney had been a player on my staff I'm sure there would have been an occasion when I had to give him a clip round the ear! I would have made him aware of the responsibility he had to the young people who idolised him.

Rooney is a terrific player, one of the best I've seen in my time in football. But he could have done more in the early days of his career to enhance his reputation. I think he's realised now that he is an influential member of society and as such has responsibilities. I'm sure his parents, his club managers and his agents did all they could to help him in his formative days but sometimes an independent voice can be more beneficial. I will always be grateful to my long-time friend Terry Hopley, who I met first when he was a football writer in East London. His was the independent voice I turned to over the years if I needed advice about, well, almost anything. I knew he would never let me down, nor would he ever advise anything that might compromise my reputation. In today's football world there is an even greater need for that kind of counsel.

I was asked once or twice in the past whether I would help with the mentoring of young players but turned down the invitations. I simply didn't have the time to devote to it. If you're going to do a job like that it should be done properly. I'm not promoting myself as a role model for anyone but I believe that it would help many of today's young footballers if they had their own role models. Once upon a time players looked up to Bobby Charlton or Bobby Moore, both gentlemen of the game. I wonder if today's stars look up to anyone.

Well, I suspect I know of at least one player from my era who is a role model for one of today's stars. That man, of course, is my old West Ham team-mate Frank Lampard whose son, Frank, has become one of the great midfield players of the modern generation. Young Frank could hardly have a better role model than his father who played more than 600 first team games for West Ham. He was just 19 games into his career when he broke his right leg. It was a terrible blow at such a stage in his career. He went into a tackle with Sheffield United's Willie Carlin just four minutes from the end of our 2–1 win at Bramall Lane. The cracking sound was heard all round the ground.

What impressed me was the way Frank recovered. He let nothing stand in his way. He was very single-minded and determined to play again at a time when a bad break could end a career. I remember the hours he spent day after day running up and down terracing at Upton Park to regain his fitness and build up the muscle in his legs. It was so boring that he used to have a portable radio halfway up the incline to cheer himself up. He was out of action for a year but returned to enjoy a fabulous career with West Ham. His son has demonstrated the same dedication in building an even more impressive career with West Ham, Chelsea and England.

As a youngster at Upton Park Frank jr. had to contend with claims of favouritism because his dad was a coach at the club and his uncle, Harry Redknapp, was the manager. Nepotism had nothing to do with it. The boy could play. For me, he became the complete all-rounder and perhaps the best goalscoring midfield player of his generation. He proved that beyond doubt when he moved to Chelsea and played such a key role in their Premiership success in 2004–05.

When I watch him play now I can see that he has much of his dad's mental strength. It must have been a help, too, for him to have his dad to call upon whenever needed. There may be one or two moments from his teenage years that he regrets but, by and large, young Frank has emerged as a fine role model for kids and I think he would agree that his dad has played a part in this.

I was delighted when the football writers voted him 'Footballer of the Year' in 2005. It was a prize he richly deserved after Jose Mourinho's first extraordinary season at Stamford Bridge. Young Frank flourished under the Portuguese coach, though I suspect he feels he owes a debt to the previous Chelsea manager, Claudio Ranieri, who signed him from West Ham. Happily England are now also benefiting from Lampard's emergence. If he and Steve Gerrard can maintain the kind of form they have shown for their clubs England could have one of the best midfields in the world.

Gerrard's consistently good form attracted envious glances from Chelsea and Real Madrid last summer while Frank has clearly reached the point in his career where he must feel he can do no wrong. I remember a similar high point in my own career just after winning the World Cup in 1966. I had the physique, the energy, the confidence. Everything I touched turned to gold – and goals. Young Frank must feel the same and I hope he carries that self-assurance into the World Cup because, forty years after 1966, England have a real chance to make a big impression.

The curious thing about fathers and sons who have played for England is that in all three cases the sons surpassed the achievements of the fathers at international level. George Eastham, for instance, won just one cap in 1935 but his son George – famous for his fight to win freedom of contract for players – won 19 caps between 1963 and 1966. Perhaps the most famous father was Brian Clough, who was to enjoy a distinguished managerial career with Derby and Nottingham Forest. But he played only twice for England. His son Nigel played 14 games for his country. Similarly, Frank Lampard senior played just twice for England while his son is heading towards his 50th cap.

Young Frank and Gerrard, a super athlete in midfield, are critical to England's prospects. So, too, are Michael Owen and Wayne Rooney. I think these four players provide England with an attacking impetus that could prove irresistible in Germany. Owen has a proven goalscoring pedigree and is slowly closing on Bobby Charlton's record of 49 England goals. Rooney doesn't have the same level of experience but he demonstrated at Euro 2004 that he can cope with the demands of football at the highest level. Two goals against Switzerland and another two against Croatia announced his arrival on the global stage. He is one of the world's most exciting players and we're all waiting to see what he does in Germany – provided we qualify.

There is always a sense of optimism accompanying England when they travel abroad for a major tournament but this time I think it is wholly justified. Sven-Goran Eriksson believes his squad is now stronger than at any time since he took charge in February 2001. He has a glut of top-quality centre backs with Rio Ferdinand, John Terry, Jamie Carragher, Ledley King and Sol Campbell the leading challengers for the two places in the heart of the defence. Gary Neville and Ashley Cole are two of the most experienced full-backs on the world stage. Add to this the vast experience of David Beckham and you can easily see why Sven is so confident. The England captain may not wield quite the same level of influence on the pitch as he once did but he remains an iconic figure whose contribution on the right and delivery from corners and free kicks will be an important part of England's armoury.

This will probably be Beckham's last chance to add a major international title to the honours he has won at club level. He's had a fabulous career and is arguably the most famous sportsman in the world. He's learned his lessons well in his career, though he still occasionally puts his foot in it. I thought, for instance, that he was foolish to get himself deliberately booked during a World Cup qualifier against Wales in 2004 – and then confess publicly.

A few days after that incident at Old Trafford, England played another qualifying tie against Azerbaijan in Baku. I was there because I had been invited to unveil a statue to one of Azerbaijan's most famous sons, Tofik Bakhramov, the linesman who had indicated that my shot off the underside of the bar had indeed crossed the goalline in the 1966 World Cup final. I was honoured to be asked to attend the ceremony outside the little stadium named in memory of Bakhramov, who had become a national hero. He died in 1993, a month after Bobby Moore. I was pleased to meet his son who chuckled at the tee-shirts some of the England fans were wearing. Inscribed across the back were the words – 'Cox Sag Ulan, Bakhramov, 66'. This means 'Thanks very much'! I often relate this little story as part of my after-dinner routine. People usually laugh when I tell them that I agreed to unveil the statue as a means of repaying the debt to Tofik!

England, without the suspended Beckham, beat Azerbaijan 1-0. It was good that day to see an old sparring partner – the legendary Carlos Alberto, captain of Brazil in 1970 and the manager of Azerbaijan. He's since quit the job. Carlos made an interesting observation to the media during that trip. He was recalling the 1970 World Cup and Brazil's 1–0 win over England. 'That result determined who would win the World Cup,' he said. 'The winners stayed near sea level. The losers went up into the mountains to face Germany.' He also came up with an illuminating answer when asked if any of Sven's men would have earned a place in the Brazil team of 1970. 'I like Frank Lampard,' he replied. 'For me he is the best midfield player in the world. He plays total football and wherever he has the ball on the field he knows how to play it.'

The press, who'd travelled from England for the match, turned up for the unveiling ceremony in the Azerbaijan capital but all the questions that day were about Beckham. 'Should he be stripped of the captaincy?' was the tenor of the inquisition. Such a thought never occurred to Eriksson, the man whose opinion mattered most. There has never been any doubt in his mind that Beckham is the best player to lead England. He has remained defiantly loyal to his captain throughout his reign as coach.

Some might argue that Sven has considered keeping the players happy to be the most important element of his job. A happy dressing-room is certainly a critical factor, though we need to judge the success or otherwise of any England coach on a deeper basis. In this sense World Cup 2006 is very important to Eriksson. It's his third major tournament as England coach. In the first he salvaged a disastrous qualifying programme following the sudden resignation of Kevin Keegan and led England to the last eight of the 2002 World Cup. Defeat came at the hands of Brazil in Shizuoka. In the second he led England, undefeated, through the qualifying programme and to the last eight of Euro 2004. Defeat came against Portugal in Lisbon in a penalty shoot-out.

In both tournaments I thought we missed good opportunities to progress further, so I was left with a feeling of disappointment. I believe that after two quarter-final finishes Eriksson will be expected to do better in Germany. Anything less will be deemed a failure. If we go out before the quarter-finals it will mean that in three tournaments we have failed to learn our lessons and make any real progress. I'd love to see England get to the final but I have to say that we often struggle against the very best in the world. For four or five years after 1966 we were able to match the top teams, but it's not often in recent years that we've been able to pull off a truly big result in competitive football. Perhaps this time, with a player like Rooney in our ranks, we will be able to offer something that the opposition cannot legislate for successfully. Brazil are one of the nations able to regularly produce special players – Ronaldinho for instance – who can conjure up a surprise or a moment of genius that turns a game.

As the defending champions and five times winners, Brazil will be high among the favourites to lift the trophy in Germany. They are the only South American nation to have won the trophy in Europe – Sweden in 1958 – and will be highly fancied to repeat the feat this time. What I have learned over the years is that, just like us, other nations believe they have the best young players and all the technical ability needed to win the World Cup. The trouble with Brazil is that they usually do have just that. Robinho, a 22-year-old striker who made his name with Santos, Pele's old club, is reckoned to be the best player in Brazil. This doesn't mean the best Brazilian, but the best one playing in Brazil. He, of course, has yet to reap the benefits of playing against top-class opposition in Europe in the way that

Ronaldo, Ronaldinho and Kaka have. Nonetheless, I look forward to seeing him in action.

As hosts, our old friends from Germany will probably be the number one favourites. Three times winners, beaten finalists in 2002, anything less than a semi-final place would be considered a national disaster. Because they have not had to qualify, coach Jurgen Klinsmann has not had the benefit of a competitive programme of matches in which to prepare his side. But it doesn't have to be a big problem as Terry Venables showed when England hosted Euro 96. His team reached the last four, before losing to the Germans in that ill-fated penalty shoot-out.

With typical German efficiency Klinsmann has left no stone unturned in preparing his squad. He summoned all his World Cup hopefuls to Frankfurt last year for two days of fitness tests with the emphasis on speed, endurance and agility. The Germans have traditionally favoured experienced players at tournament time, but Klinsmann has looked long and hard at a lot of youngsters like Fulham's Moritz Volz, Chelsea's Robert Huth and Aston Villa's Thomas Hitzlsperger.

Argentina, twice winners, are also expected to unveil an outstanding young player who many have already compared to Diego Maradona. That may be a bit far-fetched at this stage but Carlos Tevez is clearly a young man with a big future. He plays in Brazil for Corinthians, and is frequently linked with big-money moves to clubs like Real Madrid, Bayern Munich and Chelsea. Apparently he's already had a few unsavoury ups and downs in his career and for that reason may also be a player who would benefit from some sound advice.

France, winners as hosts in 1998, are not the force they were. They made an embarrassingly early exit in Japan in 2002 after finishing bottom of their group in the opening stage. The European Championship in 2004 was only a little better. They beat England 2-1, of course, but then lost 1–0 to Greece in the quarter-finals. The Greeks were the surprise winners of the European title and while I was delighted to see one of the underdogs do so well I don't really envisage them sustaining a challenge for the World Cup. I think

England and Germany will be the big hitters from Europe with Spain and Italy also serious contenders.

The beauty of international football is that it remains largely free of the financial influences that now dictate winning and losing in club football. There are no Abramovich figures shaping the outcome of the World Cup. Sure, the rich nations have the best training facilities and hire the best coaches but, ultimately, success and failure on the international stage depends on the ability of players. Greece demonstrated the truth of that in spectacular fashion in Portugal in 2004.

You cannot buy overnight success on the international stage as Roman Abramovich did with Chelsea. He spent something like £300 million on players and won the Premiership title. Some queried his motives but had I been the Chelsea manager I would have had a wonderful time building a team with that kind of money. I had two years in charge at Stamford Bridge and in that time spent absolutely nothing. In fact, I was told to save money and, by selling players, earned the club around £200,000. It all seems very insignificant compared to the economics of modern football.

When I was offered the job at Chelsea, Dave Sexton, a former manager, told me that in the right hands the club could become a major force in Europe. I think he was probably right. When I was there the club was in a real mess financially. Although I only just missed out on promotion to the First Division in my first season, I was sacked in 1981 and replaced by John Neal. A few months after my departure Ken Bates became chairman and the story of the modern Chelsea began to unfold. Personally, I was delighted that they won the Premiership title in 2004–05 because we needed a club to break the duopoly of Manchester United and Arsenal. I thought it would be Liverpool, but it turned out to be Chelsea.

After their title win, people were predicting a decade of Chelsea domination. I'm not so sure. Chelsea have set a new standard but, when that happens, it tends to enhance the level of competition. Others will want to knock them off their pedestal. Look at Tiger Woods in 2000 for instance. He was such a dominant figure in golf that year that people thought he would never be beaten. People were wrong. Tiger's rivals simply raised their game. In the same way Olympic records are broken every four years. Sir Alex Ferguson won the title for Manchester United year after year and when people complained he would argue that his team was setting a standard for others to emulate. 'The option is for us to lower our standards,' he would say. 'What good would that do?'

I'd certainly like to see a more level playing field in the Premiership with a greater number of clubs becoming realistic challengers for the title. At the moment only three or four have a chance of winning. Perhaps the fact that Chelsea broke the United–Arsenal dominance might inspire others to follow suit.

Liverpool's epic triumph in the 2005 Champions League suggests they're on the way back. It was good to see them winning again in Europe where they dominated for so long in the seventies and eighties. They, like all the big English clubs playing in Europe, have suffered to some extent from changes to the Laws of the Game. Once the Continental clubs feared the tackling and physical commitment of the English game. We considered tackling a strength and an integral part of football. Slowly, though, the value of tackling has been diminished and we have reached a point now where influential figures like Michel Platini are supporting proposals to remove tackling altogether.

In my day a player who could tackle was almost as important as a player who could score goals. Tackling was a traditional part of the English game. As a striker I suffered from over-zealous tackling but the authorities began to address that problem when they outlawed the tackle from behind. Now, though, practically any physical challenge is considered borderline. I think that's a shame. Referees often blow their whistle not because they consider a challenge to be technically a foul but because they consider the challenge unacceptably aggressive. I think if you remove that type of commitment you would seriously undermine football as a spectator sport.

Football must retain a degree of aggression to remain competitive and I point this out to the many coaches I have helped during my association with McDonald's. They may be best known for their hamburgers but, since 1998, I've worked with them to help in the recruitment and training of football coaches. The initial aim was to train 10,000 coaches to work with children between the ages of six and 12. The scheme has been so successful that my contract has been extended and my involvement is to be broadened. I've been working closely with Kenny Dalglish and Eric Harrison, the former youth coach at Manchester United, and now McDonald's have invited Olympians like Sharron Davies and James Cracknell to get involved and help their sports.

I've enjoyed my work with McDonald's and have taken some satisfaction from helping football at grassroots level but, as I approach bus pass age, I realise that sooner rather than later I will have to begin to slow down. I hope, though, to be among the England fans in Germany for the World Cup. The intensity of England's support in foreign fields has never diminished and simply illustrates the love we have for the game. It's remarkable, for instance, that 40 years after we beat Germany at Wembley, the 1966 World Cup final still holds the audience record (32.3 million) for British television. As much as I enjoy watching football on TV it doesn't quite match being in the stadium for the big occasions. Fortunately I don't have too many business commitments these days so I fully intend to be in Germany for the finals. Funnily enough, I was invited over there in 2005 to give a talk on motivation to a German business audience.

I still have a few business interests. I have, for instance, an involvement with a property company, the Royal Group, helping them market their developments in Portugal and Spain, and I've dabbled a bit myself in property in a small way. I also make a few personal appearances and fulfil after-dinner engagements. A source of continuing pleasure are the reunions with the 1966 team. We still get together on a regular basis for golf days and dinners and, whenever a World Cup comes round, the demands on us increase. The fact is, of course, that we are unique in English soccer history and will remain so until another England team win the World Cup.

One other project dear to my heart has been the redevelopment of Wembley Stadium, a place that has figured prominently in my life. We should be proud of the fact that we now have the most magnificent stadium in the world. Yes, it's cost a lot – but the best always does. The old Wembley meant a great deal to me but it was well past its prime. I was sorry to see the twin towers go, but thought it essential that they kept the stadium at Wembley. After all, you wouldn't move Lord's or Wimbledon to another part of the country, would you?

Wembley is football's spiritual home and crowning the new stadium is the famous arch, big enough to be seen right across London and the longest single-span roof structure in the world. The arch isn't there just for show. It supports a large part of the weight of the roof as there are no holding columns inside to interfere with the fans' view. It also allows for a sliding roof. The new Wembley is the largest football stadium in the world with each of the 90,000 seats under cover. I've been involved in helping the Football Association with marketing and promotion. It's a shame that I'll never get to play in it but, hopefully, Sven or one of his successors will discover other heroes to emulate Moore, Hurst and Peters at some time in the future.

Nothing would give me or my 1966 colleagues more pleasure than watching Beckham lift the World Cup. As national team coach Sven has a vital role to play, but it's always been my contention that the most important people in the equation are the players. If the players are good enough they will win more than they lose, regardless of who fills the coaching role. In 1966 Sir Alf Ramsey had the considerable advantage of having five world-class players in his squad: Gordon Banks, Ray Wilson, Bobby Moore, Bobby Charlton and Jimmy Greaves. How many does Eriksson have available to him? Not so long ago England internationals of this quality were thin on the ground but I like to think that, in recent seasons, players like Lampard and Gerrard have elevated themselves to world-class status. Rooney could join them if he maintains his current progress and listens to good advice.

Over the years many of those responsible for the development of the modern game seemed to lose sight of the importance of football at grassroots level. This, after all, is where England's international players begin their journey to the top. But there are so many distractions for modern youngsters and those keen on football often have nowhere to play. The sale of school playing fields has been a national disgrace and has, in my opinion, played a role in the decline of England's global reputation. Fortunately we appear to be address-ing some of these problems. The McDonald's initiative is producing encouraging results and I was delighted when the Prime Minister launched The Football Foundation with the aim, among other things, of putting in place a new generation of modern facilities. The Foundation's Grassroots Advisory Group has an annual budget of £45 million and a remit to invest in schools and park pitches and to revolutionise the entire funding process for grassroots football.

More than that, of course, my old West Ham team-mate, Sir Trevor Brooking, is now in charge of development at the Football Association. His role covers the well-being of football at all levels and I know he is particularly keen to ensure that the sport at schools and youth level has the support it needs. I've met him officially in my McDonald's role to discuss the way ahead and he and I agree on the importance of football at grassroots level.

Trevor, of course, was a product of the schoolboy game. Schools football has always provided the professional game with talented youngsters. My World Cup and West Ham team-mate Martin Peters, for instance, was an outstanding England schoolboy player. Sadly, many clubs sacrificed the development of youth for the quick-fix solution, preferring to spend in the international transfer market rather than invest time and money on a youth development system. But someone with the vision, patience and energy of Sir Alex Ferguson realised years ago the long-term benefits of encouraging youth. Underpinning all the Manchester United success in recent years was the development of youth players like Beckham, Paul Scholes, Nicky Butt, the Neville brothers and Wes Brown. I was disappointed when Scholes announced his retirement from the international scene but the others remain members of Eriksson's squad.

Alex devoted much of his time in his first seasons at Old Trafford to finding and encouraging young players. I remember one season early on, when United were flirting with relegation and there was mounting pressure on the Old Trafford board to sack him. They stood firm and he has rewarded their patience handsomely. Sir Bobby Charlton, a Manchester United director for more than 20 years, told me at the time that Alex was steering the club in the right direction even if the results in the old First Division didn't reflect this. I recall him telling me that Alex would happily drive 250 miles to see a young kid play. That kind of devotion to the long-term well-being of the club has paid spectacular dividends. Manchester United is now one of the world's greatest sporting institutions, a fact firmly underlined by the £800 million takeover of the club by the American tycoon Malcolm Glazer who promised to give Alex all the financial support he needed to compete for the best players in the transfer market.

Although some Old Trafford fans were seriously concerned and pledged to wage a guerrilla war against the Glazer family, they must have been reassured by the comments of Bobby Charlton after his meeting with Glazer's sons last summer. Bobby told the fans that he was relieved that the Glazer family had no plans to make significant changes. It's hard to imagine what you could do to make United very much more successful than they are already. Under Alex the Old Trafford empire dominated the domestic game for a decade. At one time their stranglehold on the title reduced some elements of the Premiership race to farce. Can we claim that the Premiership is the most competitive league in the world if the same team keeps winning? Of course not. But Arsene Wenger's Arsenal, outstandingly brilliant at times, were able to sustain an authentic challenge and then, of course, along came Mourinho's Chelsea to claim the title in such emphatic style in 2005.

In my playing days at least a dozen of the clubs in the old First Division always believed they had a chance of winning the title. This generated enormous excitement with the championship changing hands season after season. In the ten years from Burnley's title triumph in my debut season of 1959–60, the winners were Tottenham, Ipswich, Everton, Liverpool, Manchester United, Liverpool, Manchester United, Manchester City, Leeds and Everton.

To be successful in the long term the Premiership must remain competitive. For many of the big clubs the race is to secure a

Champions League place the following season. In this sense the Premiership has simply become a feeder league for the Champions League. Any future expansion of the Champions League will, in my opinion, further dilute the value of winning the Premiership title. The financial rewards in Europe are now such that finishing second or third in the Premiership is as good as winning the title itself. But winning the Premiership should be *the* prize each season. Champions League places are a motivating factor but surely no substitute for being crowned Champions of England. We shouldn't lose sight of this. What is encouraging to know, though, is that the Premier League can still produce teams good enough to win the Champions League, as Liverpool did so spectacularly in 2005.

The Champions League, of course, is hugely lucrative and enables the big clubs to meet the extraordinary wage demands of the players at the top end of the game. So, inevitably, money has become the great motivator in professional football and in some ways the pursuit of cash has turned the sport into a graceless, charmless business. In the last 15 years football has almost reinvented itself with the biggest and most powerful getting the lion's share of the profits. Some will argue that clubs that generate most should be allowed to keep most, but there is a downside for the smaller clubs, just as the growth of vast superstores has all but erased the corner shop from our high streets. Money doesn't automatically make the quality of the product better just as, in my opinion, paying referees a full-time salary won't improve their judgement. To suggest that it would is surely offensive to referees who already do a difficult job to the best of their ability.

One of the benefits of having such high salaries in the Premiership is that many of the world's best players now want to ply their trade in England. Of course not all these imports are of the highest quality but those that are help enhance technical standards. Who can say, for instance, that Cristiano Ronaldo hasn't had anything but a positive effect on the English game? Manchester United have traditionally attracted many of football's great entertainers like George Best and Eric Cantona. I was a big fan of Cantona but couldn't understand how Old Trafford fans could vote him the greatest United player of all time. However good his touch and vision, in my opinion his contribution didn't rival that of Bobby Charlton, George Best, Denis Law or Bryan Robson. In the era in which they played all four were more productive for United than Cantona in his brief spell at Old Trafford.

You can only judge players in the context of their time but I do feel that a lot of great footballers from my day no longer enjoy the recognition they deserve. The modern-day hype in football tends to embrace only contemporary players and overlooks the contribution of many of those from past years. Bobby Charlton, for instance, was one of the greatest players of all time and certainly the best to wear the famous red shirt of Manchester United. Others may have scored more goals, but none scored better goals. His achievements set him apart from Cantona and everyone else: 49 goals in 106 England matches, 198 goals in 606 league games in 17 years with United, a World Cup winner, a European Cup winner and three times a League Championship winner. On top of all that he played with a modesty and honesty that is rare in the modern game.

His is the first name in my personal all-time England line-up. Only one of Sven's present squad would get into the team, but three more of today's young stars are very close to winning places. In goal? There's only one choice for me – my 1966 team-mate Gordon Banks. But I'd have Peter Shilton among my five substitutes. My back four includes two World Cup winning colleagues – Bobby Moore, of course, and Ray Wilson at left-back. I'd give the centre-half role to Tony Adams, the former Arsenal captain, and United's Gary Neville gets my vote at right-back.

Midfield? Well, here Frank Lampard and Steve Gerrard are contenders. As I've said, they are exceptionally talented players and vastly influential in the England team. But for me they need a little more experience of tournament football. So three of my four midfield players are from Old Trafford – Bobby Charlton, Bryan Robson and the late Duncan Edwards. I never played against Duncan, who died so young and tragically in the Munich air crash in 1958, but Bobby Charlton has told me all I need to know. He was, according to Bobby, the best midfield player he ever saw. My other midfield choice is Tom Finney, the legendary winger who scored 30 goals in 76 England appearances and spent his entire career with Preston North End. He was good enough to play on either wing and twice won the Footballer of the Year award.

That just leaves the two front players. My old pal Jimmy Greaves – 44 goals in 57 matches for England – was the finest marksman of all time and so walks straight into my favourite England team. I'd partner him with Alan Shearer, the nearest England have had to the complete centre forward in recent times. I thought he and Teddy Sheringham forged the last truly successful England strike partnership during Euro 96. They complemented each other brilliantly. Manchester United's Wayne Rooney may well be worthy of one of those places in a year or two, but not just yet. He has all the physical qualities for the job. I thought he was exceptional during his first big tournament, Euro 2004, and but for his injury against Portugal England may have gone further than the quarter-finals.

So, my favourite England line-up is: Banks, Neville G., Adams, Moore, Wilson, Finney, Charlton, Robson, Edwards, Shearer, Greaves. Subs: Shilton, Butcher, Mullery, Peters, Keegan. That team, I believe, would do justice to the new Wembley and ensure sell-out crowds. They all played in the old stadium, even Duncan Edwards, who was just 18 when he made his debut there in a 7–2 win over Scotland in 1955.

Even though it's a brand new stadium my attachment to Wembley remains as firm as ever. It's just a shame that the new stadium will not host the 2006 World Cup as was envisaged back in 1997 when the Prime Minister launched the FA bid to stage the tournament. The Germans were victorious in the bid process and, as host nation, will be expected to do even better than in 2002 when they lost 2–0 to Brazil in the final in Yokohama. They have finished runners-up four times, never more graphically than when they were beaten 4–2 by England after extra time in 1966. Of course, they would love the chance to avenge that defeat in the final – and I'm sure Sven would like to give them the chance too!

Perhaps his most memorable result as England manager came in Munich in September 2001 when an Owen hat-trick helped secure a 5–1 win over Germany in the qualifying programme. That was their most humiliating defeat since losing 6–3 in Berlin in 1938 against . . . England. But I've learned never to write off the Germans. They recovered from that 5–1 defeat to qualify and then which of us did better in the finals? The Germans, of course.

Their squad of players in 2002 was generally accepted to be among the poorest they had sent to the finals yet their discipline, work rate and tactical acumen were sufficient to propel them almost all the way. Of course, we shouldn't underestimate the quality of players like Kahn, Frings, Ramelow, Jeremies, Ballack and Linke. The fact is that when it mattered the Germans probably gave Brazil a better game than England.

Based initially on the island of Kobe to prepare for the finals, Sven's men secured two draws – 1–1 with South Korea and 2–2 with Cameroon – in warm-up matches. These results helped keep expectancy levels back home at something like a realistic level. This was just as well because the opening match against Sven's country-men, Sweden, in Saitama produced a 1–1 draw. Sol Campbell's headed goal after just 22 minutes promised great things but England failed to capitalise on their early dominance.

Argentina were next. This was one of the tournament's most eagerly awaited games and while never a classic it produced 90 minutes of absorbing, competitive football. Although forced to defend desperately near the end, England clung on to David Beckham's 44th minute penalty and claimed a famous victory. A point was all that was then required to ensure progress. A goalless draw with Nigeria in Osaka secured a second-round match with Denmark while Argentina, having been held 1–1 by Sweden, were out of the tournament, much to everyone's surprise.

For the first time England began to look like serious contenders when they met the Danes in Niigata. Rio Ferdinand's forceful header after four minutes set the tone for the match and later goals by Owen and Emile Heskey put the match beyond the reach of the Danes. Then came Brazil. Even on their off days they could be brilliant. But, for much of the first half in a thrilling quarter-final in Shizuoka, England looked in control. Owen provided a priceless lead after 23 minutes and Sven's smothering tactics were working well until, just before the interval, Scholes missed a midfield challenge and with a series of swift, precise passes Brazil cut through the England defence for Rivaldo to equalise.

Five minutes after the re-start, with England's dejection still apparent, Ronaldinho, way out on the right, hit a devilish free kick that looped over poor David Seaman and gave Brazil a 2–1 lead. It was an extraordinary goal. Some thought Ronaldinho meant it. I didn't think that at the time and I don't think it now. It was a fluke and I find it difficult to understand how anyone can suggest otherwise. David played a couple more games but in reality the Brazil defeat was the match that signalled the end of his long international career. Although he was at fault, the fact is that Ronaldinho was sent off a few minutes later and, disappointingly, England were unable to exploit the one-man advantage. They lost 2–1 and Brazil progressed to the semi-finals.

The Germans, narrow 1–0 victors over the USA in the quarter-finals, then beat the gallant South Koreans 1–0 in the semi-final in Seoul. The prize for their steady, if unspectacular progress, was a place alongside Brazil – 1–0 semi-final winners over Turkey – on football's greatest stage. The final was more entertaining than expected but after Germany's initial domination the Brazilians gradually took charge, scoring two late goals through Ronaldo to win 2–0. What was ironic was that Franz Beckenbauer, who had been highly critical of the Germans, said that this had been a tournament that England could have won! In the aftermath of England's failure there were the usual calls for a reduction in the number of matches played and for a winter break to rest the top stars. Four years on, little has changed. If England fail again in Germany the same excuses will be offered afterwards.

One thing you can be sure of is that the FA will have researched the training facilities, stadia, hotels and climate thoroughly in Germany. They know the importance of a happy, healthy squad of players. It helps, too, if they can stay in one place for the duration of the tournament. The players value familiar surroundings and the prospect of having to move camp midway through a tournament doesn't have much appeal. Apart from one or two overnight trips, the bulk of the time in Japan in 2002 was spent at a luxurious complex on Awaji Island.

I was a spectator in Mexico in 1986 when Bobby Robson had to move the entire party from their cool mountain retreat in Saltillo to the heat and smog of Mexico City. Having secured an epic 3–0 win over Poland, they progressed to round two where they were due to play Paraguay in Mexico City seven days later. They flew to the Mexican capital the morning after the Poland match and moved into a hotel, surrounded by motorways, in the middle of an industrial estate. It wasn't ideal but it was close to the training ground, a critical consideration in a city choked with traffic. They stayed three nights but the complaints of senior players like Ray Wilkins, Peter Shilton and Peter Reid, none of whom had slept much because of the traffic noise, persuaded Robson to move them all again. England were bidding for a place in the quarter-finals and the manager knew that this was no way to prepare for a big match. So they moved to a quieter hotel. 'The players are smiling again,' said Bobby once they were in their new quarters.

Like Robson, Eriksson knows that the atmosphere and spirit generated by the players is what they take into the dressing-room and out on to the pitch. Good team spirit is essential. That's why I've always felt that those in the squad not playing are as important as those named in the starting line-up. There are always six or seven players in a squad of 22 who know that their chances of playing are almost certainly dependent on other players either suffering injury or missing games through suspension. It's often these players who establish the climate in which the entire squad works and plays. If they're miserable or mischievous they can cause problems for a coach. These players can undermine the feel-good factor within the entire group if the team spirit isn't right. That's why Sir Alf Ramsey picked his players so carefully. It wasn't simply a matter of skill but also temperament. Remember, a successful World Cup squad can be away from home and family for the best part of two months.

I must say, though, that I have been impressed with the team spirit since Eriksson arrived. It seems to me that the players have responded positively to his leadership. I think his rapport with David Beckham has been important in setting the tone within the squad. Sven certainly seems a very relaxed, amiable kind of coach. I'm told the players genuinely like him and enjoy his company. This is good to a point. Personally I'm not sure it's a good thing to be *too* close to your players. I'm always a little suspicious when I read that players *like* their manager. You hear that Manchester United players respect Sir Alex Ferguson but I wonder how many actually like their manager? I think it's better for the relationship between manager and players to be businesslike rather than friendly. That's the way it was with Sir Alf in my playing days.

Strangely I'm sometimes accused, unfairly I think, of boring the public with recollections of 1966 and my own playing career. All I'm doing is answering media questions and the truth is that I'd far rather a new generation of players have the opportunity to recall their World Cup winning exploits of 2006. Hopefully, Beckham's team will get the chance to establish themselves as our successors as the best team on the planet and then in 40 years' time they might be referred to as 'The Bores of 2006'!

I don't think people today find England's team boring any more than they found Sir Alf's team boring 40 years ago. At least England now seem to have a team in the real sense of the word. Every player has a job and knows exactly what he's supposed to do within the framework of the team. Eriksson doesn't ask his players to fill unfamiliar roles. He clearly favours a 4–4–2 formation, which is good because this is what the players are used to. It's the system that suits them and which most play at club level every Saturday of the season. Knowing your job and knowing you can do it breeds confidence, an essential quality when competing against the best in the world.

Eriksson's job is to ensure that confidence remains high among the players without transmitting wholly misleading messages of hope to the public at large. The media build-up to the World Cup becomes more and more frenzied and this inevitably fuels unrealistic levels of optimism. I have my own personal barometer of public interest in the months before a World Cup. For three years out of four everyone asks me about 1966. But in the fourth year I get stopped in the street with growing regularity and asked: 'How do you think we're going to do?'

Eriksson's task is to keep the entire build-up process in perspective for the players and the public because disproportionate levels of expectancy are damaging and create unnecessary burdens. Since his arrival there has been a sense of calm and quiet confidence within the squad and I hope he can retain this throughout the run-up to Germany. He has to hope his team survive the qualifying process and that his big stars emerge unscathed from the domestic season. He must also know the importance of not losing the opening match.

The first game in a tournament is always difficult. A draw wouldn't be a disaster. Chile qualified for the second stage with three draws in France 1998. The Republic of Ireland qualified with three draws in 1990. We drew with Uruguay in our opening match in 1966. We wanted to win but Sir Alf Ramsey had stressed the importance of avoiding defeat that day. Getting through the first stage can be a cat-and-mouse procedure and it doesn't really matter how you do it. What matters is qualifying for the later stages. There's plenty of opportunity then for stylish attacking football. In my opinion the winners of the 2006 World Cup will be the team with the most in-form top-quality players in the key positions. Most of the great World Cup teams had great strikers – Pele of Brazil, Muller of West Germany, Kempes of Argentina, Rossi of Italy and Ronaldo of Brazil in 2002 are just a few examples.

After his exploits in Portugal we know that young Rooney has the potential to fill this role for England. But he must realise that from now on he is a marked man on the international stage, just as I was when we defended the World Cup in Mexico in 1970. Eriksson must pray that Rooney and his other key players like Owen, Beckham, Lampard and Gerrard remain free of injury because the loss of these talismanic-type of players can seriously diminish a team's sense of well-being. I remember the dilemma facing Sir Alf Ramsey when Gordon Banks collapsed with food poisoning on the morning of the quarter-final against West Germany in Mexico in 1970. His understudy Peter Bonetti was an excellent goalkeeper but we all knew that Gordon was the best in the world, playing at the peak of his ability.

Some influential figures, like Eriksson, believe that many players have become regular victims of the physical demands of the modern game. Personally, I don't think they play too many games but the recovery rate of injured players is becoming an increasingly important consideration for the big clubs. A player who can stay free of injury – Beckham has been a prime example – can become a vital component in a manager's plans. Beckam's dependability put him in this category with, first, Sir Alex Ferguson and then with Eriksson.

It was Peter Taylor, now manager of Hull City, who gave Beckham the England captaincy during his brief period in charge of the England team before Eriksson's arrival. It was an inspired move. Beckham rose to the responsibility and became a more complete player because of it. He's done the job magnificently. His delivery of the ball from corners, crosses and free kicks has become an essential part of England's attacking force and the zeal with which he pursues lost causes is an inspiration to those around him. Sometimes I feel I'd like to see him adopt a more dominant stance on the field because the big tournaments require strong leadership and resolute personalities. Some questioned his tactical awareness and his ability to motivate during England's low moments in Japan where I felt he was short of full fitness.

Beckham will be 31 by the time the 2006 World Cup comes round so unless he's remarkably lucky with his fitness his chances of competing in the final of the tournament at some future stage are remote. It would be sad for him to retire from international football without making a really big impression on the World Cup. At least Eriksson, or his successor, has the consolation of knowing that future England captains are already emerging. Gerrard has shown the necessary maturity and I believe Lampard may also be a challenger for the captain's armband.

These two players, along with Rooney, give me great hope for the future. But do we really have the resources to sustain a successful World Cup campaign? Can we win it? Yes, I think we can, if everything falls into place. But we may have to improvise and react to the unexpected and that has not always been easy. Bobby Robson, who led England into two World Cup tournaments, said that a coach needed a card up his sleeve if he wanted to be successful in the finals. I remember him saying: 'A World Cup coach needs to be flexible. He might need another way of playing. He might need a little refinement.'

As one of Ron Greenwood's coaches at the 1982 World Cup I remember him telling us the value of being able to improvise at the highest level. Do England have enough quality players to be able to fulfil these criteria? If there are no problems we've got a good chance. But if things go wrong do we have the resources to improvise? Players are always injured in the big tournaments. Others need to be rested. In these circumstances the coach sometimes needs to dig deep into his resources. Sometimes, from moments of adversity, you extract the most unexpected triumphs. When the great Jimmy Greaves was injured against France in 1966 gloom and despondency descended upon the nation. Jim was *the* great goalscorer of the day, a natural match winner. Would England be able to recover from such a loss?

Well, as everyone now knows, we did recover and from Jim's bad luck came my opportunity as his replacement. Those three goals in the final against West Germany were to change my life. Yet a month earlier I couldn't have envisaged such a scenario. Having lost his star striker, Sir Alf Ramsey had to improvise and he did so with spectacular success. Forty years on, I'm still fit and healthy and determined to retain some contact with football in the years to come. I don't get to West Ham so much because Judith and I have now moved to Cheltenham to be near the children. I devote more and more of my time to our three daughters and the grandchildren. As you go through life you realise what is important. The health of my children and grandchildren, for instance, is far more important to me than whether England win the World Cup again, though I must confess that I got a great thrill from West Ham's return to the Premiership, their 2005 play-off win against Preston evoking memories of the 1964 FA Cup final.

Of course, it would be nice at some stage during my retirement if Sven or a future England coach picked up the World Cup. Sven has said that he hopes his successor is English. I was never against the appointment of a foreign national coach, but I hope the next one's English too. Sadly, there are not too many candidates. Steve McClaren, Alan Curbishley, Bryan Robson or Sam Allardyce would figure in anyone's list but after that you're struggling for realistic contenders. That, I believe, is a matter the FA must address.

But you never know. Perhaps one of my McDonald's graduates might one day become a big-time coach and . . . England manager!

Career record

SIR GEOFFREY CHARLES HURST

- Born Ashton-under-Lyne 8 December 1941.
- First team debut for West Ham United 15 December 1958 v Fulham (Southern Floodlit Cup).
- League debut 27 February 1960 v Nottingham Forest.
- FA Cup winner's medal 1964.
- European Cup-Winners' Cup medal 1965.
- League Cup runners-up 1966.
- England debut 23 February 1966 v West Germany.
- World Cup winner's medal 1966.
- Transferred to Stoke City August 1972 for £80,000. Loaned to Cape Town City.
- Transferred to West Bromwich Albion August 1975 for £20,000.
- Played for Cork Celtic, Seattle Sounders 1976.
- Telford United (player-manager) August 1976–79.
- England coach 1977–82.
- Coach to Chelsea April 1979 and manager from October 1979 to April 1981.
- Coached Sporting Club (Kuwait).
- Knighted in 1998.

SUMMARY OF APPEARANCES AND GOALS

Season	League		FA Cup		League Cup		Euro Cups		Internationals	
	Apps	Goals	Apps	Goals	Apps	Goals	Apps	Goals	Apps	Goals
WEST HAM UNITED										
1959–60	3	–	–	–	–	–	–	–	–	–
1960–61	6	–	–	–	–	–	–	–	–	–
1961–62	24	1	1	–	2	–	–	–	–	–
1962–63	27	13	–	–	2	2	–	–	–	–
1963–64	37	14	7	7	6	5	–	–	–	–
1964–65	42	17	1	2	1	–	9*	–	–	–
1965–66	39	23	4	4	10	11	6*	2	8	5
1966–67	41	29	2	3	6	9	–	–	6	3
1967–68	38	19	3	1	3	5	–	–	7	2
1968–69	42	25	3	2	3	4	–	–	9	8
1969–70	39	16	1	–	2	2	–	–	11	3
1970–71	39	15	–	–	2	1	–	–	4	1
1971–72	34	8	4	4	10	4	–	–	4	2
STOKE CITY										
1972–73	38	10	–	–	3	2	2†	1	–	–
1973–74	35	12	1	–	4	1	–	–	–	–
1974–75	35	8	1	–	4	3	1†	–	–	–
WEST BROMWICH ALBION										
1975–76	10	2	–	–	2	–	–	–	–	–
Totals	529	212	28	23	60	49	18	3	49	24

*European Cup-Winners' Cup
†UEFA Cup

Other matches: West Ham United – Essex Professional Cup: 1958–59 1; Southern Floodlit Cup: 1958–59 1; Southern Floodlit Cup: 1959–60 1; Charity Shield: 1964 1 (1 goal); American International Soccer League: 1963 10 (9); Seattle Sounders: 1976 23 (8)

ENGLAND YOUTH
1959 Wales, Scotland, East Germany, Italy, Romania, Greece

ENGLAND UNDER-23
1963 Wales
1964 France, Israel (1), Turkey

FOOTBALL LEAGUE
1966 Irish League (2)
1967 Scottish League (1), Belgian League
1968 Scottish League, Irish League (1)
1971 Scottish League
1972 Scottish League

Career record

ENGLAND INTERNATIONALS

1966 West Germany, Scotland (1), Yugoslavia, Finland, Denmark, Argentina (1), Portugal, West Germany (3), Northern Ireland, Czechoslovakia, Wales (2)

1967 Scotland (1), Spain, Austria, Wales, Northern Ireland (1), USSR

1968 Scotland, Sweden (sub), West Germany, USSR (1), Romania, Bulgaria (1)

1969 Romania, France (3), Northern Ireland (1), Scotland (2), Mexico, Uruguay (1), Brazil, Holland

1970 Holland (sub), Belgium (1), Wales, Northern Ireland (1), Scotland, Colombia, Ecuador, Romania (1), Brazil, West Germany, East Germany

1971 Greece (1), Wales, Scotland, Switzerland (1), Switzerland, Greece (1)

1972 West Germany

Index

Note: 'GH' denotes Geoff Hurst. Unqualified references to countries, cities and towns are to football teams unless otherwise directed. Subheadings for individuals are in chronological order.

331